My Soul is Filled with Joy

A HOLOCAUST STORY

To Diane —
Lets Keep the stories alive!
Karen Treiger

My Soul is Filled with Joy

A HOLOCAUST STORY

KAREN I. TREIGER

Stare Lipki Press
Seattle, Washington

STARE LIPKI PRESS
340 15th Avenue East, Box J
Seattle, WA 98112

www.karentreiger.com
starelipkipress.com

The name of the Wilk family have been changed to protect their privacy.

Library of Congress Control Number: 2018908602

ISBN: 978-0-692-11579-4

Maps by Robert Cronan, Lucidity Information Design, LLC
Book and Cover Design by Vicky Shea of Ponderosa Pine Design

Printed in the United States of America
10 9 8 7 6 5 4 3 2

*T*his extraordinary book enables the reader to see the Holocaust through two different lenses. Each lens gives us a compelling view of a world, far from our present reality, which we need to know. Each lens opens a gate and leads us into a reality from which we return transformed. This book which started as a gift of love from the author to her survivor parents-in-law, turns out to be a gift of seeing life anew to every reader. It enables us — no, it compels us-to see our everyday lives in a new dimension of appreciation, meaning and purpose. I urge everyone to look deeply into this book and accept its priceless gift of a new life.

The first lens reveals the remarkable story of Sam Goldberg and Esther Wisznia Goldberg who survived the cruelest and darkest depths of the Holocaust. Their stories are told separately and parallel until they come together, to hide in a dugout pit in forest ground, abutting the farm of a Polish family that agreed to hide them and try to feed them (all in secret, lest they be discovered and executed for helping Jews). By this time, every member of Sam and Esther's family had been killed in various ways.

Esther and Sam enjoyed warm, loving childhoods as they grew up in observant Jewish homes. Sam survived German air bombings, flight to Russian-occupied Poland, draft service in the Russian army, Nazi P.O.W. camps for Russians (where hundreds of thousands were murdered), escape, recapture, and being sent to build Treblinka death camp. He spent thirteen months in this place of extermination as supervisor of the laundry. At several critical moments, he was kept alive by the arbitrary whim intervention of the deputy Director of Treblinka, Kurt Franz an SS officer who shot prisoners for sport but somehow decided to keep this Jew alive. Sam took part in the prisoner uprising in Treblinka. In the subsequent chaos, he and tens of others fled but most were caught and killed. Of about 875,000 Jews sent to Treblinka, about 65 survived the war. Sam was one of them.

Esther survived German air bombing of her home town, Stoczek, her home burning down, flight to Bialystok and then to Slonim, Einsatzgruppen killing of her entire family (She was spared because she was in the hospital recovering from typhus). She returned to Stoczek, survived random selections, months of hiding with her husband under a haystack in the barn of a sympathetic Polish family, the murder of her husband when he went out to seek for food, the birth and death of her first child -until the final twelve months in the pit in the forest.

Each of these stories is told with breath-stopping matter of factness, with a heart-breaking eye for the telling detail, with restraint and accuracy, compounded of extended conversations with Sam and Esther and meticulous research on the background and *circumstances by the author. This section puts the volume in the immortal ranks of survivor accounts which tell the story of the Shoah with fidelity, sanctity and unforgettable power.*

The second lens reveals how the author, Karen Treiger, a third/fifth generation American who grew up in Seattle, Washington, galaxies away from the death planet of Treblinka, takes up the task of telling the story of Sam and Esther, after their death. She and her husband and various friends and family members go back and visit the scenes of the Goldbergs' lives. They also visit Auschwitz, Treblinka, Majdanek and other scenes of the total destruction. Alas, the Jewish presence is mostly buried in the ruins. The depressive effects of these revelations are tempered and somewhat overcome, in the encounter with the families of those who risked their lives to hide and feed Jews. We learn how in the deepest rings of hell, where mass murderers ruled and flourished, there were a precious handful of righteous Gentiles who risked all to save Jews. In the worst moments of the Holocaust, there were humans who chose life, both Jews and non-Jews who upheld the sanctity of human life and honored ethics and human responsibility. They also meet people who fan the sparks of rebirth in Polish Jewry.

Gradually, the author reveals to us how the encounter with pure evil and death of the Holocaust has the paradoxical effect of opening our eyes to the preciousness of life, to the miraculous goodness of everyday living, of the difference we can make by caring for others and not standing idly by the blood of our neighbor. This section teaches us that we must confront and remember the Shoah, even if our family was never there.

Reading this book is an invitation to live a fuller life - to become the children and grandchildren of those martyred and of those who preserved their image of God and Jewish identity under impossible circumstances. One can only bow one's head, out of an unutterable gratitude, to the author for her contribution to the sacred narrative of our people. I call this book sacred, for (as with all forms of scripture) it tells not only what happened - but how to live in light of the story.

—Rabbi Yitz Greenberg, President Emeritus,
CLAL: the National Jewish Center for Learning and Leadership;
chairman, the United States Holocaust Memorial Council, 2000-2002.

"Karen has written a powerful and personal account of Sam and Esther Goldberg. This book is a must read for those interested in the greatest crime in the history of mankind." —Chris Webb, Author/Historian, Founder of the Holocaust Historical Society, Whitehill, UK

"It is vital that this book—as well as other accounts of the Holocaust—be preserved and disseminated widely to future generations to help prevent anything similar from ever happening again." —Marion Blumenthal Lazan, Holocaust Survivor and Co-Author, *Four Perfect Pebbles*

"This story, of survival, faith and family, will fill your soul with sadness, but ultimately with joy." —Timothy J. Boyce, Editor, *From Day to Day: One Man's Diary of Survival in Nazi Concentration Camps*, by Odd Nansen

"We are haunted by the question of inexplicable evil. If you want to be inspired in spite of the horrors one human being can do to another human being, read this book." —Rabbi Michael Schudrich, Chief Rabbi of Poland

"In Karen Treiger's important book she tells the story of her in-laws. Their suitcases were filled with only tragic and bitter memories. Yet, they had the courage to pick themselves up by the bootstraps, wipe away the tears, turn despair into hope, and rebuild Jewish life." —-Rabbi Marvin Hier, Founder and Dean, Simon Wiesenthal Center

"Impeccably researched, well-crafted, and profoundly felt, this is a tale of hope and promise that emerges from horror and destruction, as well as one of the powers of the human spirit." —Steve Steinberg, Author and Baseball Historian, *Urban Shocker, Silent Hero of Baseball's Golden Age*

"In capturing the storied lives of Sam and Esther Goldberg, Karen Treiger confronts the darkness of war and brings readers into the light, as we witness her grief transformed into gratitude, self-understanding and yes, joy." —Barbara Mackoff, Author, *The Inner Work of Leaders*

"The author's quest to preserve this legacy yields a portrait of a multigenerational family with a passionate commitment to active and transformative remembering." —Katke Reszke, author, *Return of the Jew: Identity Narratives of the Third Post-Holocaust Generation of Jews in Poland*

DEDICATION

To Sam and Esther Goldberg (Z'L), whose strength of spirit, kindness and resilience inspires me each day.

And to my father Irwin Treiger (Z'L), who taught me to follow my dreams.

Table of Contents

"The Holocaust did not define what it is to be a Jew. The Holocaust defined what it is to be human. Any assault on Jews becomes, very rapidly, an assault on our shared humanity. That is why we must continue to remember, not for the sake of the past, but for the sake of the future."
—Rabbi Lord Jonathan Sacks. January 27, 2017.

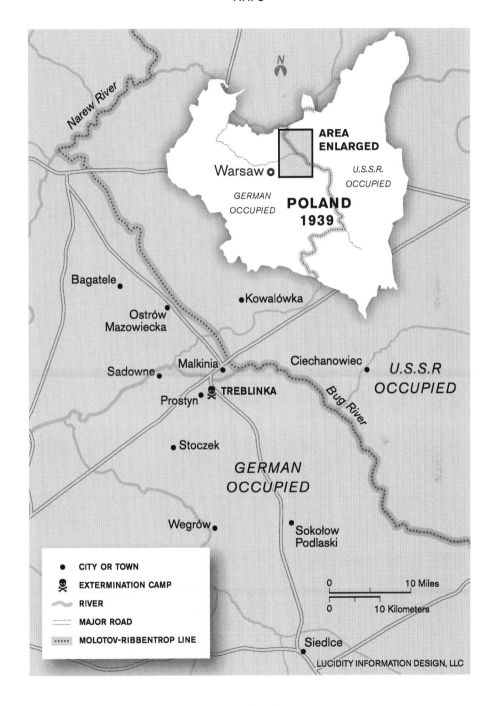

Dear Reader: May 2018

I am a member of the Goldberg family and I consider it an honor. Sam and Esther Goldberg are no longer with us. This book has been written to honor them and their legacy. I hope my life as I live it will continue to be one that makes them proud. Sam is one of approximately 65 to survive the Death Camp Treblinka and Esther is one of the few who survived years of hiding in the Polish forest. Part One is their story. Part Two is my story of marrying into the family and learning what it means to live after the Holocaust. I journey to Poland to talk with families who knew Sam and Esther and to see Treblinka.

❋ ❋ ❋

Sam and Esther Goldberg never gave up. They watched as millions were slaughtered. The earth was drenched with blood. There were times when Sam and Esther felt they could not go on, when death would be a release. But then someone, another human, reached out to help, whether it was with a sugar cube, wire cutters, supportive words, a barn to hide in, or food to keep starvation at bay. Sam believed that he survived in the *zechus,* the merit, of cooking food in the Treblinka laundry pots and sneaking it to the sick. Esther did not think twice before saving Sam after he escaped from Treblinka.

When I married Shlomo, some 34 years ago, I knew little of what people went through during the Holocaust and I knew less about the ongoing trauma of survivors and their families. As I learned Sam and Esther's story and got to know and love them, my world changed. I was challenged with the question of what it means to be human. I made a conscious decision to try to stop taking things in my life for granted. Then, I went further — I decided to try to be the person willing to help, willing to lend a hand, to show kindness. Finally, I learned that there is no absolute truth — there is only the truth as each person experiences and remembers it. The story told in these pages reflects the truth as told by Sam and Esther, interpreted through my experiences and my eyes. Others have different truths and they too are valid.

In Europe people paid with their lives for being Jewish. What had I paid? Nothing. But I can pay it forward. I hope Sam and Esther's story will reach out to you as it has to me.

Hate and murder seem to be part of the natural order. But I want to live in a world where goodness wins over evil. I believe that we can each make a difference in this world. We can strive never to take things for granted and to live in a world of kindness.

Karen I. Treiger

The Dream

AUGUST 1943

Esther Wisznia* was dreaming of the simple wooden door to her small home in Stoczek, 90 kilometers (55 miles) from Warsaw. The door had the number 4 on it. As she approached the door, she held a red crayon in her hand. In her dream, she traced over the 4 with the crayon. The 4 stood out now — bright and easy to see.

Upon waking, she found herself not at home in Stoczek,** but hiding in the Polish forest. It was July 31st, 1943 and she was 23 years old. She was surrounded by stick-like trees, tall with full green leaves. Low-lying brush and dead leaves carpeted the ground. This bit of forest she now called home was just a few kilometers away from the door in her dream. Nothing had made sense since the war started in September of 1939.

Esther and her teenage "roommate," Chaim Kwiatek, had been hiding in the woods outside Stoczek for nearly a year, living life day by day, hour by hour. They were constantly hungry. With her light brown hair, square jaw and strong, compact body, Esther could pass as a non-Jew as she searched the woods for mushrooms and berries. Their Polish saviors — the Styś families — brought food to

---

*   Pronounced Vishniu.
** Esther called Stoczek — Stok. To avoid confusion, the Polish name, Stoczek, will be used throughout.

7

their hiding spot. When it was too dangerous to bring food to Esther and Chaim, they would leave it in the dog's dish. Esther or Chaim would collect the food from the dog's dish after dark. With Poles scouring the woods looking to deliver Jews to the Nazis for their reward — a kilo of sugar for every Jew — her fear of being caught was palpable.

"Chaim," Esther said, "listen to my dream. I saw the door to my house and there was a four written on it. I drew over the four with a bright red crayon. I think this means that something is going to happen to us in 4 days."

"If you are right," said Chaim, "and something is going to happen to us in 4 days, it's not going to be anything good."

The third day after the dream was August 2, 1943. Gazing out beyond the woods and past the open fields, Esther saw a big ball of fire shooting straight up. The gray smoke menacingly filtered out into the sky. The fire was from the Nazi death camp Treblinka.

On the fourth day after the dream, Esther awoke with a pit in her stomach and not just because it was empty. In the dim light of the early morning, she

Smoke rising over Treblinka on August 2, 1943. Credit: Yad Vashem

began searching the forest for berries and mushrooms. A Polish woman, whom she didn't know, approached her.

"Do you want to see some Jews from Treblinka?" the woman asked her, assuming she was a Jew.

"Yes," Esther answered.

Esther did everything in her power to avoid talking to non-Jews — it was too dangerous. But this time, because she had seen the smoke yesterday, she knew she must meet these Jews. Leading her out of the woods, to an open field, the woman brought Esther to the two men. They were exhausted and anxious. She recognized the taller one, Velvel Schneiderman, from her town, Stoczek.

"Velvel," Esther cried, "you're alive. What happened to you, where did you come from?"

"We ran away from Treblinka," Velvel said. "We made a revolt. We blew up the gas tanks, killed some guards, and blew a hole in the barbed-wire fence with a grenade. Some were killed, but many got out through the hole and ran to the forest."

"Was the smoke I saw yesterday from the revolt?" Esther asked.

"Yes," said Velvel, "the whole camp was on fire." Pointing to the man with him, Velvel continued, "This is Shmulke (Sam) Goldberg. He's from Bagatele. He also escaped during the revolt. We met up in the woods as we were running."

Sam stood just over five feet, not much taller than Esther. He had light brown hair and his face was soft with a strong chin. His eyes startled her. They shone a translucent blue. Looking into those eyes on that August day, she was sure she got a glimpse of his soul.

"I think I have seen you before," Esther said. "Were you in Stoczek before the Nazi round up?"

"Yes," answered Sam. "I was taken to Treblinka in the very first round up in June last year."

To Esther, as she stood there in dirt-crusted, tattered rags, these two men looked like princes. Their clothes were clean; not a single tear. Sam explained that they took them from the mountain-high piles of discarded clothes from Treblinka's murdered Jews. As soon as the Jews came off the trains they were forced to disrobe and run down the "Road to Heaven" into the gas chambers.

As the supervisor of the laundry for 11 of his 13 long months at Treblinka, Sam had his pick of the finest. But now, Nazis, Ukrainians, and Poles, with guns and machetes, were hunting down the Treblinka escapees like animals.

The name — Treblinka — made her tremble. While Esther escaped by hiding in an attic, other Stokers* were captured a year ago and she had heard from Helena Styś that they were taken there. The Nazis herded the 400 remaining Jews of Stoczek into the town square. Anyone trying to run was shot. The Jews were surrounded by trained dogs and SS men "who were worse than dogs," Esther later said. From her attic hideaway, Esther heard the screaming, the crying, the barking, the shooting, as the Nazis went from house to house. She also learned from Helena that many were taken to the Jewish cemetery, forced to dig a pit and were then shot, one by one, into the pit. The rest were marched out of town — to Treblinka.

"It is not safe here — out in the open," Esther explained to Sam and Velvel. "Go into the woods and meet me back here at noon, when the Polish people have their dinner."

The nervous escapees faded into the dense trees and then reemerged from the forest at noon. Sam later recalled how a year of hiding in the woods had transformed this beautiful young woman.

"She looked terrible," Sam later said. "*Nebach*,** she suffered. The vermin crawled from her. She looked very bad, *Oy*, how she looked, it was *geferlach* (unbelievable)."

Notwithstanding her desperate appearance, Esther exuded inner strength. Sam believed that there was no one better to help him and Velvel. He looked her straight in the eyes.

"Where can we hide out?" Sam asked.

Esther took Sam and Velvel to Helena Styś, Esther's Polish "angel."

"These men escaped Treblinka," she told Helena, "you must hide them."

Helena's eyes narrowed, and Esther saw the fear in them. If she was caught

---

*   People from Stok or Stoczek are referred to as Stokers.
**   Yiddish word meaning an unfortunate one, though these English words do not capture the full meaning.

hiding Jews, her whole family would be killed. She knew there was a massive search going on.

"If someone does something, not for money, just to help, God helps them," Esther pleaded. "All day, I pray that nothing bad will happen to you because if you will be ok, then I will be ok."

"Go to hell," Helena said, "you must have learned that talk from the Gypsies. OK, quickly, go into the barn. Hide in the animal stalls in case the Germans open the barn door."

All four of them — Sam, Velvel, Esther and Chaim — hid in the barn for three days. Esther's plea to hide them "not for money, just to help," did not stop Sam from paying Helena for the great risk she took.

"I paid her all the money I had" Sam later said. "Money was worth nothing in Poland. If someone informed that she was holding us up, they would have killed her too."

"Where did you get the money?" Esther asked bewildered.

"From the shirts," Sam explained. "It was sewn into the shirts. When I worked with the shirts in the Treblinka laundry, I took it out."

The four of them hid for three days — just enough time for the mass prisoner hunt to run its course. Of the Treblinka prisoners who were at the Death Camp on August 2nd, only about half got beyond the camp's barbed wire fence. As for those who made it through the fence, most were caught and killed. Indeed, the Jew hunt was so successful that the German SS, the Ukrainian guards, and the local Poles, found Jews hiding in the woods and ultimately caught more Jews than had escaped.[1] By allowing Esther, Sam, Chaim and Velvel to hide in her barn for those few days, Helena saved, not just Sam and Velvel, but Esther and Chaim as well.

After three days, this group of four ventured into the dense woods. Velvel decided to move on and made his way through the forest. Sam decided to stay and hide with Esther and Chaim. They knew that the Soviet army had defeated the Germans at Stalingrad six months earlier and that the army was driving the Germans back. Would they live to see the Red Army liberate their patch of Polish woods? They didn't know.

Part I

Bagatele — the Early Years

1920-1930'S

"**G**ood morning little brother, it's time to get up," Raizel whispered as she entered the bedroom where Shmulke (Sam) slept with his three older brothers. Sam opened his eyes and seeing his beautiful sister, he smiled and wrapped his arms around her neck. As she did each morning, Raizel helped Sam wash his hands and face and dress in simple short pants and a cotton shirt. Together they smelled their way to the kitchen where their mother, Chaya Faiga, was holding baby Henya in her left arm and frying eggs with her right. Fresh bread and milk, still warm from the cow's udder, were ready for the morning rush. Yankel, a few years older than Sam was already seated at the table, buttering his bread. Helping Sam onto a chair and pushing him up to the large wood table, Raizel filled his plate with bread and eggs and poured him some milk. Sitting down next to him she helped herself while keeping close watch on her youngest brother.

Within five minutes, the others joined the breakfast chaos. As usual, Itche entered the kitchen singing and dancing. He made everyone laugh. His voice was so melodious that after his *Bar Mitzvah*,* he was often the *Chazan* (Cantor) for *Shabbes* (Sabbath) services. Hersh Mayer, the oldest came in next. He was

---

* A boy becomes *Bar Mitzvah* at age 13 and he is then obligated to follow the commandments, including reciting prayers in the morning and again in the afternoon and evening.

their father Zelig's best help on their large farm. He would often go with Zelig to nearby towns to sell grain or farm animals and to Polish estates to buy timber. Zelig did a brisk business trading in wheat, domesticated animals and timber, throughout the district. Zelig also did business in Ostrow Mazowiecka,* the big town, 15 kilometers (9.3 miles) away.

Zelig, while not a physically tall man, was broad shouldered and energetic. He carried himself as if he was six feet tall, full of confidence. His short-cropped hair contrasted with the *Peyes* (sidelocks)[2] he grew on each side of his head. On the top, back of his head, sat a *Kippa* (skullcap). Wearing his weekday work clothes, he strode into the kitchen bellowing in Yiddish "*a goot free morgen tzu alle myne kinder*" ("good morning to all my children"). He surveyed the scene and took his place at the head of the table. He was indeed hungry, as he had risen before dawn, already *davened* (said morning prayers), and prepared the farm for the day ahead.

After breakfast, Raizel washed Sam's hands and then set him loose. As a young boy living on a big farm with cows, chickens, goats, horses, dogs, cats and other assorted animals, there was plenty of work to be done. Unless it was the deep freeze of winter, Sam ran outside and played, sometimes under the big tree that stood full and tall next to their home. The bark of the tree was a dark brown and the branches extended out and upward toward the sky. In the spring, large green leaves filled-in the branches.

Because the Goldberg farm was located towards the end of the village of Bagatele, not many buggies passed by. But when they did, Sam loved to watch the horses with their manes flowing and tails waving as they passed by on the narrow dirt road, pulling an open-air cart behind them. Sometimes he was lucky enough to go with his father or brother in the horse and buggy to Wąsewo, just two kilometers (1.2 miles) away, or the *Shtetl*** of Goworow (pronounced Goverov), or even the big city — Ostrow. In these places and others, they sold grain, traded in animals and bought supplies. Sam loved how his father, well-known in the region, would wave to people and sometimes even stop the horse to chat and catch up on the news. When they traveled to other towns, they would hear of the

---

*   Ostrow in the Mazowiecka district of Poland.
**   A *Shtetl* is a village that is majority Jewish.

16

happenings in Warsaw, the big city, 70 kilometers (43 miles) away.

His father's renown was such that he was simply known as Zelig of Bagatele. He was thought of as a kind and generous person. Before Passover those in need of wheat for *Matza,* the unleavened bread eaten on this holiday, found an open heart and open silos on Zelig's farm.

But one day in the early 1930's tragedy struck Zelig's family and they were the ones who needed help. The Goldberg house caught fire. Zelig ran inside and grabbed the *Sefer Torah* — the *Torah* scroll that had been passed from father to son for generations. This they saved, but much was lost in that fire. They gathered the remnants of their belongings and wondered where they would live while they rebuilt.

They did not wonder for long. One of the Goldberg's non-Jewish neighbors, the Załęski family, invited them to live in their home. Andrzej Załęski, was the Mayor of Bagatele, and he lived at the other end of town, just next to their cousin — Mottle Goldberg. Zelig took him up on the offer and was so grateful to the Załęski family.[3] After the insurance money was received, they rebuilt their home. They moved back in, placing the *Sefer Torah* back where it belonged in an *Aron* (Ark).

The Goldberg home thrived with the rhythm of the Jewish year. *Shabbes,* the celebration of the biblical command to rest on Friday night and Saturday was central to their lives. As spring arrived, the family cleaned the home to rid it of leaven food before Passover, and in the fall, they enjoyed the sweet Bagatele honey on *Rosh Hashanah*. Even at the young age of four, Sam knew that *Yom Kippur* (Day of Atonement) was unique among all the holidays. The adults didn't eat or drink on that day and they swayed in prayer all day long. On that *Yom Kippur*, when Sam was four, his paternal grandmother, Malka, was sick. Prostrated on a bed of straw, she lay outside all day. Refusing to eat or drink because it was *Yom Kippur*, she died before sunset, when she would have been permitted to eat. Her refusal to eat, even as she lay dying, left Sam feeling that *Yom Kippur* is a day like no other.

As Sam grew older, he began public school and *Cheder* (Jewish elementary school). Though Raizel was still his wakeup call, Sam was now able to wash and dress on his own. His day now began before breakfast, with his own morning prayers that he learned in *Cheder*. After breakfast, he walked, by himself, out of the big house, turning left down the dirt road to the Polish public school. For the first four years, he attended school in Rząśnik Włościański, one and a half kilometers (.9 miles) away and for grades 5 through 7, he studied in a small schoolhouse in Wąsewo, a two-kilometer walk (1.2 miles). The Wąsewo school house was a wooden building with low door frames, just next to the red, brick church. Sam learned enough Polish to manage his schoolwork and talk with his Polish friends.

On his way, he often met his friend Fishel Kusher. Jabbering in Yiddish, the boys passed the time as they walked to school. They would walk past homes, some Jewish, some non-Jewish, lots of barns and wheat silos. They would see barns filled with animals and enjoy listening to the sounds of the horses, cows, and chickens. As they inhaled, they enjoyed the fresh, crisp farm air, perfumed with a tinge of manure.

After a morning in school learning Polish, history, and arithmetic, Sam walked, together with thirteen other Jewish boys, back down the dirt road to his home where the *Cheder* was held. There the *Melamed* (teacher of Jewish elementary children) was waiting for them. He settled them on hard benches pulled up to the long wooden table that dominated the room. They had already mastered the *alef-beis* — the Hebrew letters — learning to read. The *Melamed* instructed the boys to open their *Chumash* (Hebrew Bible). He told them the stories of the lives of their biblical ancestors — Abraham greeting the three angels, Jacob tricking in his brother Esau into selling him the right of the firstborn in exchange for a bowl of red soup, and of course, the terrifying story of Abraham binding Isaac on the altar and Isaac's narrow escape from death. In the singsong chant used at *Cheders* throughout Eastern Europe, the boys carefully translated the ancient Hebrew to Yiddish. The *Melamed* spent hours teaching them the prayers — the morning blessings of thanksgiving, the central prayer of *Shema Yisroel* and the *Shmone Esrei* (Eighteen Benedictions), said standing and in silence. Of course, once the students were old enough, *Mishna* and *Gemorah* (together — the *Talmud)* was studied.

The Goldberg farm was so large and Zelig was so busy buying and selling animals and timber that the family could not do all the work necessary to keep the farm running. The Goldbergs employed six full-time non-Jewish workers to help run their 25-hectare farm (62 acres). The farm reached all the way to the forest, far in the distance. They grew wheat, potatoes, and vegetables, selling the produce in nearby towns on market days. The non-Jewish workers were important on *Shabbes* because the Goldberg family stopped all work on Friday before sunset and did not resume until Saturday, at nightfall.

As Zelig and his family wound down their work on Friday afternoon, the smells of baking *challah*, *gefilta* fish, roasted chicken, and potato *kugel* filled the house. Friday afternoon around 2 o'clock, Sam, his father and his three brothers went to Wąsewo to the *Mikve* (ritual bath) to bathe. Walking down the road they would pass their cousin, Mottle Goldberg's home. Sometimes they would stop to say hello to one of Mottle's seven children on the way. At the end of road, they turned right and went another few blocks to Wąsewo. The *Mikve* was a small house on the corner, just a stone's throw from the school and the church. Upon entering the *Mikve* building, the men got undressed and walked down a few steps into the stone-lined bath. The water, warm and inviting, dripped from the cracks between the gray-colored stones. The *Mikve* was large enough to fit Sam, his father and his brothers all at once. They returned home, clean and ready for *Shabbes*.

As the sun lowered in the sky, Zelig changed from his work clothes into his black, double-breasted silk *Kapote* that reached down, just below his knees. Some men of Bagatele, like Zelig, wore a *Kapote* on *Shabbes,* while others wore the more modern short jacket with a tie. The women of Bagatele saved their most stylish clothes for *Shabbes*. Some wore mid-calf length skirts or silk dresses — some with bows around the neck, others with large lace collars. While the women remained at home on Friday night, the men gathered in the large main room of the Goldberg home to welcome *Shabbes* with song and prayer. They sat at the same long wooden table that Sam and his friends sat to study with the *Melamed*. Faiga, Raizel and little Henya enjoyed listening to the men as they sang *Lecha Dodi*, a poem welcoming *Shabbes*.

After services, the house quieted down, and the Goldberg family was left to enjoy their *Shabbes* meal. Sitting at the head of the table, Zelig chanted the *Kiddush*, sanctifying the day and shared sweet wine with the whole family. In between the gossip of the week and thoughts on the weekly *Torah* Portion,* Itche led the family in *Zmiros*, ancient multi-verse songs in honor of *Shabbes*.

Saturday mornings, the Jews of Bagatele once again joined together in the Goldberg home and raised their voices in prayer and song. During the morning services, Zelig removed the *Torah* scroll from the simple wooden *Aron* (Ark) and laid it out on the *Shulchan* (the table). Yossel, their neighbor, chanted the weekly *Torah* portion. Zelig beamed with pride. This *Torah* scroll had been passed down through so many generations of Goldbergs that no one could remember who the first was to obtain it. When the reading was complete, the *Torah* was held aloft for all to see the Hebrew letters, hand-written in special black ink with a quill. The two sides of parchment were rolled back together, and the *Torah* was wrapped in its velvet dressing and placed back into the *Aron*. The women also came to the Goldbergs on *Shabbes* morning, wearing embroidered shawls and scarves imported from Turkey. They purchased the scarves in Ostrow and called them "*Shul* (Synagogue) scarves." After services, other families filtered back to their homes and the Goldberg family gathered for lunch of *Challah, Gefilta* fish and *Chulent* (traditional warm stew, made of potatoes, beans and meat, left to cook all night).

After *benchin* (grace after meal), lunch was cleared and Sam joined his father and brothers at the big dining room table. The afternoon passed as they studied the weekly *Torah* portion or a section of *Gemorah*. Some days their neighbor, Yossel, would come and join in their lively discussions of ancient texts. With the setting of the sun marking the end of *Shabbes*, the busy farm life resumed. The animals were hungry and there were chores to do.

Sam was not yet *Bar Mitzvah* when his oldest brother — Hersh Mayer — got married and moved to a house across the small, dirt road. The Goldberg farm stretched out on both sides of the road. On one side — all the way to the forest

---

* Each week a portion of the *Torah* (Genesis, Exodus, Leviticus, Numbers, and Deuteronomy) is read in *Shul* (Synagogue) on *Shabbes*, such that the entire *Torah* is read over the course of a year.

— and on the other side, another 300 meters. Hersh Mayer and his wife shared their wooden house with the Goldberg cows. One half of the house was home to the new couple and the other half, separated by a thick wall, was home to the Goldberg cows.

Bittersweet emotions raced through Sam when Raizel was the next to get married. She married a barber from the town of Długosiodło, just 16 kilometers (10 miles) away. When Raizel moved to Długosiodło, Sam missed his beloved sister. For as long as Sam could remember, Raizel was a loving, ever-present figure in his life. Raizel promised to visit often and invited "her Shmulke" to their new home.

Itche, not yet married, kept the rest of the family entertained. He danced and sang his way through the day of farm chores. He was good at everything. Itche began trading like his father, but he traded in mushrooms. He traveled to Germany and bought a special kind of mushroom and brought them back to Poland selling them at a profit. When Itche married, he didn't move far. He rented a home from the Kazimierczyk family, two doors down from his parents.

At age 14 or 15, Sam began to help his father full time. With a natural head for business, Sam went with his father to nearby towns to buy and sell cows, chickens, and other farm animals. Often Sam and Zelig went together to negotiate the purchase of a stand of timber from a nearby estate.

One of Zelig's business deals was a partnership with the Polish Army. There was a military base in Komorow, near Ostrow Mazowiecka, and Zelig provided the army with a steady supply of animals for food. One day, Zelig gave Sam 1000 Złotys* and instructed him to go to a nearby town, where his brother Yankel lived to purchase cows for the Polish army.

"If you pay too much, you pay too much, don't be afraid," his father told him. "Just go buy animals and Yankel will help you out."

Sam did the deal and brought back the cows. He learned how to bargain and get a good price. This skill served him well in many a situation.

Sam was in his late teens when his younger sister, Henya, was married. It was

---

*   Polish currency.

a celebration to remember. His aunt, Miriam Schloss, came from Jasienitz (pronounced Yashinetz) and his *Tante** Esther Fleisher, from Komorow. Henya married a man named Idul** from a town nearby.

Meanwhile, Raizel was having a hard life in her new home. She and her husband had children, but many of them died young. It broke Sam's heart to see the pain of these children and the sorrow in the face of his beautiful, kind sister.

During those years, Sam and Zelig often went to Ostrow, a town of 20,000, of whom 8,000 were Jews. It was perhaps on a sunny spring day that Sam and Zelig filled their buggy with grain and set out on the dirt road. Their first stop was to pay a visit to Kalman Kagan and the Trejster brothers — owners of the "Automat" — a steam mill that produced some of the finest flour in all of Poland. The "Automat" transformed wheat into flour, fetching top dollar on the Warsaw, Canadian, and even Australian markets. Upon entering the mill, the deafening noise of the steam engine made it hard to be heard.

"*Shalom Aleichem*,"*** Zelig shouted.

Kalman was the first to hear him. His face broke into a smile. He was always happy to see Zelig of Bagatele. He gestured to Zelig to step outside to talk.

"*Aleichem sholom*,"**** Kalman responded. "Good to see you *Reb* Zelig. I see you brought us some of your excellent wheat."

After the small talk was out of the way, they bargained a fair price. Within days Kalman and his partner would turn Zelig's wheat into fine flour. It would be shipped to markets near and far.

With a pocketful of cash and an empty buggy, father and son headed into town. It was Monday, a market day in Ostrow. Faiga, Sam's mother, sent them with a long list of things to buy. Entering Ostrow from the outskirts where the Automat was located, Sam saw boys trying to catch fish in the local pond. The blue of the water matched the blue sky on that spring day. They passed the brewery, which supplied the people of Ostrow with "Das Bier" one of their favorite beverages and filled the air with that unique smell of brewing yeast.

---

*   Yiddish for Aunt.
**   Idul is diminutive for Yehuda and is pronounced "Edu".
*** Meaning "peace to you" — a common Hebrew/Yiddish greeting.
****The common response meaning "unto you peace."

Entering the main part of town, their buggy rambled along the cobblestones. The flat stones with grass planted between, provided a smooth ride. Sam noticed the low, simple wooden houses, built close together. He couldn't imagine living so close to his neighbors. In Bagatele, the houses were spread out along the dirt road and among the farms, barns and silos. Plenty of space.

The cobblestone road led to the town square, their horse just had to follow behind the other buggies. Some buggies were empty — driven by people coming to purchase, like Zelig and Sam. Others, driven by peasants from nearby villages, were overloaded with grain, fruit, vegetables, cabbage, geese, turkeys, hens and eggs, ready to sell to the eager buyers. They passed villagers heading to the market on foot, carrying empty baskets, ready to fill them with butter, cheese, sweet cream, cherries, strawberries, or a whole chicken.

Craftsmen's booths filled the square. Each type of merchant had a distinctive look and a special location in the market. The tailors' stalls looked like houses with linen walls. Near the tailors' shops were smaller stalls where the cap makers sold their goods. These stalls were full of caps with "all sorts of lacquered brims."[4] You didn't have to walk far to reach the stalls where shoes and boots were hanging from poles. Tables were filled with loaves of bread, white rolls, sugar beets, pails and bottles of soda water with syrup, sour pickles and herring. Glasses and dishes were laid out on the ground for purchase.

Zelig and Sam tied the horse up on the side of the square and headed into the happy chaos. Paying close attention to Faiga's list, they visited the fruit merchants and bought apples, pears, and Sam's younger sister Henya's favorite — green gooseberries. The vegetable stalls had small wooden barrels or round, deep baskets that overflowed with red beets, yellow carrots, black and red radishes, and mushrooms of many shapes and sizes. Sam helped his father pick the best to take back to the family.[5]

Just on the other side of the street, permanent shops were scattered among modest wooden homes. There were shops to buy clothing, leather goods, kerosene, paint, and groceries. They made a quick stop at the kerosene shop to keep the lamps at home burning at night. In the 1930's Ostrow was powered by electricity, but this new technology had not yet made it to the countryside.

After the items on Faiga's list were strapped into their buggy, Sam and Zelig stopped by a small café to grab some lunch. After lunch, they visited the *Shtiebel* of the *Gerrer Hasidim* to daven *Mincha* (afternoon prayer). There were many *Shuls* in Ostrow, the larger ones were populated by *Misnagdim,* traditionalists who focused on textual learning and intellectual prowess. They were adamantly opposed to the changes made by the *Hasidim* and viewed them as a danger to traditional Judaism.[6] The smaller *Shtieblach* were populated by the *Hasidim,* who were followers of the Baal Shem Tov, the 18th century Hasidic master. They believed "faith and emotional expression to be more important than learning."[7] *Hasidim* would sing and dance during prayer to express their belief in God and Judaism.

The *Hasidim* and the *Misnagdim* constantly battled for control of the Jewish community of Ostrow. These feuds led to battles over who should be the town Rabbi. But for a few exceptional Rabbis who garnered support from all sectors, either the *Hasidim* would make the *Misnagdishe* Rabbi's life miserable or the *Misnagdim* would make the *Hasidishe* Rabbi's life a nightmare. With such strife, the Rabbis didn't last long in Ostrow.[8]

Before heading home, they drove their buggy to the nearby town of Komorow to visit *Tante* Esther Fleisher and her husband Yankel. *Tante* Esther, Faiga's sister, was a successful businesswoman. There was a military school and base in Komorow and *Tante* Esther sold military uniforms to the graduating officers. Many a young man passed through *Tante* Esther's shop, walking out well fitted in a crisp new uniform. Though *Tante* Esther and her husband had no children she loved her nieces and nephews and was always happy to see them.

During the late 1930's Jewish life in the Ostrow area continued to blossom. One movement that expanded rapidly was the Zionist movement. With the death of Theodor Herzl, the Hungarian-born founder of modern political Zionism, people throughout Europe took up the mantle. There were many stripes of Zionism in towns such as Ostrow. For example, the religious *Mizrachi* party believed that Jewish nationalism was a way to achieve religious objectives. *Poalei Tziyon* (Workers of Zion) had a Marxist — class struggle ideology, believing that an independent Jewish socialist-national state should be created in Palestine.

There were of course, anti-Zionist groups in Ostrow as well. For example, the *Bund,* a secular group, was devoted to Yiddish language and culture and secular nationalism in Poland, not Palestine. On the other side of the religious spectrum, there was the *Agudah,* ultra-orthodox Jews who would never recognize a secular Jewish State.

These movements and other Jewish and Yiddish organizations strengthened the Polish Jewish communities in the 1920's and 1930's. While the 1930's brought persecution and turmoil to German Jews, Polish Jews lived in relative peace. But war was on the horizon. On August 23, 1939, the German Foreign Minister, Joachim von Ribbentrop, traveled to Moscow and signed a non-aggression pact with the Soviet Union. Politburo member, Viacheslav Molotov, signed the pact on behalf of the Soviet Union. Germany and the Soviet Union secretly agreed to attack Poland from opposite sides and split control of the country. The line drawn on the map, setting the border was called the "Molotov-Ribbentrop Line."

The German invasion of Poland occurred on September 1, 1939.[9] It did not take long for the war to reach the people of Ostrow. Bombs fell, shattering windows, sending layers of thick dust through the air and terrifying residents. Eight days later Nazi tanks rolled into town. Within a few days of their arrival, the Nazis ordered the Jewish merchants to open their shops. The Nazis went into the shops and warehouses and handed out all the goods to the local Poles, who were eager to receive their booty of sugar, salt, rice — to name a few.[10] The first week saw the destruction of Jewish businesses and the torture and killing of many Jews.

Yom Kippur, the holiest day of the Jewish calendar, fell on September 24, 1939. The Nazis had already destroyed most of the *Shuls* and *Shtieblach* in Ostrow. Most Jews went down to their cellars to pray. But there was one *Shtiebel* still standing — the *Gerrer Shtiebel.* On the evening of *Yom Kippur,* the *Gerrer Hasidim* waited until dark and then made their way to the *Shtiebel.* Wearing the traditional *Kittel* (white robe) and *Tallis* (prayer shawl), they began to intone the *Kol Nidrei,* the opening prayer of *Yom Kippur* eve. As soon as the prayers began, the Nazis stormed the *Shtiebel* and surrounded it, cutting off all means of escape. "The Jews were dragged out and thrown into the trucks," described Jakob Widelec. "They were driven down ulica Warszawska to the *sadzavka* [natural

Siedlce, a town near Ostrow Mazowiecka after Nazi invation. Credit: Chris Webb Private Archive.

water basin or pond]. A lot of dirty trucks were parked there and the Jews were given the honour [sic] of cleaning them. They were forced to remove their white robes, prayer shawls and even their clothing and go into the dirty water halfway, wet all their things and wash the trucks with them. When the work was done, all the men were ordered to go into the water again, until it was over their heads. When they came out from the filth, the Germans cut off all their hair. Some of the men had half their beards ripped from their faces. Then they were photographed and ordered to go home."[11]

While Ostrow was in the German-controlled area of Poland, the border designated by the Molotov-Ribbentrop Line was only sixteen kilometers (10 miles) away. The Nazis forcefully suggested that the Jews leave town. They left in droves, many heading to either Slonim or Bialystok, both well-established Jewish communities on the Soviet side of the border.

The Jews who remained in Ostrow did not survive. In November of 1939, a Jewish home caught fire and the fire spread to other parts of town. The Germans blamed the Jewish homeowner, saying he burned down his own house and caused all this damage and must be punished. With the Poles pointing out which homes belonged to Jews, the Germans broke down the doors, grabbed the Jews, and forced them to march to the forest. There, the Nazis shot three to four hundred people. Such was their punishment.[12]

When the war broke out, the Jews of Bagatele didn't know what to think. In the last war, the Germans weren't so bad to the Jews. But that was a different kind of war.

"The Germans are coming," Mayor Załęski, told Zelig, "and when they come, they will take the young men into the army and they will burn and kill all the Jews."

Terrified, Zelig and his family gathered to discuss what to do.

Stoczek — the Early Years

1930'S

As the early morning sun shone through the window, Esther Wisznia awoke on a fall day in the late 1930's. It was cool in Stoczek, Poland, but not yet cold. The window was open, and the morning breeze flowed through the house. It was quiet. Their house was at the end of a narrow, paved street. No one ventured down to the end of this road unless they were coming to their house — or the neighbor's. The road was so narrow that only one horse-pulled wagon could travel on the road at a time — no room to pass.

Esther glanced to her left and saw the familiar face of her little sister, Sheina, lying next to her in the bed. As they got out of the bed, their feet touched the smooth wooden floor. They tucked the sheets and blankets around the pull-out bed and pushed it back up on the wall where it would remain until nighttime. It was very convenient because the house had just one large room with an alcove. Stored for the day, the bed took up very little space. Their oldest brother, Yisroel Yoseph, was still asleep on a cot in the middle of the room. He was home from *Yeshiva*, a place of Jewish learning for older boys. He spent his days studying *Mishna, Gemorah, Chumash* and other Jewish texts.

On the opposite side of the room was a long wooden table. Esther loved that table. When she ran her fingers over the surface, it felt smooth and somehow comforting. The light brown color reminded her of the milk chocolate in the candy store. It was where they ate, studied, sewed, played cards and other games, and did just about everything. During the day, the family table transformed into a desk for the young, elementary school children who came to her father's *Cheder*. Shlomo Zalman Wisznia was a *Melamed* and he welcomed his students to his home daily. At 5 feet, 3 inches, Shlomo Zalman was not tall, but his slim body filled his *Kapote* (long silk black coat), conferring a regal appearance. He wore a large black *Kippa* (skull cap) that took up his whole head — the kind often worn by old-style *Chazanim* (cantors). His black hair, cropped short, was visible on the sides and back of his head. His black beard was short, reaching just a few inches down from his chin. The children spent hours in his home learning to read Hebrew and Yiddish, studying *Chumash* and praying in the way of their ancestors.

Bracha and Reb Shlomo Zalman Wisznia. Reprinted from Pinkas Stok – Stoczek Yizkor (Memorial) Book, 592.

Sheina and Esther went to the alcove to see if their parents were awake. Their father shared his bed with their brother Leizer Yitzchak and their mother slept with the baby — Shimon. They found their mother, Bracha, awake, dressing the baby. She was a trim, petite woman, standing a few inches shorter than her husband. Her hair was covered by a simple wig, as was the custom of religious women and she wore a practical plaid smock dress that gave her a look of simple preparedness for what the day would bring.

"Go get dressed girls and then we'll prepare breakfast," Bracha said as she saw her daughters.

But, what to wear? Esther touched each of the handmade weekday dresses in the small closet. She made them all herself. They were simple, but stylish, reaching down below the knee, with a flare at the bottom. The plaid one was nice, but the gray one with buttons down the front was more practical for the day ahead — studying at *Beis Yaakov*, helping her mother with cooking and household chores and finding some time to sew a few shirts to sell in the Stoczek market. She longingly looked at her more stylish and beautiful *Shabbes* dresses. The blue one, with rounded white lace collar, showed off her brown hair. The maroon one with buttons down the front was a favorite — it had a long ribbon attached to the collar that turned into a bow, just above the buttons. They would have to wait until Friday night or Saturday. Their mother entered the big room and saw Yisroel Yoseph sleeping.

"Wake up," she whispered, "it is time to go to *Shul* for *Shacharis* (morning prayers). Your father will be ready in a moment."

The *Shul* was not far — they just had to step out of the door, turn left, walk past seven or eight houses to reach the big road. At the corner, just where Chana's bakery stood, they turned and went down two blocks. This street was wider — two horse-pulled wagons could easily pass. At this hour of the morning, the foot traffic was headed towards the *Shul* — a large two-story brick building, covered with white stucco. Esther's younger brother, Leizer Yitzchak, also walked with his father and Yisroel Yosef. His destination was not the *Shul*, but the town well, which stood just next door. He dipped the bucket down the dark deep well and carried home water for breakfast. Sometimes the Wisznia family got water delivered to their house by the *wasser treiger* (water carrier). But he charged for his services, so they took turns making the trek to the well.

As Shlomo Zalman and Yisroel Yoseph entered the large wooden doors of the *Shul*, they first passed through the section reserved for women and then found themselves in the large space where the men sat. Clasping their worn *Siddurim* (prayer books), they strapped their *Tefillin* (phylacteries) on their heads and around their arms, counting seven wraps of the leather straps up and down their arm. Shlomo Zalman wrapped himself in his *Tallis* — the woolen prayer shawl worn by married men. He glanced at the *Aron* (Ark) at the front of the room, such a large beautiful *Aron* made of dark wood. He could almost see the *Torah* scrolls inside — beyond the curtain, beyond the wooden door. He visualized the *Torah*, dressed in velvet cloth and adorned with silver breastplates. Just in front of the *Aron* stood a *Shulchan (*table*)* also covered with velvet cloth. This was where the *Torah* was laid, unrolled, and the weekly portion read each *Shabbes*. A shorter section was read on Monday and Thursday mornings. But today was Tuesday and Shlomo Zalman would not hear the chant of the words of the *Torah* — it would remain sequestered in its treasure box.

Back at home, Esther and her mother were busy preparing breakfast, while the younger children played. The kitchen took up an entire wall of the big room. They had all they needed to prepare meals for their family of seven — a small counter, pots and pans, and eating utensils. They fried some eggs and put some brown bread with butter on the table. When Shlomo Zalman and Yisroel Yoseph came home from *Shul*, the family sat down and ate together. The chatter was about the day ahead. The younger children were off to school — Polish public school. Esther had already completed the seventh grade — the highest grade she could attend. She wanted to attend High School, but it was out of her reach — it cost too much and besides, Jewish children had a hard time getting in. Esther did continue to attend *Beis Yaakov* — a school for girls where she received a formal Jewish education, learning Hebrew, Yiddish, and *Chumash*.

Informal education abounded. Esther's cousin taught her to sew. She learned to sew shirts, underwear, brassieres, and dresses.

"Don't make dresses," her mother, Bracha, told her, "there is not enough money in it for the time it takes to make them. There are too many headaches."

Heeding her mother's advice, Esther made shirts and underwear and sold them on market days in the Stoczek town square. When she sewed dresses, she kept them for herself and her sister, Sheina. Her mother also taught her to cook and take care of the home.

After breakfast, Esther and her mother cleaned up and pushed the large table against the wall — ready for the students to arrive. Perhaps it was time for Esther to walk to *Beis Yaakov*. She closed the door of the house and turned her head for a last look at their small wooden home. Noticing the slanted roof, she recalled the time she and Leizer Yitzchak climbed up to the triangular space in the attic.

There wasn't much room, but there was enough space to play a game of cards. The chimney protruded out of the sloping roof where smoke escaped the *pripichik* (hearth). She looked forward to winter just so she could sleep on top of the *pripichik*. It kept her warm, even after the embers extinguished.

She walked to the corner where Chana's bakery stood. Oh, she loved to walk by Chana's bakery. The sweet smell of yeasted breads, buns, and other delicacies, hit her nostrils as she turned the corner. She could almost taste the sweet cinnamon and vanilla. Of all the family chores, the one Esther loved the most was to run to Chana's bakery and buy fresh bread, a sticky bun, or a *mandel broit,* a hard-crusted almond cookie. As Esther passed by the bakery on her way to school, she often looked in the window and saw Chana bending down to give her son, Moishe, a roll with butter. When she saw the love in Chana's eyes as she leaned over her young son, Esther would smile and think of her own mother.

On Fridays, Esther delighted when her mother would ask her to take the twisted loaves of unbaked *Challah* down the street. Chana welcomed the women of Stoczek to bake their *Shabbes Challahs* in her large oven. Then, just as the sun was setting and *Shabbes* was about to begin, Stokers would stop at Chana's bakery — sometimes on the way to *Shul,* sometimes just before lighting the *Shabbes* candles — and place their sturdy *Chulent* pots, filled with beans, potatoes, and meat, into Chana's large oven where it would cook all night. On the way home from *Shul,* someone in the family would stop by the bakery and, wrapping the pot in a heavy towel so as not to burn themselves, would carry the warm *Chulent* with its smell of *Shabbes,* home for the afternoon meal.

Turning the corner, Esther hit the big road leading to the town square. At this early hour, it was quiet, but in her mind's eye she saw the square on market days — filled with people and tables piled high with fruit, vegetables, chickens, pots, and clothing. She would come and set up a table, selling the clothes she made. Market days were exciting — Christians and Jews together — buying and selling, yelling and *handlin* (bargaining/trading). She crossed over the empty square to her teacher's home where the *Beis Yaakov* school was located. It was just a block off the square near the red brick Catholic Church. The Church had two large steeples rising high in the air and a huge round stained-glass window in the front. She had never been inside — it was forbidden for Jews. But she had a few Catholic friends from school who attended this Church.

As she walked, she passed some of her fellow Stokers. The men were mostly dressed in suits and fashionable skinny ties. Many wore a cap, others wore a *Kippa,* and yet others were bare-headed. A few were dressed, as her father, in a *Kapote.* As she passed, she nodded to the many people that she knew.

After school, Esther stopped for a drink at the soda factory owned and operated by the Kwiatek family. Her parents gave her a coin each day to buy a soda. The soda factory was a favorite place for everyone in Stoczek, but especially the young people. The soda was bubbly and cold, tickling her nose. Flavors, such as watermelon or strawberry, could be added. With a flavor added, the sweet wetness hit her lips and a bit of heaven ran down her throat.

Having quenched her thirst, Esther crossed the town square, heading home. She spent the afternoon helping her mother with chores and sewing. As evening approached, the house filled with the smell of dinner simmering on the stove. The family sat around the big table and told each other about their day. It made the small house feel warm, even when the temperature dropped outside. In the evenings, the home was illuminated by candles and kerosene lamps. Esther and Sheina pulled their wall bed down and used the water in the basin to wash themselves. To use the toilet, they had to venture outdoors, which was most unpleasant in the cold weather. There were no bathing facilities in the home, so she and Sheina went with their mother once a week to the *Mikve* where the women of the *Shtetl* would bathe. The men had a turn to wash themselves at the *Mikve* as well, but on a different day.

Though their home was small, Esther's paternal grandparents lived with them until 1932. Rivka, her grandmother, died when she was seven or eight and Mordechai Gronim, her grandfather, died when she was twelve. Esther's father, Shlomo Zalman, was an only child. His parents raised him to be an educated, hard-working man. His work as a *Melamed* and a *Shoichet* (ritual slaughterer) didn't make him rich, but there was enough for the family to make do.

Esther's maternal grandparents lived in the nearby town of Wengrow, twenty-three kilometers (14 miles) away. They had no horse and buggy, so travel was hard. Esther only met her grandfather — Moshe Nisim Silvernagle — once. Esther was named for her maternal grandmother who died before she was born. On her mother's side, Esther had two aunts and three uncles, but she didn't know them well, as they lived in different Polish towns.

In the small house, the *Shabbes* candlesticks sat ever-ready on the mantle, waiting for the 7th day to arrive. When it came, activity would slow as they put on their best clothes. On Friday at sundown, the men went to *Shul*. The house was filled with the soft glow of the candles and smell of chicken and *kugel*. The two *Challahs*, baked to a perfect golden brown at Chana's, sat waiting, covered, on the smooth brown table, to be eaten only after the family gathered and made the blessings on the sweet red wine and then thanking God for bringing bread forth from the earth. As the family slept, Bracha's *Chulent* simmered in the communal oven at Chana's. The arrival of the *Chulent* after *Shul* in the morning was a moment of delight for the whole family. The rich aroma, sweet and savory in the same inhalation, filled the small home with a comforting bouquet that could only mean that *Shabbes* day arrived and the meal would be hearty, warm and filling. On *Shabbes* they would sit around the table a bit longer, singing *Zmiros* and talking about the weekly *Torah* portion. No work was done; it was a day to enjoy family, food, and friends.

Esther loved to sing. Singing together with her brothers and sister at the *Shabbes* table was one of the joys of her life. In the afternoon, she would get together with friends, walk and converse about the things teenage girls talk about — fashion, school, parents, and of course boys. Esther, now in her late teen years, had a boyfriend — Moishe Kwiatek — of the soda factory family. Moishe was short — just a bit taller than Esther's towering four feet, eleven inches. He was broad and stocky, with a full head of dark hair. He dressed in fine modern clothes. They took long walks in the forest and often went to the town library to get books. Their library had many books translated into Yiddish, even books by Tolstoy.

They may have known each other from their youth group — *Hashomer Hatzair*. They both loved attending their youth group. They had special uniforms to wear — light colored skirt for the girls and pants for the boys. A scarf was tied around the neck — scout-style. *Hashomer Hatzair* was a socialist/Zionist group. Esther loved hearing the speakers who traveled 90 kilometers (55 miles) from Warsaw. They seemed so sophisticated. They talked about Palestine and what it would be like to settle on a *Kibbutz* and work the land. Along with Zionism, the speakers emphasized personal fulfillment and education. There were of course, rival youth groups, such as the *Bund*, *Poalei Zion,* and the Scouts. Only the Scouts and *Hashomer Hatzair* had special uniforms worn to each meeting.

Sometimes there were parties. To celebrate the end of 1938 and the beginning of 1939, some of Esther's friends planned a New Year's Eve party. She had just turned 18 and was desperate to go, but her father forbade it. After dark, she snuck out of the house and went to the party. When it was over, she reentered her home and slipped into bed with Sheina. Her parents never found out. Esther was sure that when the Germans attacked Poland on September 1, 1939, it was her fault. She should never have disobeyed her father and gone to the New Year's Eve party. She was the cause of this terrible event.

The war hit Stoczek when bombs started falling on September 1, 1939. Esther learned that one of the first bombs fell into the house of Hershel Skerupke and killed him and with his wife, Itte Rosa. Their three children survived by exiting through the *hinter tier* — a kind of back or trap door that was in their kitchen. No one could say how many died from these early bombing raids, but houses and buildings were destroyed all over town.

German troops stormed Stoczek just a few days after those first bombs fell. The Jews of Stoczek were defenseless against the overwhelming power and might of the German army and the terrors they wrought. The Polish army was nowhere to be seen — not a single Polish soldier came to help the residents of this *Shtetl.*

The Nazis came into the town square shooting and screaming at the people to get out of the stores, into the open square. All the Jews the Nazis could find were forced to gather. The Nazis began burning down shops and homes. Then, the Nazi yelled *"raus"*— "get out." As they ran, the Nazis began to shoot. Half of them were shot dead before they could reach the safety of their homes. There was no safe place to run. Then the Nazis began burning down homes.

Esther, her parents, and her siblings heard the Nazis yelling outside. At first, they smelled smoke and burning; then they saw flames and realized that their house was on fire. They each grabbed a few things and ran out of the burning house. They tried to hide from the Nazi marauders as they watched their home burn. Smoke and ash filled the air, it was hard to breath. Stunned and shocked, Shlomo Zalman and Bracha were at a loss; they didn't know what to do or where to go. So many in town were now like them — without a home, without anything. Running to a neighbor's home that was still standing, they were welcomed. That evening, they sat together and through the tears, they discussed what would happen with the Germans now in control of their *Shtetl*. They had no idea what the future held, but they feared that life under the Germans would not be easy.

Flight from the Farm

SEPTEMBER 1939-JUNE 1941

German bombs exploded. Polish cities and towns were upended by the destruction. Nazis attacked Western Poland, by air and by land, killing Polish intelligentsia and Jews. Homes and buildings were burned, destroyed. Bagatele, a small farming village, off the beaten path, was not a German target in the opening week of the war. But the Mayor's warning was ringing in Zelig Goldberg's ears.

It was decided. The children would leave — head to the German-Soviet border that now split Poland in half. Hersh Meyer, Raizel, Itche, their spouses, and children prepared for the journey. Henya and her husband, Idul, had already left for Russia. Packing some clothes and food — only what they could carry — they got ready for the journey. Their goal was to travel 260 kilometers (161 miles) to Slonim, a town of 15,000. It had a strong and diverse Jewish community. There was a good timber industry there and the Goldberg children knew about timber.

Within days, they loaded the buggy and said their goodbyes to Faiga and Sam. Zelig gave a shake of the horse's reins and headed east. The border wasn't far, maybe 15 kilometers (9.3 miles). Zelig watched as half of his family walked across the border, making the German-controlled territory just a bit more *Judenrein* (clean of Jews).

Zelig was adamant that he didn't want to leave his home. And he especially didn't want to cross the border and live under the Soviet Bolsheviks. He opposed the Communist collectivization of farms. Also, he was a *Kulak* — one who owned a small farm and animals. Zelig knew well that the Bolsheviks hated *Kulaks* and killed them or sent them to Siberia. After a *Kulak* was sent away, the Communists stole his land. Even though Zelig's land was under German control and the Communists couldn't take it, he didn't want to voluntarily put himself in the hands of the Bolsheviks.

Yankel came home to Bagatele, from the nearby town where he lived with his wife. He and Sam also decided to heed the Mayor's words. They jumped on their bikes and rode towards the Soviet border. They got as far as the *Shtetl* Bodke. But Sam developed a kidney stone and was in so much pain, he could travel no further. Yankel spent "a fortune" and bought a horse and buggy to get Sam back home. Yankel loaded Sam and their bikes onto the buggy. Worried that German troops or armed Polish civilians would steal his horse and buggy, Yankel hammered a nail into the foot of the horse. No one would want to steal or confiscate an injured horse. With a handicapped horse, they hobbled their way home, arriving just before *Yom Kippur*. Relief flooded through Faiga and Zelig when Sam and Yankel returned. They had worried that the worst had happened. Yankel headed back to his wife to regroup and decide what to do next. Sam passed the kidney stone and, feeling better, stayed with his parents on the farm. That *Yom Kippur*, their prayers were mixed with tears, uncertainties and worries.

Soon, letters arrived from Slonim with descriptions of how thousands of Jews were flooding the city. They told of how they shared an apartment with other refugees. Food was in short supply, even on the black market.

"Please send food and especially sugar," they wrote, "with sugar we can get anything."

Sam knew that the border was still open, but it was illegal to transport food across the border. He had heard that if the Soviets caught you smuggling food, they would send you to Siberia. Sam was not afraid. At first, he took the train to Slonim with packages of food hidden in his bag. But then the trains were confiscated by the German army and were off limits to civilians. His only way to Slonim was by horse and buggy. It was a long and dangerous path, through both

German and Soviet-controlled lands. Sam built a secret compartment under the floor boards of his buggy where he placed food and sugar — "as much as I could fit" — he later explained. In this way, Sam delivered the goods to his siblings.

At first, the decision to stay on the farm in Bagatele seemed like a good one. Life was peaceful, and Zelig continued to manage his farm and trade with the locals. As October turned to November, Zelig and Faiga could not stop thinking about the Jews murdered in Ostrow and they wondered how long they would be safe in German-controlled land. They sat up late one night talking and decided that it would be wise to move to Soviet-controlled territory. Faiga had relatives in Kowalówka (pronounced Kovalovka) — not far from the border.

"Let's go to Kowalówka," Faiga said. "At least we will be with family."

Faiga spent hours deciding what to take and what to sell. They sold many things but decided not to sell the farm or the house; they hoped to return to it after the war. Then, one day in late November or early December, a German soldier arrived on the farm. Terrified, Zelig and Sam went outside to see what he wanted.

"Can I help you?" Zelig asked.

'Jid (Jew)," the Nazi soldier responded, "you must leave. Go to the Soviet side."

"Why must we leave?" Zelig asked.

"Because you are smelly Jews," the Nazi replied, "and we don't want you here. Fill your buggy and go. You can take the horse — that's it."

"Let us take our cows," Sam pleaded.

"No," the officer replied.

"Let us take just one cow!" Sam said beginning to cry.

"Ok," the officer agreed, "which one do you want?"

"I'll take this one," Sam said.

The cow was tied by rope to their buggy and they loaded their boxes and suitcases into the cart and Zelig tucked all the money he had deep into his pants. Although the Nazi didn't search Zelig's body, he searched the buggy before they departed. He found something he liked — the sterling silver Passover cutlery. It was beautiful. The German removed it from the box, but he left the rest of their things. Everyday utensils and pots were not fine enough for the Nazi to bother with.

As Sam, Faiga, and Zelig left, they said goodbye to their farm, their other cows, chickens, their silos filled with wheat from the summer harvest, and their sacred *Torah* scroll left alone in the house, inside its wooden Ark. With Sam walking by their side, Faiga and Zelig drove the buggy down the dirt road, heading east. It took only three hours to travel the thirteen kilometers (8 miles) to the border, but it was as if a lifetime had passed. They sighed in relief when they crossed the border into Soviet-controlled territory, without incident. The three newest Goldberg refugees continued for another four or five hours, traversing another 20 kilometers (12 miles), to reach the *dorf* (farming village) of Kowalówka.

Faiga was sad and scared to leave the farm and all she and Zelig had built in Bagatele. The future was so uncertain. However, this territory was familiar. Kowalówka, was only two kilometers (1.2 miles) from the town where she grew up — Jasienitz. Her father, Avrohom Mischler and his brother had settled in Jasienitz. Her sister, Miriam, married Reb Yankev Schloss and they settled in Jasienitz. They had run a small general store out of their home. The Goldbergs often visited the Schloss family on holidays, especially *Chanuka* and the children visited each other during the summer holiday. Shaya, one of the Schloss's sons was friends with Sam.[13]

At the start of the war, the Germans living in Soviet-controlled areas were ordered home by their government in Berlin.[14] Soviet officials moved into most of the empty houses in Kowalówka. But a few homes remained empty and were taken by displaced Jews. By the time the Goldbergs arrived, a month or two later, all the empty houses were occupied. So, they rented a large room in a farm house belonging to a Christian "*Volksdeutsche*" family, who were Soviet citizens of German ancestry.[15] The Christian couple had three daughters. Knowing that the Goldbergs were Jews, the couple allowed them to keep their kosher food separate and cook in the kitchen. The father took a liking to Sam right away.

"I want you to marry one of my daughters," the father told Sam.

Sam was astonished that this Christian man wanted him, a Jew, to marry one of his daughters. They were good looking women, but Sam was not thinking of marriage in these troubled times. He was happy to be friends with these young women, but he had no intention of marrying any of them.

Picture of Schloss Family taken in Jasienitz, Poland in 1934. Top Row – Left to Right: Yitzchak Schloss; Pola (Paya) Schloss; Shmulke (Sam) Goldberg. Middle Row: Bubbe Sheina Ruchel Mischler; Miriam Mischler Schloss; Yankev (Jacob) Schloss. Bottom Row: Shaya Schloss; Klara Schloss. Credit: Shaya Schloss.

The Soviets didn't allow Jewish refugees, who lived so close to the German-Soviet border, to become Soviet citizens. The only way Jewish residents of this area could be granted citizenship was if they could produce a witness to testify that they lived in this area before the war. A Christian woman who knew Faiga's relatives testified on their behalf and said that the Goldberg family had lived in Kowalówka before the war. So shortly after they settled in Kowalówka, Zelig, Faiga, and Sam applied for and received Soviet citizenship. With Soviet citizenship and passports secured, they had some assurance that they would not be shipped off to Siberia and Sam had a chance to get a job.

Sam secured a job as a postman. Using his family's horse and buggy, he delivered mail in Jasienitz, Kowalówka, and the surrounding towns, even in the bitter cold. He got paid by the Soviet government and supported himself and his parents.

The spring of 1940 arrived and the frozen earth thawed. Just before Passover, Sam, along with other young Jewish men, received a draft notice from the Soviet army. Most Jewish boys who went into the Soviet army never returned home. Sam's father, Zelig, went straight to the army officials and tried to bribe them to remove Sam from the list. No luck. The best he could do was to extract a promise that when Sam's first tour of duty was over, he would return home. Sam had no choice. He put on a Soviet army uniform and joined a unit. Three-quarters of the young men in the unit were Jewish. Sam was *sapion* — building and repairing bridges.

For over a year, Sam built and repaired bridges for the Soviet army. He thought about his parents all the time. He had never lived away from them. Now, he lived in dirty, ugly barracks and ate food that he wouldn't have served to the animals on his farm.

"A yellow kasha," Sam later explained, "*fershtunkina* (putrid) yellow kasha. It was lying around for twenty years. It stank from a distance and we had to eat it because they had no better."

Then without warning, the Germans breached the nonaggression pact they had signed with the Soviets. On June 22, 1941 they launched Operation Barbarossa, [16] the largest German military operation of the war. It was swift and brutal. While the German planes flew low, dropping bomb after bomb, infantry and tanks arrived to multiply the force effect. Sam's unit was in Ciechanowiec,* just a few kilometers from the German-Soviet border, so it was one of the first to be attacked. He and his fellow soldiers were completely unprepared; they had no armaments to counter attack. Sam was building an unfinished bridge with two or three hundred other soldiers. The bombs fell all around him.

"It was *geferlach*, (unbelievable)," said Sam.

The sounds were deafening and the earth shook. The air was thick with smoke from bombs and blasted earth. The smell of burning trees and human flesh was something Sam had never experienced before and would never forget. Sam hid under the bridge and prayed. He gambled that because it was not a completed bridge, the Germans wouldn't bomb it. His hunch paid off and his half-finished bridge-shelter was spared. He hid there until the guns and bombs died down. When he emerged, he saw so many dead soldiers that they covered up the survivors. All the survivors, including Sam, became prisoners of war.

The Germans built a makeshift Prisoner of War (POW) camp[17] in a wooded area near Zembrow. The camp held hundreds of POWs — Poles, Soviets, and Jews. The first German order to the POW's was to dig graves and bury the thousands of dead soldiers. Then, without food for two days, the exhausted, filthy Soviet soldiers, stood in row after row in a state of shock. Before the attack, the Soviet soldiers believed that Germany was their ally — they had an agreement. But here they stood, facing a new reality.

"All Komosavoltziz [Officers] step out," yelled the German officer.

The Soviet military officers stepped forward and were shot — "ta ta, ta, ta, ta."

"All Politrupin (Political Officers) step out," yelled the officer.

The political officers stepped out of line and were shot — "ta ta ta ta ta."

"All Jews step out," was finally yelled.[18]

Sam stood in line, exhausted, starving, and as he later described, his "life was ugly" and he "didn't want to live anymore." He was ready to step out knowing full well that the shot would come. He hoped it would be quick. But then, Sam's

---

* Ciechanowiec was 34 kilometers (21 miles) from his parents in Kowalówka and 66 kilometers (41 miles) from his family farm in Bagatele.

friend, a large non-Jewish soldier from Kavkaz, Ukraine, forcibly held Sam's arm.

"No, don't go." The Kavkazer said. "Whatever happens to me will happen to you."

"I am too hungry, I want to die," Sam said to the Kavkazer, as he looked at him with his tired, clear blue eyes.

The Ukrainian had a sugar cube in his pocket and slipped it into Sam's mouth. Sam let the sweetness run down his throat and revive his soul. He did not step out.

"Now what?" Sam asked the Kavkazer after the killing was over, "what will happen?"

"At night," 'he whispered," we'll get out. They will be sleeping."

Those left alive after this "liquidation," were miserable. The Germans held them for days without food or water. Then "*jelov*" arrived.

"*Jelov* was broth that was so disgusting, ordinarily we would not have touched the outside of a vessel containing such a thing," Sam later explained. "But now we drank it with a hearty appetite — and we were refreshed by it."

While the Soviet prisoners laid around in a weakened and starving state, the German soldiers ate meat and drank wine, laughing at the prisoners who watched in desperation. It was miserable. But then one night, just as the Kavkazer had promised, he woke up Sam at 2 a.m.:

"Tonight, now, let's escape," the Kavkazer said.

They walked through the throngs of sleeping men to the barbed wire fence at the edge of the camp. The Kavkazer had wire cutters! He cut a hole in the fence and together, with two other Jewish prisoners, they ran out into the woods. Sam knew these woods; he had traveled here with his father to buy timber. He led the way.

Running until they reached an orchard, they stopped — hungry and tired. Shaking a tree, some of the precious fruit fell to the ground. Though it was not yet ripe, they devoured it. Then the owner of the orchard saw them and came over. He saw four men in Soviet army uniforms and was unsure of how to greet them. But then, his eyes flickered with warmth and recognition when he saw Sam.

"Are you perhaps the son of Zelig of Bagatele?" the orchard owner asked.

"Yes, yes, I am," Sam replied.

This man was a Jew and was Zelig's good friend. The orchard owner saw Zelig in Sam's youthful face. He "right away" brought them milk and bread, admonishing them not to eat too fast or too much, since they had not eaten in days. The relief of having food in his stomach could not be measured. Sam looked around and saw a scarecrow in the garden. In the spur of the moment, he switched clothes with the scarecrow, thus creating the first scarecrow dressed as a Soviet-soldier.

Back in the POW camp, dawn arrived and the Germans saw the hole in the fence. Realizing that four prisoners were gone, some officers ran out to try to find the escapees. In the light of the new day, as Sam and his companions sat eating and drinking, they saw three machine gun and grenade-carrying German soldiers running towards the orchard. Terrified, they didn't know which way to run or what to do. The Kavkazer and the two other Jews ran out into the orchard to get away. Sam, realized that there was no way out and he was about to be killed.

"Please, tell my father what happened and take my body out of here," Sam pleaded with the orchard owner.

But Sam did not follow the other soldiers. Instead he hid by a tree, pressing his body so close to the trunk that his flesh memorized every knot and bump. The Germans saw the three running soldiers — easy to spot in their Soviet army uniforms. They threw grenades and killed them. At the sight of these killings, the orchard owner's daughter, standing near Sam, began to wail. Her screams were so loud and desperate that the German soldiers came running over to help her. She fainted. The Germans grabbed a bucket of water and poured it on her face to revive her. Sam stayed pressed next to the tree, dressed in the scarecrow's clothes. The Germans paid him no heed. Their only concern was rescuing the damsel in distress. They told the girl and her father to go into the house. After doing their good deed for the day and finding and shooting the escaped soldiers (or at least three of them), they headed back to the POW camp to report their success.

Sam stood in silence and terror, his breathing low and shallow, as he watched the Nazi soldiers walk away. He couldn't believe the miracle that just happened.

Thanking the orchard owner and his daughter, Sam said he would return to Kowalówka, to find his parents. As he began his journey, he saw Poles running towards a mill that had been set afire by the Germans. This was a wonderful diversion — he joined the running mass of people, drawing no attention to himself. He detoured just before reaching the mill and headed toward Kowalówka. He hoped he would find his parents still alive.

The Eastward Journey

SEPTEMBER 1939–SUMMER 1941

Esther, a young woman of 19, stood with her family, looking at the charred remains of their home. Gone, their house was gone. She was stunned and couldn't name the emotion she felt. Was it anger, fear, sadness, bewilderment? No, it was all of them. For 19 years, this house had been her anchor, her refuge, her home. She could still see the frame of the big room that was at once their home and her father's *Cheder*. It was no more and the Germans were in control of her beloved Stoczek.

They knew they had to leave. But where to? For a few days, Esther and her family stayed with a neighbor whose house was still standing. Esther heard that the Kwiatek soda factory and home were not destroyed. She walked over and found her boyfriend Moishe and the Kwiatek family all alive and indeed, their house and soda factory had been spared. This bit of good news was a welcome relief.

"We are going to leave Stoczek," Esther told Moishe, "and go to Prostyn where we have relatives. It is seventeen kilometers (10.5 miles) away. I will write and let you know what happens to us."

Esther and Moishe didn't know when they would see each other again. They said goodbye and Esther returned to her parents to bundle up the few articles of clothing she had managed to grab from her burning house. Then, she walked with her parents and her siblings away from their town, meeting other refugees on the road. There were no smiles, greetings, or small talk. There were tears and some words of comfort, but otherwise they walked in silence. As they walked out of Stoczek, they passed many burnt-out homes and stores. They passed the *Shul*; it stood empty and cold. Reaching the outskirts of town, Esther walked through the forest where she had played as a child and walked with Moishe, with the stick-like trees standing as tall and green as ever. The forest smelled clean, but there was a hint of decay from the dead leaves that scattered the forest floor. The mushrooms were sticking up among the brush. Esther was sure she heard the trees whisper goodbye.

"I hope to see you again, my trees," she whispered back.

Some people they met on the road were heading to the German-Soviet border to cross and search for safety on the Soviet side. Others like the Wisznias were searching for shelter closer to home. Arriving at Prostyn, Esther was relieved to see that the Germans had not yet attacked here and her relative's home was still standing. The door opened and the warmth of the home flooded her senses. It was hard to believe that normal life could still be happening. They went in and told their tale of horror.

"You are welcome here," their relatives said, "as long as you need."

Poland was now sliced in two, with the Molotov-Ribbentrop Line dividing German-controlled Poland from Soviet-controlled Poland. The German-Soviet border was a mere seven kilometers (4.3 miles) from Prostyn — so close. Esther's brothers, Israel Yosef, now a man of 21 and Eliezer Yitzchak, 17, decided to head east.

"We will cross the border to Bialystok,"[*] they said. "We will write to you from there."

Bialystok, a city approximately 100 kilometers (62 miles) away, was a well-known center of Jewish life. Before the war, it had a population of 100,000, about half of whom were Jews. The Wisznias had heard that many Jews were crossing the border and making their way to Bialystok.

---

[*]   Bialystok is the name of a town in Poland. Bialystok was used by Mel Brooks and Thomas Meehan as the last name of one of the characters in 1968 movie — *The Producers*.

"I will miss you both," Esther said, hugging them.

But life in Prostyn was difficult. There was nothing for the Wisznia family to do. As gracious as her relatives were, her father had no students, her siblings had no school and she had no sewing machine. So, a few days after their arrival, it was decided that Esther and her father, Shlomo Zalman, would travel to Bialystok to find her brothers. They would determine whether the rest of the family should relocate. Her mother, Bracha, would stay in Prostyn with the younger children, Sheina and Shimon.

It was a Friday. Esther and her father packed up some clothes and a bit of bread for the journey. They set out early, as they wanted to arrive in Bialystok before *Shabbes* began with the setting of the sun. Crossing a bridge over the Bug River, they soon reached the town of Malkinia, where there was a border crossing.

Approached the crossing, Esther was shaking, but she tried not to show her fear. She passed through, but her father was pulled out of line.

"*Jid*, you want to cross? Work for us before we will let you cross," the Nazi yelled, grabbing Shlomo Zalman's belongings, including his food.

Shocked, Esther hid and watched as the Nazis forced Shlomo Zalman to lay train tracks to the Malkinia station.* Unsure what to do, Esther ran to the nearby town. There she found other Stokers. She told them what happened and some of them conveyed a similar experience. They too had to wait and watch for their loved one.

The day was spent watching and worrying. What had happened? Was her father still alive? As the sun set and *Shabbes* began, Esther was crazy with worry. Where was her father? It was forbidden to work on *Shabbes*. Why had he not yet arrived? It was well into the evening when she finally saw him. She ran to him and they embraced. She cried with relief. He was alive, but soot and dirt covered his clothes. He explained how he worked all day and into the evening with no break and no food. The Nazis screamed — "Jewish pig, vermin" — at him all day as he built the tracks. It was nightfall — *Shabbes*. They had to find a place to sleep. But,

---

* These train tracks were used three years later to transport hundreds of thousands of Jews to their death at Treblinka. At this time, September of 1939, the death camps were a distant dream.

there were not enough beds for the many travelers in this town. There was much discussion as to who would sleep on a bed and who would lay a blanket on the floor. Esther, barely five feet, stood up tall and spoke with a strong and determined voice as she insisted that her father get one of the beds. It was granted.

Over *Shabbes* they learned that the Soviets allowed people to travel deeper into Soviet territory but didn't permit them to travel back over the border to the German side. Esther and her father decided that on Sunday, he would continue to Bialystok by train and find her brothers, while Esther would find a way to cross back over the border, avoiding Soviet and Nazi soldiers. She would return to her mother in Prostyn and explain what had happened and would convince her that she and her younger siblings must travel to Bialystok. The Nazis would never let the Jews live in peace. If they went to Bialystok, under Soviet control, they could live and work and the family could be together and safe.

The twelve-kilometer (7.4 miles) journey back to Prostyn took Esther days because she was on foot and she had to hide and evade the Soviet and German soldiers. She finally found a bridge over the Bug River where there were no Soviet or Nazi guards. She snuck across, arriving in Prostyn tired and hungry, but safe. Her mother and siblings flung their arms around her. They expected her back on Sunday or Monday and when she didn't return, they thought the worst. Esther told them what happened and that they should pack up and head to Bialystok. Her mother, Bracha, agreed.

Esther slept fitfully, worried about the journey ahead. When the sun rose, Esther, Bracha, Sheina and Shimon said goodbye to their kind and generous relatives and set out for Bialystok. Esther didn't want to go to the Malkinia border crossing again. She didn't want to risk the Nazi harassment, the confiscation of their few belongings, or worse. To hide from the Germans, they went by foot to the Bug River and got a ride over the bridge from a passing buggy driver. They crossed the border at the place Esther had snuck through just the day before. Once safe on the Soviet side, they boarded a train to Bialystok.

On the train, Esther met David Dennberg, a young man from Stoczek. He had been in Bialystok and told them that a group of Stokers had rented a building. It was crowded, but her father and brothers were living there and had their own apartment. Her brothers, he said, were working on the railroad.

Stepping off the train in Bialystok was a surreal experience. Esther had never been in such a big city. With all the refugees flooding in, the population had swollen from 100,000 to 200,000. As they walked down the main street, Esther wanted to look up and stare at the clock tower and three-story buildings, but she dared not. There were too many people walking on the sidewalk. She had to watch every step and jostle her way between the crowd. She held Shiena's hand and her mother held tight to Shimon and they tried to stay together. They couldn't walk in the road itself, too many buggies, going in both directions — packed with people, produce and merchandise. Young men on bikes whizzed by. There were even automobiles driving in the street.

On the way to the Stoker building where her father and brothers were staying, Esther realized that Bialystok had many kinds of Jews. Just on their short walk, she saw long-bearded *Hasidim* with *Peyes* (side locks), more modern observant Jews with trim beards and fashionable short jackets, ties and hats. She also saw secular Jews with no head covering at all. Some of the women appeared to be observant, wearing wigs or head coverings and modest dresses, but others wore the latest fashions from Warsaw. Shaken, Esther also saw poor people, with tattered clothing, begging on the street corners.

After a few short inquiries, they found the apartment building where her father and brothers were living. Her mother knocked. The door opened and seeing them standing there, Shlomo Zalman's face lit up. He ushered them into the apartment, hugged them all, and brought out the bit of food he had. Esther realized how lucky her family was to have a room in a building with beds, heat and even electricity. With the money her brothers made working on the railroad, they could pay the rent and buy food.

Other refugees were not as lucky. They had nowhere to live. Every house, every room, every corridor in Bialystok had refugees bunking down. The Bialystok Jewish community did all they could to help the newcomers. *Shuls* and schools were transformed into shelters. Public kitchens were opened, providing daily free lunches to thousands.

It was a good thing that over the past century of Jewish life, the Bialystok

Jewish community had built a strong infrastructure. The dedication to assisting the poor and those in need was deep and strong. By the late 1930's Bialystok had: a Jewish hospital; a *Linas Hatzedek* — a free clinic where physicians cared for the poor and medications were provided free of charge; an old age home; orphanages; aid societies; lending institutions; over one hundred *shuls*; *batei midrashoth* (schools of higher Jewish learning) and strong *Cheders*. "The poor were also provided with wood and coal for heat, food for the Jewish holidays, money to help pay their rent, and marriage dowries for their daughters," wrote I. Shmulewitz. "All of this was done quietly and with the greatest discretion to preserve the dignity of the recipients."[19]

Esther was aware that other new arrivals were dependent on the charity of the community for food and shelter. She was grateful that her family could support themselves. But she wanted to help. So, her top priority was finding a job. Esther knew that her mother stood in the bitter cold, waiting for hours in long lines to buy bread, milk, and other basic commodities at Soviet-controlled stores. She had a little Polish money, which early in the war was still legal tender. Later when Polish money was no longer accepted, she exchanged her remaining *Złotys* for Russian *Rubles*. Not understanding the importance of the exchange rate, Esther exchanged her *Złotys* at the official Soviet government rate, which was much lower than the black market.

Bialystok was a center of industry with silk and textile manufacturing, but because there were so many refugees, jobs were scarce. Word was going around in their apartment building that Yoel Lande, a Stoker,[20] was looking for workers who knew how to knit. Mr. Lande had acquired wool to make hats. Esther went straight to him.

"I know how to knit — well," Esther told Mr. Lande.

"You're hired," he said. "Report to work in the morning."

Esther arrived at Lande's "factory" (a rented room) the next day ready to make hats. Mr. Lande gave her a strange tool with which to make the hats. It was not a knitting needle and she had no idea how to knit with it. Nonetheless, he expected her to make top quality hats with this inferior tool. Esther told her father about the problem and he had an idea. He took a *rittle* (a twig) from a broom and made a knitting needle that was far superior to the terrible tool Lande had provided. Esther was ecstatic. With her father's *rittle*, she made attractive hats that Mr. Lande could sell. She got paid for her work and helped her family.

Her father had more trouble finding work. Most of the factories were now under Soviet control and employees were required to work on *Shabbes*. Shlomo Zalman refused to take any job that required him to violate the prohibition against working on *Shabbes*. So, he stayed home and helped with the younger children. He taught them their lessons and kept them busy.

The Soviet regime was not considerate of its new citizens' religious needs, even beyond making people work on *Shabbes*. They closed many *Shuls* and *Shtieblach*. One of the few that remained open was the Great Synagogue, located on Suraska Street.[21] With its three Byzantine-style domes over the main and side halls, the Great Synagogue gave people comfort that God had not abandoned them. The lights were left off, except for holidays, because the Soviets charged high prices for electricity.[22] But even without lights, people gathered daily and on *Shabbes* to pray together.

The Soviets also closed the public bathhouse, which included the *Mikve*. Some members of Carpentry Cooperative — a group of religious Jews who worked as carpenters but did not work on *Shabbes* — built a new *Mikve* in the home of one of their members. This *Mikve* was open to all Jewish residents of Bialystok.[23]

The city was so crowded that a few months after Esther's arrival, Soviet officials ordered certain people who were not working to relocate to other cities. Esther's parents and her two younger siblings were part of this forced exodus. They were sent to Grodno, eighty kilometers (50 miles) away. Esther didn't know whether to stay in Bialystok or leave with her parents. She had never been separated from them before. But in Bialystok she had a job and who knew what she would find in Grodno. She decided to stay with her two brothers in Bialystok.

After her parents left, Esther kept making hats for Mr. Lande. But after a few months, her cousin, Altschuler, found work for her with a wealthy family who had raw material and machines. This was a much better job because Esther lived with the family and they provided her meals and paid her a wage. With the food shortages in the city, having daily meals was critical. Esther corresponded with her parents and heard how they had settled into an apartment in Grodno. Her father took jobs in the Jewish community, serving as a *Shoichet* and *Melamed*.

Esther, on her own for the first time in a big city, had the time of her life. There were so many young people. She went to the movies and the Yiddish theater, and "*farnbrengt* (partied) in such a way that in Stok one could not imagine," she later reported. The city was filled with Yiddish culture and things to do. Esther visited the Sholem Aleichem Library, which she had heard was the largest Jewish library in Poland, containing the most Yiddish books and publications anywhere.[24]

With the influx of Jewish refugees from large Polish cities like Warsaw and Łódź, the cultural smorgasbord only became more exciting. Adding to the Yiddish cultural offerings already in place, "[a] Jewish theater sponsored by the government was formed, as well as a Jewish vaudeville company," described Awrom Zbar, in the Bialystok Yizkor (Memorial) Book. "Some of the best Jewish actors in Poland, who were in Bialystok as refugees from the Nazis, performed in these two newly established theaters. . . . A fine choir was formed under the direction of the famous choirmaster from Warsaw, M. Sznejur. A jazz orchestra, art exhibits and concerts surfaced in the city. Also, gambling casinos went into operation. They attracted quite a few patrons."[25]

The Soviets created a Yiddish daily newspaper — The Bialystoker Stern. Though refugee writers were hired to work on the paper, the top officials were all from the Soviet Union. Strict controls were imposed on what could be published. Because of the nonaggression-pact between the Soviet Union and Germany, this official paper was silent about the persecution of German Jews and Polish Jews in German-occupied lands. "To be sure," writes Zbar, in the Bialystoker Yizkor Book, "the Bialystoker Jews knew what was going on through the grapevine, every morsel of news disseminated by whisper. But the Jewish newspaper dared not publish anything critical about Germany, much less expose how the Nazi murderers beat, tortured, robbed, humiliated, and persecuted Polish Jewry."[26]

Walking on the street in Bialystok, Esther often saw teenagers wearing the tan uniforms of her Zionist youth group — *Hashomer Hatzair*. She was too old to participate in the youth group now, but when she saw them she felt an immediate connection. The Soviet regime tried to suppress Zionist activities and sent many of the movement's activists to Siberia. Before the war, Hebrew-speaking schools and Hebrew theater thrived. The Soviets, however, saw the speaking of Hebrew as subversive. They forced the *Tarbut* school, whose language of instruction was Hebrew, to switch to Yiddish. They even required the Hebrew words that are part of the Yiddish language, to be spelled phonetically, thus secularizing the language.

Spring came to Bialystok and that meant that Passover was near. The air warmed and flowers bloomed. Esther missed her parents and wanted to be with them for the holiday. She decided to travel by train to Grodno. Arriving in Grodno just a few days before the holiday, Esther found her father busy baking *Matzas,* flat unleavened bread, eaten on Passover and her mother busy ridding the home of *Chametz* (Leaven).*

Their father brought home plenty of hand-made *Matzas* for the *Seder.* Esther rolled up her sleeves and jumped into the preparations. The traditional *Seder* is a series of readings, songs and symbolic food and drink (wine) commemorating the freedom and exodus of the Hebrew slaves from Egypt. Bracha, Esther's mother, did the best she could under the Soviet coupon system to find ingredients to make the *Charoses*, the mix of apples, wine, and nuts, representing the bricks that the Hebrew slaves made in Egypt. They also obtained potatoes, which represent the spring harvest (*Karpas*), which are dipped into salt water at the *Seder* to recall the tears of the Hebrew slaves.

They wondered whether they were obligated to eat *Maror* (bitter herbs), representing the bitterness of slavery, this year. But they had been through their own exodus from Stoczek and it had been plenty bitter. They ate it, burning with the bitterness of it all.

On the Wisznia's *Seder* table, three *Matzas*, stacked one on top of the other, were placed before Shlomo Zalman, who led the proceedings. At an early point

---

* Jews are forbidden to eat leaven products on Passover. This prohibition extends to having any leaven product in your home. So, before Passover, Jewish families clean the home to rid it of all leaven.

in the *Seder,* he took the middle *Matza* and broke it. The breaking of the *Matza* expresses the idea that *Matza* is *Lechem Oni* — Poor Man's Bread or Bread of Affliction — and how the Hebrew slaves were broken by the hard work in Egypt. This year they thought of their own afflicted, broken lives and mourned that their family was exiled from their home and that Yisroel Yosef and Leizer Yitzchak were in Bialystok and not sitting at their table. The larger of the two broken pieces of *Matza,* called the *Afikomen,* was wrapped in a cloth and hidden while the smaller piece was put back between the other *Matzas* on the table. At the end of the *Seder,* after the fun of searching for the *Afikomen,* each of them ate a bit of this last piece of *Matza.* It was the last taste in their mouths before they retired for the evening.

In the middle of the *Seder,* as tradition dictates, dinner was served. Esther's favorite part of dinner was the chicken soup. The steaming, yellow liquid was eaten with bits of floating carrot and chicken. The best part of the soup was the thin egg noodles that substituted for flour-based noodles. Her mother had taught her how to fry a thin layer of egg, making a type of crepe and then how to cut it into thin strips to look like noodles. The soup made the small apartment in Grodno smell like home. The eight-day holiday passed without incident. They were filled with uncertainty about the future, but the joy of being together chased away the dark shadow, if only for an evening or two.

Esther's return trip to Bialystok was smooth; she didn't encounter any difficulties. She returned to the wealthy family and her comfortable work there. But a few weeks after Passover, Esther heard rumors that anyone without Soviet citizenship would get sent far away to the "White [Polar] Bear." Esther and her brothers applied and were granted Soviet citizenship and passports. The rumors were indeed true because not long after that, the Soviet officials came at night and gathered people who didn't have Soviet passports and put them on a train. Later they found out they were sent to Siberia, with its barren and frozen terrain. But at the time no one knew where they went.

With so many Jews sent away, families were separated, and people were lonely. Sadness crept into everyday life. Esther continued to work for the wealthy family, but as summer drew to a close and *Rosh Hashanah* (the Jewish New Year) approached, Esther missed her parents more than ever. She discussed it with her brothers and they all agreed to leave Bialystok and move to be with their parents and younger siblings. They would work in a new city.

Just then, Esther and her brothers received a letter from their parents. They wrote that the Soviets had, yet again, forced them to move. This time to Slonim. So, in September of 1940, Esther and her brothers packed up and boarded a train for the 150-kilometer (93 miles) trip from Bialystok to Slonim. Finding their parents proved easy because Slonim was smaller than Bialystok. Their father was already involved with Jewish communal affairs, serving as a *Shoichet* and *Melamed*. Bracha and Shlomo Zalman were thrilled to have the whole family together and just in time for Rosh Hashanah. The apartment was small, but at least they were together.

Esther learned that Jews had lived in Slonim for over five hundred years. In the late 1800's many moved to America and Palestine, due to rising antisemitism.[27] The city's Jews had suffered from pogroms[*] and blood libels[**]. But now, their numbers were on the rise. Since the beginning of the war, 15,216 refugees arrived, swelling its population to 31,467, of whom 23,821 were Jews.

Walking around town, Esther saw the many *Shuls*. The Soviets had not closed them as they had in Bialystok. Esther's favorite was one of the largest, called the Wooden House of Prayer. Esther loved the irony of the Wooden House of Prayer, because it was made of brick. The people of Slonim explained that in 1881 there had been a fire that burnt down the entire town, including the Wooden House of Prayer. It was rebuilt with brick, so it wouldn't burn down again, but they didn't want to change its name.[28]

There were also small *Shtieblach*. Most of the craft guilds had their own *Shtiebel*. For example, just across the alley from the larger Wooden House of Payer, stood the tailors' *Shtiebel*. The shoemakers also had their own *Shtiebel*.

Slonim reminded Esther of Bialystok, just smaller. A variety of Jewish schools, ranging from small *Cheders* to a Yiddish high school, were still open. There was

---

[*]   An organized massacre of Jews.
[**]   The false accusation that Jews murdered Christian children to use their blood to bake *Matza*.

a Jewish hospital, which was impressive, but not as large and prestigious as the one in Bialystok. She saw a home for the aged and many charity institutions that helped Jews in need. Esther was pleased to find that Slonim had a small Yiddish theater and a Jewish library. It was told that Eliezer Ben Yehuda, the man who revived Hebrew as a spoken language, published his first dictionary in Slonim.

Soviet officials were in firm control of Slonim's industry, including its thriving lumber trade and banking industry. Esther and her brothers quickly realized that there were no jobs available through the Soviet government. So, she and her two brothers Yisroel Yoseph and Eliezer Yitzchak started *handlin* — transporting and selling goods on the thriving black market. They moved goods to White Russia and the Ukraine. After the sales were made, they bought flour, kasha and other food stuffs that were scarce. They brought it back to town, kept what they needed for their family and sold the rest on the black market. With the profits, they would head back to White Russia or the Ukraine and start the process again. Working in this way, they had enough to survive and their mother was even able to bake *Challah* for *Shabbes*. Luxuries were not part of their life, but they had enough.

Slonim was no Stoczek, but Esther and her family were getting used to it. They thought that they would make a new life here and that they would live in Slonim, under Soviet control, forever. Esther's life improved when her boyfriend, Moishe Kwiatek, arrived in Slonim. Moishe reported that his family members were well. But Stoczek felt empty with so many Jews having left. But his father didn't want to leave and he continued to run the soda factory and was making enough money to keep the family going. Moishe and Esther spent time together walking by the river and visiting the Jewish library.

April of 1941 saw a second Passover that the Wisznia family was exiled from their home. But it came and went without incident. Thanks to the *handlin* of the oldest three children, the Wisznia family had what they needed to make passable *Seders*. However, a month later, Esther fell ill. She was plagued with a fever and chills, a dry cough, headaches, and joint pain. Her parents were worried, but when the rash appeared on her stomach, they knew it was typhus. Typhus was all over the city, passed in the crowded living conditions by lice or fleas. Esther went to the Slonim hospital for treatment.

Esther was scared. Her body was covered in a rash. She had fever, chills, and a terrible headache. But as she lay on the crisp white hospital sheets, she felt hopeful that the doctors and nurses would take care of her. Esther was so weak that she could hardly get out of bed. Her body felt like it was burning. Perhaps some medicine was administered, but under Soviet control, medicine was scarce. The best treatment may have been rest and good nutrition.

The weather warmed and on June 1st, the Wisznia family celebrated *Shavuos.* Esther was not with them; she was still in the hospital recovering. The holiday was celebrated amid worry and rumors about the Nazi persecution of the Jews of Germany and western Poland. That *Shavuos,* the Jews of Slonim lived in ignorance that in three weeks the Germans would break their nonaggression-pact with the Soviet Union and attack from the air and the ground with force, fury, and a plan to implement Hitler's "Final Solution."[29]

From Kowalówka to Treblinka

JUNE 1941–JUNE 1942

They were alive! His parents were alive. Sam was so relieved. After escaping the German POW camp and eluding the fate of his fellow soldiers in the orchard, Sam had made his way back to Kowalówka. He had last seen his parents some fourteen months ago, before he was drafted into the Soviet army. But here they were and they could not believe their eyes; happiness surged through them. But what kind of strange clothes was he wearing?

"How did you survive the German attack?" they asked. "How did you escape? Where did you get these clothes?"

Sam had no words to explain — how could he articulate what he had been through? He didn't tell them all that had happened. He ate a bit of food and went to sleep. But shortly after Sam's return, his mother suffered a stroke. She could no longer move her right arm or leg.

"*Gevalt*,"* said Sam. "What do I do now?"

My child," said his mother, "if God helped you when you got out of the [prisoner of war] camp, go away and you will stay alive. With me, you'll be lost. I want you to stay alive. Go away from me."

---

* Loosely translated as "Yipes."

"Mama," Sam said, "I will not go away from you. Whatever will be, will be."

A few days after Sam's return, they heard that there was going to be a *oblawa*, a roundup of Jews in the town. They had to find a place to hide. Zelig went to a non-Jewish man he had met in town, hoping he would help them.

"I will pay you well," Zelig told the man, "just hide me and my family."

They hid under a pile of hay in the barn. When the *oblawa* was over, and the German soldiers had left, they were told that it was safe to come out. When Zelig, Faiga and Sam heard that many Jews had been captured and shot, they realized that they could no longer stay in this part of Poland. They decided to travel to Stoczek where it was reported that Jews were living in an "open ghetto" and they were not being murdered. The Stoczek Jews wore the yellow star, but there were no walls or barbed wire around the ghetto.

Sam insisted that his parents try to go too, even though traveling would be difficult for his mother after her stroke. They found a local man with a horse and buggy and told him they would pay him a large sum if he would take them across the border.

"What do you want," the man responded, "that I should get killed for you? I don't want to. I won't do it."

So, they tried yet another buggy owner. After some negotiations, he and Zelig agreed on a sum to take them across the border. They traveled in the buggy to the border crossing, but the Germans would not let them through, so they had to return to Kowalówka. Soon after their return, some Jews that Sam knew wanted to cross the border and go to Stoczek. One of these travelers came to Sam's home:

"Shmulke," he said, "come, we'll go to Stoczek together."

Well, Sam's mother heard this and did not hesitate:

"Go, go, my son," Faiga said. "You should go and you will stay alive. We will go to Ciechanowiec. It's only 35 kilometers away. It's not far from the Bug River, but hopefully the Nazis will leave us alone there. I have a cousin there, he will take care of us."

So, Sam went with eight others including Yechiel and Rivka Chus and their two young children. They left at night, on foot and found a place to cross the border; at 1 a.m., they crossed undetected. They were in the woods, just outside the town of Sadovne. In the early morning, a couple and their teenage daughter came into the forest to collect wood for a fire to cook breakfast. Sam saw the man had a beard and he heard him speaking Yiddish. Approaching, he spoke to them in Yiddish, explaining that they had come from the other side of the border to escape the Germans and were hungry and tired.

"Could you do a *mitzva*?"* Sam asked, "and let us stay with you?"

"No," the mother said. "We are not allowed to take people in. Sadovne is an open ghetto like Stoczek, but the Germans are everywhere. If they find extra Jews in our home, they will kill us all."

"Mama," her daughter pointed to Sam and said, "take this one."

"Ok," said the mother, "if my daughter says to take you, I'll take you."

"But we are nine people," Sam responded, "I won't leave them."

"We can't take all of them," the mother said, "but, we can take you."

Sam didn't have much choice, so he went with this family. He said goodbye to the others and hoped that they could remain together and stay safe. Sam lived with this family of three in Sadovne in their one-room house. They treated Sam like one of their own. The father shared his bed with Sam while the mother and daughter shared the other bed. Sam ate his meals with them and they were kind to him. But, he didn't have much to do. That changed as soon as Sam met the woman's brother. The brother heard that Shmulke Goldberg from Bagatele was living with his sister.

"Are you the son of Zelig of Bagatele?" the brother asked.

"Yes, yes, I am," Sam replied.

"He is my good friend," the man said. "Come live with me. I will take you into my butcher business. I will give you a straight 50% of the profit."

Sam was a natural businessman and had been trading in animals and butchering with his father for years. He agreed. When the daughter heard that Sam was leaving their home to go work with her Uncle, she began to cry. She was in love with Sam and knew that her Uncle had four daughters who would vie for his

---

* A *mitzva* is a commandment from God. But the word is also used as a general term for a good deed.

attention. Her parents told Sam that they had hoped that he would marry her.

"I was thinking about getting married," Sam later said dryly, "as much as a dead person dances."

Sam moved in with her Uncle. His house was larger and Sam had a room of his own. The Uncle gave him money to buy cattle on the black market. He would *shecht* (slaughter) them and sell the meat, making three times as much as he paid. Although all Jews in the area were required to wear an arm band with the yellow star, Sam refused. He went about without the star and was not stopped. Maybe it was his clear blue eyes, so loved by the Aryans.

Four months after Sam came to Sadovne, the Nazis arrived and forced all the Jews to move to Stoczek, thirteen kilometers (8 miles) away.[30] Sam, along with the other Jews of Sadovne, including the young woman who was in love with him, packed what they could carry and moved to Stoczek. Sam had a sick feeling in his stomach. He was sure that the Nazis were moving them to Stoczek to kill them all.

Once he arrived, he found a place to stay with a man named Avram. Sam continued to trade on the black market and operate his cattle/butchering business in Stoczek. He roamed free without the yellow star. But in Stoczek, the *Judenrat*** had a quota of men they had to deliver to the Nazis each day. The Nazis said they took these men away, to "work," but no one knew what happened to them. This created tension in the *Shtetl* and a deep sense of foreboding.

Sam was worried about getting caught. He was new in town and had no family connections to protect him. Because of this, his name was often placed on the *Judenrat's* daily list of people to capture. But Avram had a son-in-law, Chaim Yankel, who was a Jewish policeman. When Chaim Yankel heard that Sam was on the list, he would send his eight-year-old daughter to warn him, giving him enough time to hide. One day, Sam came late from *shechting* animals and he did not have enough time to hide. So Avram and Chaim Yankel got their four young daughters to lay on top of Sam and hide him in the house. He was saved once again.

---

*   *Judenrat* was the Jewish Council set up by the Nazis to run the affairs of the Jewish community and do the bidding of the Nazis.

Sam's luck ran out in June of 1942. One day, the Nazis surrounded the town, closing off all escape routes with trucks lined up in the town square. The Ukrainian guards were ready. The *Judenrat* was ordered to deliver 135 men and Sam was on the list. As he was *shechting* cows in a barn, a member of the *Judenrat* brought the Nazis there. Sam saw them and jumped into a large pile of grain to hide. But they saw him jump and caught him. They dragged him back to the town square and forced him to lay down on the ground, surrounded by gun-carrying Nazis. The young girl from Sadovne who was in love with Sam saw him lying on the ground in the square. She was distraught. She came and lay down next to him on the ground and began to cry.

"It's no use," Sam told her. "I can't escape."

Sam was pushed onto one of the trucks with the other men. He couldn't believe it, but Chaim Yankel was on the truck too. He was surprised because Chaim Yankel was a Policeman, a protected status, but not today. The *Judenrat* needed to reach their quota and that made Chaim Yankel a target.

The men were told they were being taken to work. The convoy with 135 Jewish men pulled out of Stoczek and traveled the twenty kilometers (12.4 miles) to Treblinka.

Sign to Treblinka. Credit: Yad Vashem

ESTHER

From Slonim to Stoczek

MAY 1941–AUGUST 1943

Esther began to feel better. Typhus was a serious illness, but after a couple of weeks in the Slonim hospital she could get out of bed. Then, with a bit more strength, she started to take walks. During these weeks of rest and recuperation, she created friendships with the nurses, the doctor, and some of the other patients. Finally, she felt well enough that she didn't want to just lie in bed any longer.

"Can I help in some way?" Esther asked the nurse knowing that other patients were much worse off than she.

"Yes," the nurse replied, "we have more patients than we can handle."

As she regained her strength, Esther helped by wiping foreheads, cleaning bedpans, washing sheets, and feeding the patients. She missed her family and Moishe, but they came to visit and once she was strong enough to take walks outside the hospital, they would walk together in the fresh air.

Being cloistered in the hospital, Esther had little news. So, her family supplied her with a steady stream of reports about Jewish life in Slonim. It was getting harder and harder to get food and people were dying of starvation. There were many rumors that Germany was ramping up for war against the Soviet Union, but they had no way to know what might happen or when. The newspapers were silent.

After a month in the hospital, Esther's positive, can-do attitude, and her self-assured manner made her a well-loved patient. Although the doctor determined that Esther was ready to be discharged, he urged her to stay at the hospital. She could continue to help and she would be assured of having food. Esther discussed this with her father and they agreed that she should stay. Why should she suffer at home? After this, whenever she met her family, she was guilt-ridden. She knew they had so little to eat. But she could not help them as she was prohibited from taking food outside of the hospital.

Then came the "horrifying day of June 22, 1941;" breaching their nonaggression-pact with the Soviet Union, Germany launched Operation Barbarossa. Within just a few days, the Nazis were in Slonim, repeating the horror Esther had witnessed in Stoczek. Her heart was filled with dread when she remembered what had happened in Stoczek — the bombs that fell, the people that were killed and the houses, including her own, that were burned to the ground. Had it only been twenty-one months since then? It felt like a lifetime ago.

From the hospital, Esther could hear the bombs getting closer and closer. Then, the airplanes were so loud that she knew they were over Slonim. She heard the bombs fall and felt the earth shake. Her father came to the hospital and told her that the German infantry was pouring into the area.

"The Germans are ferocious," Shlomo Zalman told her, "even wilder than when they entered Stoczek."

The Soviet forces were helpless. Thousands of Soviet soldiers, including many Jewish men, were captured and taken as prisoners of war. They heard that the Germans were killing the POWs by the thousands and shipping thousands more to concentration camps to serve as slave labor.

Reports made it to the hospital about the fate of Jews in different cities. Esther heard about what happened in Bialystok. Esther had so many friends there; she worried day and night. She heard that the Nazis overran Bialystok, murdering thousands of Jews. Jewish women were raped and machine guns were set up in front of *Shuls* with Nazis shooting rapid fire bullets at anyone in the street. Over a thousand people were forced into the Great Synagogue and burnt alive.[31] Esther had no way to reach her friends there. Were they alive? Were they able to hide from the Nazis? Had they been able to run away?

What Esther could not have known is that the Nazis were not only attacking to conquer Soviet lands, to acquire *lebensraum* — living space — for the German people, but also a parallel war had begun — a war against the Jews. Hitler's earlier plan was to deport the Jews, so that Germany and German-controlled lands would be *Judenrein*. The French island colony of Madagascar[32] had been suggested as a possible relocation center, or perhaps deep in the Soviet wasteland. But moving millions of Jews was now seen as unrealistic, there were too many. They had to be "dealt with" where they were. Hitler ordered the "Final Solution of the Jewish Questions" and Heinrich Himmler, head of the police and the SS was appointed the responsible agent to carry out Hitler's commands. Together with Hermann Göring, Reinhard Heydrich, and Adolf Eichmann, Himmler was tasked to get the job done.

With the invasion of the Soviet territories, Himmler wanted to show Hitler "that he was attuned to the darker side of National Socialism, and ready to pursue policies of absolute ruthlessness. . . . [And that] shooting was easier than starvation, deportation, and slavery."[33] Four *Einsatzgruppen* killing units (A-D) followed the German infantry into enemy territory. Their job was to gather and shoot the Jews. It began with murdering the Jewish men, but it quickly escalated to include women, children, and old men. By August of 1941, these killing units had 20,000 soldiers. It was reported to Berlin that the forces were "sufficiently reinforced to kill all the Jews that they found."[34] However, they soon realized that 20,000 fighters were insufficient to carry out the immense killing operations. So, local men were recruited to help. Some joined the Germans voluntarily, while others were forced to participate.

While Esther remained safe in the hospital, terror reigned in the streets of Slonim. Even before the *Einsatzgruppen* arrived in Slonim, hundreds of men were rounded up and taken to the municipal stadium where they were beaten and killed. After this first round of killing, the rest of the Jews were ordered to wear the Star of David armband and forced to move into a *ghetto*. Esther desperately wanted to go and be with her family, but it was too dangerous. She stayed in the hospital, frantic with worry and fear. She learned from the doctor that her family was safe, for now. As June turned to July, the days were hot and seemed to go on forever.

During the heat of the summer, *Einsatzgruppen* B[35] found that they were ready to take on the Jews of Slonim. They located a remote spot outside of town and forced locals to dig huge pits.[36] It took days, but now they were ready. The Nazis created an Auxiliary Police force made up of non-Jewish Poles to show the Nazis where the Jews lived. The night before the *Aktion*, the Nazis sealed the ghetto. The Polish Police took their opportunity — they entered the ghetto in the dark of night and raped as many Jewish women as they could. When they were done, they shot them, leaving their bodies to rot, and then went to grab some coffee to compare rape stories with their fellow Police officers.[37]

It was two hours before dawn, at four in the morning, when the Police surrounded the area. In a desperate attempt to escape the round-up, some Jews dug holes in the ground.[38] Some succeeded in hiding, others were found and shot. At dawn, the Nazis and the Polish Police went from house to house screaming — "*raus*" — "get out," and "*schnell*" — "quick." Those who did not obey or were not quick enough, were shot. Whips and clubs helped to hurry the process along. There was no time to grab anything and terror gripped them as they ran into the town square, with just the clothes on their backs.

Lines of trucks and horse-drawn carts, commissioned from the local population, waited for their passengers. The Slonim Jews were forced to board, squeezing in so many that there was no room to move. It was hot and the sweat of the bodies mingled with the scent of terror as the trucks and carts rumbled along the road. They drove out of town. After some time, they turned off the main road. The bumps and jostling made it clear that they were on an uneven, dirt road. The trucks stopped and the Jews were pushed and whipped until they got out, their cries and screams pierced the air. They were surrounded by Nazi soldiers, as well as the local police and civilians. Escape was impossible. Those who ran were killed.

Back in the hospital, Esther was told what had happened. The Jews were ordered to undress and stand in lines. Then, one of two methods was used to kill them. Some Jews were forced to stand or kneel at the edge of the pit and the

Nazis shot them in the base of the neck. The force of the bullet would kill them and push them over into the pit. The other was the Jeckeln Method, developed by Friedrich Jeckeln, the head of the SS and of the Police in southern Russia. With this method, the Nazis forced the naked Jews, in groups of twenty, to walk down into the pit and lay on top of those who had come before. Then, laying down, they were shot in the head or in the neck.[39] With this second method, sometimes local girls were forced to "press the bodies down with their bare feet, as if the bodies were grapes on harvest day in wine country."[40]

Esther crawled into her hospital bed that evening and wept into her pillow for hours. Her body shook and the tears would not stop. Her whole family, her mother, Bracha, her father, Shlomo Zalman, her brothers, Yisroel Yoseph, Eliezer Yitzchak, and Shimon and her sister, Sheina, were all murdered — shot into a pit. Then there was Moishe; what would she do without him? How would she go on?

The town was quiet now. The *Einsatzgruppen* had moved on to the next town. Tomorrow she would leave the hospital, but what would she do, where would she go? At some point sleep overcame her. When she opened her eyes in the morning, she couldn't believe what she saw — Moishe was sitting by her bed — alive! Was she dreaming? No, it was really him.

"I hid," Moishe explained. "I didn't make a sound during the round-up and the Nazis didn't find me." But, he confirmed her fear: "your family was taken; they are all gone."

The tears erupted again. But this time they cried together, holding each other until they could cry no more. Esther gathered up her few belongings that she had at the hospital, hugged the nurses and the doctors, and thanked them for their kindness. Esther and Moishe left the hospital and went to the ghetto to find other Jews who had survived the massacre. They found a place to live and tried to make a bit of money. Life was filled with darkness.

Then Esther heard news that made her sick. The Nazis had entered the hospital just a day or two after she left. They shot all the patients as they lay helpless in their beds. There was no mercy, even for the sick and dying. She had left in the nick of time, but the patients who had been her friends and whose brows she had wiped, were all gone now, murdered in their beds.[41]

Those Jews who remained in Slonim were forced to live within the ghetto, a small area of the city, and were forbidden to do business or have interactions with non-Jews. A *Judenrat* was formed to govern the affairs of the remaining Jews, but Esther and Moishe knew that the Nazis intended to destroy every bit of Jewish life. They agreed that life was probably no better at home in Stoczek and if the Nazis were intent on killing all the Jews, it would be better to die at home.

That *Rosh Hashanah* was their last in Slonim. They gathered with other Jews to pray, but there was no joy, only dread. The *Kaddish*, the memorial prayer, was said by so many who had lost loved ones; the entire town was in mourning.

The big question for Esther and Moishe was how to get back home. Stoczek was 280 kilometers (174 miles) away and going on the train was out of the question. The Nazis were in complete control of the railways. Moishe and Esther agreed that they would work as long as they needed to buy a horse and buggy. There was another young couple who wanted to go back to Wengrow, a town near Stoczek. They agreed to travel together, once they had enough to buy a horse and buggy.

Esther and Moishe had no idea what the future would bring. But, they decided to get married. They had been dating since they were eighteen. It was time.

"Let's arrive back home as a married couple," Moishe said.

Esther agreed, and they likely had a small *Chuppah* (wedding ceremony) in Slonim, with little fanfare and not much more than some moonshine* for a *L'chayim*. But now they could move forward, knowing that whatever would come, they would have each other and be able to face the future together.

Esther relied on her extensive knowledge of the black markets accrued during her months working with her brothers to make money. Moishe had other contacts. And so, together they managed to make enough money in the shadow markets to buy a horse and buggy for their journey. It was around *Purim* time, early March of 1942, when they set out for home. The Nazis were everywhere. Because they had to hide along the way, the trip took a month, making it home in time for Passover. They dropped their friends off in Wengrow and traveled the final twenty kilometers (12.4 miles) to Stoczek.

---

* Moonshine is a term used to describe high-proof distilled liquor, usually produced illicitly. The main ingredient is typically corn.

Entering Stoczek, Esther and Moishe were overcome with sorrow. The *Shtetl* was in ruins. The houses, including Esther's that had been burned down two and a half years before, still lay in ruins. Some shops in the town square were open, but others were shuttered. As they passed the red brick Church, they noticed that it was still standing and well kept. They were relieved to see Moishe's home and the soda factory still standing. When Moishe's mother, Faiga Leah, opened the door, she screamed and ushered them into the house. Moishe's father, David, his teenage brother, Chaim, and his younger sister, Chana, all came running. The other two children, Yosef and Mendel were not living in Stoczek at the time. But those at home couldn't believe it. They had heard what had happened to the Jews of Slonim. They were sure Esther and Moishe were dead. But here they were in flesh and blood. They sat at the table and Faiga Leah brought out some food. Though times were hard, they still had food. The Polish farmers still came into town once a week for a market day and the Kwiateks' soda factory was still in business.

"First of all," Moishe said, "we're married."

"Oy, *mazal tov*,"* they all screamed in unison.

They told each other what had happened since the Germans invaded the Soviet Union in June of 1941. Esther and Moishe retold the horror of the Slonim massacre and how they had avoided death; she in the hospital and he in hiding. In turn, David and Faiga Leah told them that though there were 400 or so Jews left in Stoczek, the Germans were not murdering them and there was a recognizable Jewish life. The soda factory had been taken over by a German, but it still churned out bottles of bubbly water and the German paid the Kwiatek family to run the business. Life was not simple, but they carried on.

They were relieved to see, that indeed Stoczek was an "open ghetto." The Jews had to live in one part of the town, but there were no walls. While the Jews were subject to other laws, including wearing the Star of David armband, their freedom of movement was not restricted. Of course, the Nazis established a *Judenrat* and a Jewish Police force to carry out their orders.

---

* *Mazal Tov* means good luck, but this phrase is commonly used as an expression of congratulations.

Moishe and Esther jumped right in to help with the soda business. They might have used the horse and buggy they bought in Slonim to make deliveries to the non-Jewish customers who lived just outside of town. They noticed a distinct difference in their interactions with many of their non-Jewish neighbors. Before the war, they had a friendly and warm relationship with them, but now, many were cold and distant. The non-Jewish Poles felt that they were better than the Jews, and some were verbally abusive and refused to buy from them. This was hurtful.

There were of course, non-Jews who remained friendly and kind. One such family was the Styś (pronounced Stish) family who were long-time customers of the Kwiatek soda factory. For years on Sundays, the Styś family walked to town to attend Church. After Church, the entire Styś family walked the block and a half to the soda factory for "acid" or "*kwas*" water. The children were allowed to buy a sweet, sparkling drink. It may have been the promise of the sweet bubbly treat that kept them quiet during the Church service.

There were three Styś brothers. Two of the brothers, Stanisław and Aleksander, were married, had children, and lived next door to each other. The third brother, Edward, lived with Stanisław's family. He had suffered from Polio as a child and was disabled. They were excellent customers and friends to the Kwiateks before the war and unlike some of their neighbors, they continued to buy soda and interact with the Kwiateks during the Nazi occupation.

Spring arrived in Stoczek and the flowers bloomed. Esther and Moishe were hopeful that the Nazis would leave Stoczek alone and they would not see the murder and devastation they had witnessed in Slonim. They were looking forward to the holiday of *Shavuos*, which would fall on May 21, commemorating the giving of the *Torah* on Mount Sinai. It would be good to have something to celebrate. Esther's love of cooking was on full display as she helped Faiga Leah prepare the holiday meals. *Blintzes*, a traditional *Shavuos* food, was high on the "to do" list. They fried crepes, one at a time, then made a mixture of cheese, eggs, and a bit of their precious sugar, placing a dollop in the middle of each crepe. Each crepe was wrapped around the cheese and refried. The family ate every blintz that Esther and Faiga Leah made. They gathered in the *Shul* to pray with the other Jews of Stoczek. They prayed that God would keep them safe.

But, not long after *Shavuos*, the Nazis came back. Nazi officers, "armed from head to toe," surrounded the town. The order was issued "produce 135 young men." The Jewish Police were dispatched to do the dirty work. Word spread and Moishe ran to hide. But, Chaim was caught. It may have been because of his bandaged hand which slowed him down. He had cut himself on a glass bottle in the soda factory and the bandages hindered his mobility. He was held at gunpoint in the town square. There was no way out.

Then the German, who now owned the Kwiatek soda factory, heard that Chaim was captured. He went to the town square and found the Nazi in charge. He insisted that Chaim be released.

"He works for me," the German said. "He is an essential worker in my soda factory."

The Nazi relented and Chaim was freed. He ran back home. The Nazi knew they would be back for him later, when "things" were up and running.

The Jews of Stoczek watched as a caravan of trucks drove out of town with 135 young Jewish men packed in like sardines. Wives, parents, siblings, and friends cried for those who had been taken. From that day on "there was terror in the *Shtetl*," Esther later explained. They felt like they were "standing under a tree that had been cut and was about to fall. It was waving in the breeze, and as it rocked, a great misfortune was about to befall everything." No one knew where the Nazis were taking the young men or what would happen to them.

SAM

Treblinka

JUNE 1941-SUMMER 1942

"You — to the left," the Nazi officer shouted, pushing Sam off the truck laden with the 135 men from Stoczek.

After traveling twenty kilometers (12.4 miles) from Stoczek in the back of a truck, Sam was disoriented. He was in the middle of nowhere — a field, surrounded by trees with no houses in sight. The only building at Treblinka in the beginning of June 1942 was a wooden shack. [42]

"Those to the right will be going home soon," the Nazi officer announced. And "those to the left will stay here for a while."

Sam wanted to leave and find his parents. So, he slinked over to the right. Joining the line, he hoped he had not been noticed.

"What are you doing, you disgusting swine?" the Nazi screamed, pushing him back to the group on the left with a smack to his head that blurred his vision.

Sam was in shock. Was this nightmare real? He began to cry and his throat closed — no words could form. A friend from Stoczek, Yankel, the Jewish policeman, grabbed him and whispered in his ear:

"I left behind a wife and a child, I'm not running, you see how we are, stay here, you stay here!"

His whispered words penetrated Sam's consciousness, refocusing him. Sam watched as the Nazi officer aimed his machine gun and killed every single man in the group on the right. The survivors who had remained on the left stood shaking. They tried to get their bearings and take in their loss of freedom and new status as prisoners. At that moment, Sam thought "I am not killed now, but I will be killed later." Any hope of staying alive vanished. The task given to those standing on the left was to build the death camp Treblinka. *SS Hauptsturmführer* Richard Thomalla from the Construction Office of the Waffen-SS *Und Polizei* in Zamosc, supervised the construction of the camp.[43] Thomalla looked at Sam, a strong man of 22 and asked:

"What do you know how to do?"

"I'm a farmer. I can do anything, everything that has to be done," Sam answered.

"Everything?" *Hauptsturmführer* Thomalla asked.

"Yes, everything," Sam said.

"Good, make roofs out of straw," *Hauptsturmführer* Thomalla ordered.

Thus began Sam's thirteen months at Treblinka. Each second was terrifying — would he be shot, hit over the head, or hung by his feet in the open square? Would he live to see the next hour, the next day, or would he join the other corpses in the pit? The killing was random and Sam learned to keep his eyes and nose down and work as hard and as fast as he could. For weeks, he lived in the barracks he first saw when he arrived at the camp, ate stale, moldy bread, the slop they called soup, and drank the brown, fetid liquid they called coffee. He furiously made bundles of straw, binding them together and turning them into roofs for the buildings that seemed to spring up overnight.

Sam had never made straw roofs. But he had seen the non-Jewish workers on his farm in Bagatelle make such roofs. He dug into his memory, recreating what he had seen as precisely as he could. Like the Hebrew slaves of ancient Egypt, he transformed straw into building material. Tied together in tight bundles, he created roofs for shelter in a place where 870,000 innocent people would be murdered.

He could see right away that they were not building a concentration camp. He had heard about those — imprisoning tens of thousands of people for months or years. The 3-4 meter-high camouflaged, barbed wire fence, built to enclose the camp, made it obvious that this was no concentration camp, it was too small. The enclosed area was maybe 600 meters long and 400 meters wide.[44] New wooden sleeping barracks for the Jewish workers were built with rows and rows of wooden planks for beds and a few buckets in the corner for night time relief. But they were built to house maybe 1000 people, max. No, he realized this camp was purely for the quick, efficient, killing of humans. Once the killing began on July 23, 1942, he saw that the people who arrived at Treblinka were dead within 90 minutes.[45]

Sam kept bundling straw and watching as the Jews built two distinct sections of the camp, a "Lower Camp" and an "Upper Camp." Sam lived and worked in the Lower Camp. What he saw was a huge reception area with a rail spur from the nearby town of Malkinia running along the western edge of the camp. Trains would pass through Malkinia and stop at the nearby Treblinka station. Some cattle cars were left behind, waiting their turn, because only twenty cattle cars could fit at the Death Camp's reception area.[46] It was at the reception area that victims would step off the trains for "processing." On the right side of the reception area were two store rooms for sorting the booty from the suitcases left behind. Here, people's most valued possessions — those they chose to arrange in the one permitted suitcase — were sorted, packed, and shipped off to Lublin and from there to locations throughout the Reich.

Watch towers — eight meters high — were built in each of the four corners of the camp. They had searchlights and were manned twenty-four hours a day by Ukrainian guards.[47] On the left side of the reception area, two undressing barracks were built, one for men and one for women and children. These barracks exited directly to "the Tube" also called "the Road to Heaven." The Road to Heaven was narrow (4.5-5 meters wide) and 80 to 90 meters long. It had barbed wire fence on either side. The fences were covered with branches taken from the nearby forest. This kept those running down the Road to Heaven from seeing beyond and prisoners, like Sam, from seeing in. Like rats in a maze that must follow the path built, the victims had nowhere else to go but straight into the gas chamber.[48]

The "Ghetto" was just past the undressing barracks and was where the Jews slept. Women had separate barracks. Twice daily all prisoners were subject to the dreaded roll call. If a worker looked ill or didn't stand straight or just didn't meet with the SS Officer's favor at that moment, they were tortured or removed, never to be seen again. Further, periodic selections were made at roll call, sending tens or hundreds to the gas chambers in one fell swoop. The Ghetto also included the workers' kitchen, separate living quarters for *Kapos*,* a tailor shop, shoe-repair, carpentry shop and sickroom.[49] At night, the Ghetto barracks were locked and those sleeping on the wooden planks had to endure the putrid smell of urine and feces accumulating (often overflowing) in the corner buckets.

The arsenal, living quarters, and administrative offices for the twenty-five German SS officers and their 100 Ukrainian henchmen[50] were as far away from the reception area as possible. They were separated from the living quarters of the Jews by a barbed wire fence. They had their own kitchen, barber shop, sick bay, and dentist office, with plenty of good food and *schnapps* to go around.

One of the most terrifying buildings in the Lower Camp was the *Lazaret* ("Infirmary"). It was in the far-right corner of the reception area, adjacent to a massive pit at the edge of the camp. It was here that the aged and infirm were taken straight from the trains, for "medical attention." They were escorted or sometimes even carried by "the reds" — Jewish workers thus called because they wore red arm bands. The reds were also referred to as the *Chevra Kaddishah* — the burial society. Using techniques learned at the German Euthanasia Program[51] the exterior of the *Lazaret* was painted with a large red cross and its interior was designed to look like a doctor's office. Although the German and Ukrainian killers wore white doctors' coats, the "patients" could quickly see that they were done for. They were made to sit on a bench at the edge of the huge pit. Looking down into the pit filled with dead bodies gave the victims a few seconds to realize their fate. A quick and powerful shot to the neck put an end to their psychic suffering. The jolt forced the body to topple straight into the pit. Once enough bodies were collected in the pit, they were burned to make room for the next batch of *Lazaret* victims.[52]

The "Upper Camp," where the gas chambers were built, was separated from the Lower Camp by a tall earthen embankment and high fences to conceal its existence and keep out unauthorized people. Sam never went to the "other side"

---

* A *Kapo* was a Jew, appointed by the SS to supervise other Jewish prisoners.

of the fence. But he knew what happened there. They all did. The stench of rotting flesh filled every particle of air and filled his soul with dread.

Though Sam never saw the Upper Camp, others who survived gave chilling descriptions of what they had seen. There, the Germans set up an entirely separate world, enclosed with a sapling-covered barbed wire fence. The Upper Camp was smaller than the Lower Camp — approximately 200 x 250 meters.[53] It had its own guard towers and guard station and a separate work force of Jews who had the grisly task of removing the corpses from the gas chambers and taking them to the burial pits. These unfortunate souls were called *Totenjuden* and they were kept separate from the work force in the Lower Camp. They had their own living barracks, kitchen, and laundry facility. They lived there together with the "dentists," whose job it was to extract the gold teeth from the corpses before they were thrown into the pit.

The main attraction of the Upper Camp was the three gas chambers. They were approximately 4 x 4 meters in area and 2.6 meters high. The victims entered the chamber through a door — directly from the Road to Heaven. The room held approximately 200 to 350[54] naked bodies crushed together. The room was hermetically sealed and glistened with white wall tiles and terra cotta floor tiles. The tiles were scrubbed clean between each use.

The innocent looking nickel-plated shower heads protruded from the ceilings, delivering the gas. The Treblinka gas chambers did not use the Zyklon B gas made famous at Auschwitz. Rather they used old fashioned carbon monoxide. An old Soviet tank motor would pump gas into the chambers through pipes.[55] With the door sealed the gas turned on, the victims' last shred of doubt vaporized. Terrified screams, crying *Shma Yisroel* — a Jewish prayer declaring that God is our God and God is one — was the last sound they made. Death took approximately 25 minutes. After the victims fell eternally silent, the door on the other side of the chamber was opened and the *Totenjuden* removed the dead bodies. They ran, carrying the bodies to the edge of the massive pit, pausing for a few seconds along the way to allow the "dentists" to pull out the gold teeth.

These three very busy gas chambers could not kill quickly enough. So, in late August or early September 1942 a decision was made to build more gas chambers.[56]

These additional gas chambers were larger (approx. 50 sq. meters) and could hold approximately 1,000-1,200 each.[57] The new gas chamber building was made to look like a *Shul*, adorned with a Star of David on top.[58] Upon entering, victims were greeted with a *"Paroches"* — a curtain that covers the Ark holding the Torah scrolls in a synagogue, with the Hebrew inscription from the book of Psalms — "This is the gateway to God. The righteous shall pass through."[59]

Treblinka was built primarily to receive and "process" the Jews of Warsaw and other large Polish towns. On July 23, 1942, the trains from Warsaw rolled in and the real work began. They arrived daily — sometimes two or three each day. Each transport brought thousands of men, women and children, old and young, devout and secular. Between July 23 and the end of September — 265,000 Warsaw Jews arrived, and this was only the beginning. The processing of the "pieces," required that all luggage be left in the reception area and then with no chance to get their bearings and with the help of Nazi screams and whips, the women and children were herded into the undressing barracks while the men removed their clothing, at least at the beginning of the camp's operation, in the outdoor reception area. They were forced to deposit all remaining valuables with the "Clerk," remove their clothes and tie their shoes together with the laces. In a state of shock, they obeyed. They were then sent running, naked and terrified, down the Road to Heaven. The whole way they were urged forward faster and faster by SS guards screaming — *achtung!* and *schnell, schnell*, as they hit them with rifle butts, whips, and random bullets to keep the fear level high. With this atmosphere of chaos and terror, the victims ran down the Road to Heaven into the gas chamber to escape the beatings and the bullets. Women had the added humiliation, before running to their deaths, of having their hair shorn. The Jewish locks were packed and sent to the SS Central Economic Administrative Office.[60] The hair may have been used for stuffing mattresses or making hawsers for submarines.[61]

The first Commandant of Treblinka, Irmfield Eberl, was a physician who honed his skills at the T-4, Euthanasia Program and during his stay at the Death Camp Sobibor. Eberl, wanting to impress Himmler, kept the number of Warsaw transports ever coming. He was not, however, prepared for the volume. The task of disposing of the dead bodies on the train, selecting the *Lazaret* victims, getting the rest to relinquish their valuables and move through the undressing area and down the Road to Heaven, just took too long. They couldn't all be killed in the gas chambers before the next train arrived. So, the guards were ordered to shoot hundreds of people as they stepped off the train. And there they remained — for days. Thousands of decomposing, bloated corpses, piled up together with mountains of clothing and valuables that were strewn all around the open space. Dante could not have imagined the sight and stench of rotting human flesh, lying amid gold, money and jewels, that hit those stepping out of the boxcars that summer.

In late August, the Treblinka "mess" became known to the Operation Reinhard top brass. Eberl was immediately dismissed. Franz Stangl, an Austrian Nazi with years of experience from both the T-4, Euthanasia Program and one of the other newly minted Operation Reinhard death camps,[62] Sobibor, was appointed as the new Commandant. First, all the transports were halted and the Jewish prisoners were ordered to clean up the "mess."[63] No transports arrived between August 28 and September 3, 1942. In December 1942, Stangl constructed a fake train station so that arriving passengers would be lulled into believing that they were at a transit stop, heading east for work. A tall clock (that did not change time), together with a timetable and ticket counters were built. There were arrows indicating "To Baronovich," "To Volokovysk," "To Bialystok."

When passengers disembarked they saw a sign:

Attention, Jews from Warsaw!

You are now at a transit camp, from which you will continue your journey to labor camps.

In order to prevent epidemics, clothing as well as luggage must be turned in for disinfection.

Gold, cash, foreign currency and jewelry must be turned in at the ticket office. You will be given receipts for these valuables. Your valuables will be returned to you later, on presentation of your receipts.

For reasons of personal cleanliness, all new arrivals must bathe before continuing the journey.[64]

Kurt Franz, was transferred from Belzec to Treblinka in August of 1942.

He was known as the *Lalka* — the Doll in Polish — because he was so handsome. The *Lalka* had a black and white spotted dog with the characteristics of a St. Bernard, called Barry. It was the size of a calf. "The dog," Sam later said, "was as big as I was." Though Sam was no giant at five feet, one inch, that is still a big dog. Barry was employed to encourage the victims to run down the Road to Heaven and was trained, at the command, "Man, go get that dog,"[65] to attack a man's genitals. Once attacked by Barry, even if you survived, you were in such bad shape that you would be taken to the *Lazaret* and shot.[66] It is said that the *Lalka* never strolled through the camp without killing a few Jews on the way. Just for sport. He loved sport — especially boxing. Jews were forced to box until their blood flowed.[67]

One day, the *Lalka* walked through the camp with his hunting rifle on his shoulder with his dog, Barry, following behind. He noticed a Jew, aimed his rifle, and shot. The Jew fell, screaming in pain. The *Lalka* approached him, laughing, and ordered him to get up and pull down his pants, so that he could check his aim. The man, doubled up in pain, with blood streaming from his lead-filled behind, pulled down his pants as ordered. But the *Lalka* gave a disappointing shrug, and muttered:

"Damn it! I missed the balls."[68]

Nonetheless, the *Lalka*, was Sam's savior. Sam could not understand why, except that the *Lalka* told him he liked his eyes. They were translucent blue — the blue of the sky mixed with the blue of a shallow sea. Soon after the *Lalka* arrived at Treblinka in August of 1942, Sam became the *Lalka's* "Pet Jew."

Kurt Franz, the *Lalka*. Credit: Yad Vashem

ESTHER

Stys Families

JUNE 1942-AUGUST 1943

After the Nazis carted away 135 men in June of 1942, the Kwiateks were scared. They gathered around their table to discuss what happened and what to do. Their relief that Moishe and Chaim were safe was overwhelming. They needed to make plans for when the Nazis come back. Their father, David, wanted to make a hiding place in their small, slanted attic. They could hide without leaving their home and drawing attention to themselves. Their mother, Faiga Leah, disagreed.

"The Nazis will search each Jewish home and will find us hiding in the attic," Faiga Leah insisted. "We must go to one of our non-Jewish friends and ask them to hide us if the Nazis return."

David and Faiga Leah could not agree on the best course of action for when the Nazis returned. Faiga Leah went, on her own, to the Czarnecki family and poured out her heart to them. She told them that the Nazis would return to Stoczek and take the rest of the Jews. She and Chana needed a place to hide when they came back. Her friends agreed to make a hiding place in their basement.

The summer wore on with tension in the air. As *Rosh Hashanah* approached, Esther helped Faiga Leah prepare for the holiday. They obtained some carp to make *gefilta* fish and they had a chicken to make chicken soup, but their hearts were not in it. In 1942, *Rosh Hashanah* came on September 12. The *Shuls* that were still standing were filled with Jews crying and praying for God's help in these dark times. What would come in the Jewish year of 5703? They did not think it would be anything good. The Nazis had made the lives of the Jews so difficult and now there were rumors that they would be "resettled to the east" to work.

It was not long before their worst fears were realized. It was a few weeks after *Rosh Hashanah* and the Nazis had things "up and running" at Treblinka. They came back to Stoczek with their Ukrainian henchmen. Again, they surrounded the town. This time they had no use for the Jewish Police or the *Judenrat*. Members of these elite groups were rounded up and forced to stand in the town square, just like the other 400 men, women, and children. House by house, screaming, "*raus, raus*" and "*schnell, schnell*," the Nazis hit people who refused to leave their home or just shot them. Specially trained dogs were let loose to increase the terror by barking ferociously and attacking the Jews on command.

The moment they heard the screaming and shooting, the Kwiateks knew the time had come. David and Faiga Leah still did not agree on where to hide. Faiga Leah gave David, Moishe, Chaim, and Esther a final hug and took their daughter Chana by the hand and headed out the door. Faiga Leah and Chana ran to the Czarnecki's, slipping into their basement hiding place. The rest of the Kwiatek family went up into their small triangular-shaped attic to hide. Esther had one last idea. She wrote a note in German: "This house is owned by Germans," and she put it on the front door, placing a lock on the outside of the door to make it look like no one was home.

They sat in the attic listening to the dogs barking, the Nazis screaming, their neighbors wailing, and the gun shots that pierced their hearts. No one knocked at their door or forced their way in. Perhaps the sign on the door and the lock had worked. Over the next couple of days, the town quieted as people were killed or forced to leave on foot or by truck. Esther had no idea where everyone was going, but after Slonim, she knew it couldn't be good. They stayed in the attic for three nights and days. With no food, their hunger drew them out. After dark, they climbed out of the house window, as the door was locked from the outside.

Stoczek was a ghost town — it was empty. No people, no sounds, nothing. They ran out to the woods that surrounded the town. There, they found others who had hidden and escaped the round-up. They too were frightened and starving. David looked for Faiga Leah and Chana, but they were not there. He hoped they were still hiding in the Czarnecki's basement. It was September, so the trees still bore fruit, giving them something nourishing to eat. They begged for food from some nearby Polish farmers. A few gave them something, others sold them some food, and yet others chased them away and threatened to turn them over to the Germans.

They knew that hiding with such a large group was dangerous. So, they agreed to split up into smaller groups and go their separate ways. It was better not to know where other groups were hiding. If they were captured and tortured, they would not be able to reveal the hiding places. David Kwiatek decided to separate from his children and go to the home of a non-Jewish friend in Wielga, a nearby town, and hide there. Moishe, Esther, and Chaim stayed together. But they had nowhere to go and nowhere safe to hide. They first knocked on the doors of non-Jewish farmers close to town. They were turned away. It was too dangerous to help Jews. Esther, Moishe, and Chaim decided to walk a few more kilometers, to the Styś farms. They hoped that these families, whom they knew well, would help them in their moment of desperation.

Arriving at the home of Helena and Aleksander Styś, they opened the gate and entered the yard. The small wooden house, with a low roof, stood opposite the barn with grass covering the open space in between. They knocked on the door and Helena answered. She took one look at Esther, Moishe, and Chaim and knew that they had escaped the Nazis. She had heard what happened in town. Her nephew, Jan, only eleven years old, came home from school crying and he told them how he had been in school and just below the schoolhouse window he had seen the Nazis force the Jews to dig a pit at the Jewish cemetery and then shot them into it.

Helena had heard that the rest of the Stoczek Jews were taken out of town, by foot or truck. The rumor was that they were being taken to Treblinka, just twenty kilometers (12.4 miles) away. They didn't know why. Treblinka was a small town with a tiny railroad station. There was nothing else there. Esther thought of Slonim and how the Jews were taken out of town and shot into pits.

Could this be what was happening there?

"We have nowhere to go and nowhere to hide. Will you help us?" Esther begged. "The Jews in the forest are being hunted by Poles and if they find us they will kill us or turn us into the Nazis."

"It's dangerous," said Helena. "If I am caught, my whole family will be killed."

Looking at the desperate Kwiatek at her doorstep, Helena could not turn them away. Their families have been friends for so long. They went each Sunday after Church to their soda factory with their children. Winter was just around the corner and they would soon freeze to death in the harsh weather.

"Listen, I don't want you to get caught. Hide in my barn, but don't stay in one place too long. It will be too dangerous. I will talk to Władysława (pronounced Vadislava), my sister-in-law, and see if you can hide in her barn as well. She lives just next door."

They were so grateful to lay their heads on the hay in Helena's barn. They hadn't realized how exhausted they were. They closed their eyes and slept for hours. When they woke, they found some food that Helena had left for them. They ate every morsel.

So it went, the first few nights they hid in Helena's barn. Chaim, a teenager, was not sure this was a good idea. He didn't trust the Styś family. He wanted to go back out into the forest and hide with other Jews.

"Fine, go ahead," Esther and Moishe told Chaim. "We are staying here."

Chaim left and went out into the forest. He found some Jews who were hiding. He asked if he could stay and hide with them. The Jews told him he could stay, but only if he paid them. Chaim had no money, so he came back to Helena's barn. Later, they heard that the people that Chaim had met in the forest were discovered and killed.

During the day, they mostly hid, coming out at night to look for food. Food was the main concern. It was fall, so they found some fruit on the trees, berries, and mushrooms that grew all around the forest. Helena, Edward, and Władysława brought them food, but only when it was safe. There was never enough food and they were always hungry. They knew they couldn't stay in one place for long, it was too dangerous for them and for the Polish families. They hid in Helena's barn, Władysława's barn, the barn of a family named Dobosz, as well as other farmers' barns that they entered without permission. When the weather warmed, they hid more often in the thickest parts of the forest where the brush and trees would serve to hide them.

They ventured out in the daylight to search for food when they thought it was safe. But, they never knew when a German might arrive in the forest looking for hidden Jews. There was a paved road not more than five minutes by foot from the Styś farms that Nazis used to travel to and from Treblinka. But, even more dangerous than the Germans, were the non-Jewish Poles. It was known that one of the Styś' neighbors was a "Jew Catcher" and would spend his days roaming the forest looking for Jews. If a Jew was caught and turned over to the Nazis, the catcher received a reward — a kilo of sugar. Besides individual Jew Catchers, groups of Poles would often gather in the village and organize a *Judenjagd* (Jew Hunt), combing the nearby forest for hidden Jews. If it was discovered that the Styś families were hiding Jews, the Nazis would be informed and Esther, Moishe, and Chaim and the entire Styś family would be killed. Helena and Władysława told Esther that a neighbor was hiding Jews and a non-Jewish Pole informed the Nazis. The Nazis killed the Jews and all the non-Jews who were home.[69]

Stanisław was very nervous about hiding Jews. But his wife, Władysława, was insistent, they would not abandon the Kwiateks. To do so meant certain death for them. Stanisław wanted to make hiding the Jews a bit safer — for the Jews and for his family. He built a wooden box frame — 4 by 4 meters — in his barn. He covered the frame with hay to make it look like a hay stack. Slats were cut into the wood so that they could look out into the yard to see what was happening. Esther, Moishe, and Chaim hid inside the fake haystack during the cold months. If a Polish neighbor or a Nazi was snooping around the barn, they would see a haystack, nothing out of the ordinary.

Edward, Władysława, and Helena made food and brought it to them in the fake haystack. To conceal the food under her large hooded cloak, Władysława placed it behind her neck or in the large sleeves. When it felt safe enough, Władysława would take the food into the barn and give it to Esther, Moishe, and Chaim. There were days, however, that it felt too dangerous, the food would be left in a dog's pail just outside the door of the barn. The hidden Jews would sneak out after dark and retrieve the food.

After they had been hiding for just a few months, Moishe ventured out in daylight hours to look for food in the Toporski Forest. When it got dark and Moishe was not back, Esther began to worry. Her worry grew to panic when he did not return. The next morning, she began to ask if anyone knew what happened to Moishe. She found out that he had been killed in the forest.

She could not move; she could not breathe. Moishe, her husband, her rock, was dead. Someone told her where his body lay. She went to see him and there he lay, motionless. She touched his skin, it was so cold. She knew that he had an expensive watch hidden in the crotch of his pants. She thought about reaching in to get the watch but decided that she would not desecrate his body. She left him and ran back to Helena's house. She told Helena and her 16-year-old daughter, Janina, what had happened, that Moishe had been killed in the forest and that he was dead. She cried and cried as Helena held and rocked her.

Esther could not hold back, she told Helena and Janina that she was pregnant. Now what would she do? She had only been married for a year and here she was, her family murdered, her husband shot, and now she was pregnant and hiding with her teenage brother-in-law. How could she go on? She did not want to continue living.

But she did. Her pregnancy was difficult, as she was hungry all the time and there was very little food. As the baby grew, sleeping on the hay in the barn or on the ground in the woods became harder and harder. When the time came, she gave birth in Helena's home. The baby died shortly after birth. Esther cried and cried until she had no more tears. Now what? Was there any future? Esther could not even begin to imagine. She didn't want to go on. But she was strong in body and spirit and she stored her pain in every cell of her body and concentrated on surviving one more day.

Now that it was warmer, Esther and Chaim hid less often in the Styś barns and more often in the woods. They stayed hidden during the day, but their insatiable hunger brought them out at night to forage for food. Her desire to collect more food led Esther to go during daylight hours to a nearby forest to pick blueberries. Chaim didn't come with her because he looked too Jewish. Esther covered her hair with a scarf to look like a Polish peasant and ventured to the blueberry field. She got a bucket from a Polish girl and began to pick. She chose one side of the blueberry field where there were some women picking who didn't seem to know each other. On the other side, there were women who were laughing and socializing while they picked. She didn't want anyone to ask her questions.

As she was picking the berries, a forest policeman with a dog came over to her.

"Do you have a license to pick berries?" the policeman asked.

"I do," answered Esther, "but I don't have it with me. I am sorry. I will bring it next time."

"What is your name?" he asked.

"Why do you need to know my name?" Esther responded.

"I don't need to know, I am just curious," he said.

Though among non-Jews Esther went by Krystyna, she did not want to tell him her name. The policeman confiscated all her blueberries but left her alone. Her body was shaking as she picked a few more berries, trying to appear calm. Then she left. She found Chaim and told him what happened. She didn't go back to pick blueberries any more, it was too dangerous. She gathered mushrooms instead.

The woods had a Polish *gajowy* (watchman) who knew they were hiding. Sometimes he would send a piece of meat or other food to Esther and Chaim with a small non-Jewish child who would not garner attention. They would hide all day and come out only at night to get the gift of food and scavenge for mushrooms that carpet the forest floor.

Summertime was easier because there was fruit to be found in the forest and they could bathe in the nearby river. The Styś families were still a huge presence in their lives. Edward would come out into the forest leading a cow on a rope and pushing a cart. He limped due to his polio and it was slow going. Because of his disability, the Nazis didn't bother him. He would reach the hiding place and call out to Esther and Chaim. He would reveal that under the blanket on his cart, lay some freshly baked bread. He would give them the bread and allow them to milk the cow. They had no bucket to put the milk in, so they took turns squirting the milk into their mouths — straight from the cow's teat.

One day, Helena told Esther to take as many potatoes as she wanted from their garden. She took as many as she and Chaim could carry back to the forest — both red and white potatoes. In the forest, she built a stove out of two stones with a fire underneath and a pot on top. She cooked the potatoes. After they were cooked, she put them in a sack and then cooked some mushrooms they had picked and ate them together. With a little salt that they had saved, it felt like a feast. While they had that food, they didn't have to beg. It was a moment of freedom.

It was then, in the end of July in 1943, that Esther had her dream where she saw the "4" on the wooden door of her Stoczek home. In the dream she stood up and traced over the 4 with a red crayon. When she woke up in the morning, she couldn't believe that it had only been a dream; it seemed so real.

"That is bad," Chaim said when he heard the dream. "Something terrible will happen in four days."

Treblinka — Count Down to Uprising

JUNE 1942-AUGUST 1943.

After building straw roofs at Treblinka for two months, the *Lalka* asked Sam: "Can you wash laundry?"

"*Yavall!* — Yes, indeed!" Sam answered.

So, a wash basin with a board was presented and the *Lalka* ordered Sam to show that he knew how to wash clothes.

"I like your eyes," the *Lalka* said satisfied. "I will make a laundry and you will be the supervisor."

Two days later, there was a laundry building and Sam was installed as supervisor. The *Lalka* laid down the law:

"Jewish laundry, Ukrainian laundry, and German laundry should never be mixed."

Other prisoners were assigned to work with Sam in the laundry, but they didn't last long. "They tried to fool them with stomach aches not to work," Sam later explained. "They were taken away." Every day, Sam would venture out to the reception area to collect the clothing to be laundered, still warm from the victims' bodies. One day, the *Lalka* saw Sam out in the open making his rounds.

"What are you doing?" he said, "It's too dangerous out here; you could get shot at any moment. I want you to survive. Stay in the laundry and I will have the clothing brought to you there."

Sam worked furiously, washing tons of laundry. There were twenty-four basins, twelve on either side of a large pot in which the laundry was "cooked." After six weeks, he could not keep up with the volume. "There were hundreds of thousands of shirts, hundreds of thousands of underwear, plenty," Sam later explained. "Twenty-two boxcars of people came every day."

Sam told the *Lalka* that he needed help in the laundry and twelve women were selected from the next transport and put to work with Sam. Sam said this was not enough. So, they added another twelve women. At one point, thirty-three women worked in the laundry with Sam. These women would later save Sam's life when he faced the gallows.

Sam ran the laundry as a business. He didn't know what went on in the tailor shop, shoe shop, or other Treblinka "businesses." "I had to make sure that my business was in order," Sam later said. "And if I did things in order, I would have success."

One day a *Kapo* saw some of his relatives get off the train from Warsaw. To save them from the gas chamber, he ordered Sam out of the laundry. The *Kapo* intended to replace Sam with four of his Warsaw relatives.

"I've been working here for a year already," Sam said. "You are going to take me out of here and put me in hell?"

The *Kapo* started to hit Sam with a *beitch* and a *conchik*, whips made from wire and leather. Grabbing a wooden board, Sam hit the *Kapo* over the head. Falling to the ground, blood ran from his head. At Treblinka, to hit a *Kapo* was a capital offense. The *Kapo* called the Nazi *Obersturmführer* who the prisoners nicknamed "Stinker," but Sam called "a bastard, a terrible bastard." The Stinker ordered the carpenters to build gallows to hang Sam.

"Don't hang him, hang the *Kapo*," the women of the laundry said to the *Obersturmführer*. "If you hang him, hang us all."

"Why?" the Stinker asked.

"Because the Jews are coming now from Warsaw and the *Kapo* was going to take Shmulik out of the laundry and put in four of his relatives," one woman responded.

The German asked the *Kapo* what Sam's crime was.

"He stole money and gave it to the Ukrainians," the *Kapo* said.

"This is not true, he didn't steal any money, he works very hard. But the *Kapo* wants to take him out," the women retorted.

The *Obersturmführer* saw what was going on and gave Sam his gun and gestured that he should shoot the *Kapo*.

"No, I won't shoot anybody, no sir, I don't want to," said Sam.

So, the Stinker shot the *Kapo* in the head and Sam returned to the laundry with his female saviors. This was not the last time Sam's moral judgment would be tested. The laundry workers were guarded by an older German officer. One day, Sam told him that he wanted to use the washing tubs to cook food.

"I understand, but other German guards will come in here, what will they say?" The officer said.

"It will happen to me, whatever they say, they say," Sam responded. "I'll cook here."

So, Sam cooked. He cooked potatoes he stole from the kitchen. He also cooked food he found sown in people's clothes or left out in the reception area.

"When people came to Treblinka, *nebach*, they didn't know where they were going," Sam later explained. "They told them they were taking them to work. They fried goose *shmaltz* (fat) and *farfel* (barley)."

The victims brought pots filled with this and other food stuffs. Sam would grab them and bring them into the laundry. He first fed himself and his female saviors and then he carried the food to the sick and dying in the so-called hospital. Without these additional calories, the patients were doomed. Sam knew that if he was caught, it would cost him his life. But the old SS laundry guard didn't give him away and he continued his clandestine restaurant, feeding the desperate souls of Treblinka until the uprising.

Working in the laundry had other benefits. Sam found money and jewelry sown into the lining of people's clothing. He took some of these valuables and buried them next to a tree. He hoped and prayed that he would survive and live to sell or spend these treasures on the "outside." Also, Sam never lacked for fine clothes. The *Lalka* insisted that he be well dressed. Sam didn't want to wear the clothes of his murdered brethren.

"Do you want to get hit?" the *Lalka* said. "I want you to look sweet."

So, Sam would pick out nice boots, pants, and shirts to wear. There was no shortage of fine clothes to pick from. Sam hated to wear the clothes of these dead Jews, but he obeyed.

Meanwhile, life inside Treblinka was fraught with danger. At any moment, you could be killed or tortured. One day, Sam watched while a man had his legs and arms locked to a table. As he was locked down, he received 25 lashes with a *beitch* or *conchik*. If he survived, sitting was a challenge for the next few weeks. Or another time when the Germans found someone with bread that had not been baked in the camp, he ordered a Ukrainian guard to hold his head in a pitcher of water until he drowned.[70]

"It would come into my head," Sam later said. "I would think at night, where are my mother and father, where are my sisters and brothers? Why should I be here? I wanted to be free of my life also." But, the *Lalka* insisted — "You will survive."

The only possible explanation was that "God in heaven sent them to me," Sam later explained. Besides the *Lalka*, there was another Nazi officer who wanted Sam to make it out alive. This officer was one of the Nazis who chased the victims into the gas chambers. One day, sometime in 1943, the Nazi told Sam he would take off his uniform and give it to him, so he could escape.

"He took off his coat with anger and he ordered me that I should leave there." Sam later said. "I thought, where would I go? I will be caught — A Jew wearing a German SS uniform. I will be killed instantly."

Early in 1943, Heinrich Himmler visited Treblinka. He visited the massive pits where the corpses were dumped after gassing. He began to worry that the Germans may not be victorious, especially after their defeat at Stalingrad in February of 1943. If they lose the war, the world will come here and see the evidence of their crime. The Jewish workers were locked up in their barracks during the visit. They were not allowed to see the "great man." Just before leaving the

Dredge at Treblinka. Credit: Yad Vashem

camp, Himmler issued an order — don't throw the bodies into the pit any longer. Burn them. Further, he ordered that the hundreds of thousands of corpses buried in the massive graves were to be exhumed and burned. All traces of the crime must be erased.[71]

It was the Jews who were forced to carry out this unspeakable task. Bodies were exhumed with a dredge. Train tracks were used as grills upon which the bodies were burned. By spring, fires burned day and night. It turns out that the subcutaneous layer of fat on female corpses is better developed than on males and they burn better.[72] So women were placed on the bottom of the pile and men on the top. Oil was poured on the bodies to increase the inferno. When Sam smelled the air, he knew that they were burning bodies. He remembered the sickening smell of burning flesh from Operation Barbarossa as he hid under the unfinished bridge when this awful war began.

As spring turned to summer, the number of bodies left to burn was smaller and the train transports began to slow. The prisoners heard from the Ukrainian guards that the Germans were suffering defeats on the battlefield. With well over

800,000 already murdered at Treblinka, the end of the operation was in sight. The prisoners knew that they too would soon be turned to ash. This knowledge intensified plans for an uprising. There were 50 men who were in on the plan. Sam's cell of twelve men was led by Shmuel Rajzman. Years later, Sam told how he carried a picture of Shmuel Rajzman in his wallet.

"I carry it around with me," Sam said, "because he was my best friend."

The final date for the revolt was set for August 2nd at 5 p.m. The time was chosen carefully to allow for maximum manpower. It was at 5 p.m. that a train-load of 200-300 men came back from the Treblinka work camp.[73] These men could join the uprising. A message was also sent to prisoners who worked in the Upper Camp, so they too would be ready. The prisoners in the Lower Camp wrote messages on paper used to roll cigarettes and threw the cigarettes over the fence to the Upper Camp. In this way, the *Totenjuden*, who worked in the upper camp where the gas chambers were, knew the details of the revolt.

There were two locksmiths involved in the planning. They worked with a thirteen-year-old boy who, because of his youth, could roam the camp, without German suspicion. One of the locksmiths, Sam thought was "brilliant," and he showed the boy how to make an impression of the lock on the arsenal door from soap. Once the impression was made, the "brainy one" made keys to the arsenal. Sam and a few others were given keys to take weapons out of the arsenal at the appointed time. The signal to start the revolt would be a single shot from the blacksmith's workshop. If a Nazi came into any of the workshops before 5 o'clock, he would be killed and his body hidden. This would eliminate some Nazis even before the start time. At the sound of the shot, the administration building was to be attacked and the Nazis inside murdered. The telephone lines would be cut, and the oil and gas barrels would be used to set the camp on fire. The man Sam called the "electrician," rigged the gas tank to explode at the push of a button. Other groups were tasked to disarm the Ukrainians and lock them in a barracks at the start of the revolt. At the same time, the watchtowers were to be fired on, killing the guards or at least forcing them to evacuate the towers.

Sam didn't sleep the night before, and on that sizzling hot August day the tension was palpable. Sam hid his small packet of poison, given to all those involved in the uprising, in his pocket. They were to swallow it if caught to avoid both the horrible pain of torture and the possibility of revealing details of the plan. That afternoon found the camp quieter than usual. A group of SS Officers had gone to cool off in the nearby Bug river. At 3 o'clock the boys went to the arsenal and began to take out some of the rifles and grenades. They were passed around to those with specific tasks to perform. Each group knew their task and was ready to execute.

But things didn't go as planned. The revolt started early, at 4 o'clock — before the group leaders had everything in place. The premature start came about after a Ukrainian guard in one of the watchtowers saw a prisoner dig something up and put it in his pocket. Seeing the glint of gold in the afternoon sun, the Ukrainian called Fritz Kuttner, the Chief of the Lower Camp. Sam saw Kuttner come and beat the man with a whip — over and over again. It was not long before the prisoner revealed that a revolt was planned for that very evening. Sam ran as fast as he could and told Shmuel Rajzman what he saw. Rajzman ordered the revolt to begin immediately.

Malkinia – Nazi soldiers at the Bug River. Credit: Chris Webb Private Archive

"We started the uprising right then and there," Sam later said. "It was 4 o'clock. We started to throw grenades and shoot. . . . I shot too. There was a watchtower near me. I threw a grenade at him. . . . We got the electrician and he pushed the button and blew up the whole camp from head to toe."*

Utter chaos erupted and prisoners began running towards the fence. Someone threw a hand grenade at the fence, tearing a hole big enough to run through. As hundreds of prisoners ran towards the fence, many were hit by machine gun fire. A cry of fear was heard, but, as Samuel Willenberg describes, "above the sounds of fear and terror, there rose a mighty shout: 'Hurrah! Hurrah!'"[74]

At this most painful and triumphant moment, each person was on his or her own. Those who were not killed in those early minutes, ran as fast they could — out — out into the open and to a place of hopeful escape — the woods. What would happen next, no one knew, but at last they were free.

---

* This account of the uprising is Sam's version, though some details are filled in with stories of the others listed below. Other survivors have different versions about what time the revolt started and why they were forced to start early. For other versions, see memoirs of Jankiel Wiernik, Samuel Willenberg, Samuel Rajzman, Tanhum Grinberg, Shalom Kohn, and Oskar Strawczynski. See also, accounts retold in Webb and Chocholatý, 99-113 and Sereny, 236-250. The brick gas chambers were not damaged.

SAM & ESTHER

Meeting in the Woods

AUGUST 1943-JULY 1944

Smoke had emanated from Treblinka for months — day and night. Helena told Esther what was happening there, that the Jews were being gassed and their bodies burned. But this smoke was different — a huge ball of fire with an explosion of dark gray smoke. It had been three days since Esther's dream. She had no idea what it meant, but she was scared. Would she and Chaim be alive tomorrow evening?

The fourth day after the dream, Velvel and Sam came into Esther's life. They were like a mirage in a desert. Jews who escaped Treblinka. Impossible.

After Esther's convincing plea to Helena to hide them in her barn, Sam, Velvel, Esther and Chaim found a corner, put down some hay and tried to be invisible. In the quiet of the night, Sam began to tell Esther, in whispers, of his escape. He explained how, during the prisoner revolt he threw grenades at the Ukrainian guards and then ran straight to the hole in the fence. On the other side of the fence, he could hear the shouts and the shots being fired all around him. But what rang most sweetly in his ears was sound of the prisoners yelling "Hurrah, hurrah."

"I ran for my life," Sam told her. "So many were shot as we ran out of the camp. Those, like me, who got out, were being chased by Germans, Ukrainians, and Poles. After a few kilometers, I ran right into the Bug River. I didn't know how to swim, but I decided that if I am going to die, I would rather drown in the river than be caught by the Nazis. All of us who were part of the revolt had cyanide in case we were caught. But it wasn't the time for that yet. I jumped into the river and the next thing I knew I was washed up onto the shore. I got up and ran towards Stoczek because that was the last place I lived. I thought that if I could get to Stoczek, I would be able to find someplace to hide. As I was running, I saw another man running too. I yelled to him and realized that it was Velvel. He was from Stoczek, so he knew the way. We ran together and ended up here."

All four of them, Esther, Chaim, Sam and Velvel survived the tense days following the uprising at Treblinka by hiding in Helena's barn. It was during these days and nights that Sam and Velvel told Esther and Chaim about Treblinka. They told them about the transports filled with Jews coming day in and day out, at first from Warsaw and then from all over Europe. They told them about the fake train station set up to fool the Jews into believing they were at a transit station. How they had to leave their valuables, undress, and run down the Road to Heaven straight into the gas chambers. How the outside was made to resemble a *Shul* and each gas chamber was made to look like a shower room. But once the people were inside, the chamber was sealed and carbon monoxide pumped in. They were dead within 25 minutes. Sam and Velvel explained that they had been forced to help build the camp, that Sam went on to be the supervisor of the laundry and Velvel, a carpenter, became a "Court Jew,"[75] a skilled craftsman who was allowed to walk freely around the camp and had plenty of food. The Court Jews had their own kitchen. They explained that the Jews who made up the *Totenjuden* units had the worst task of all, carrying the dead from the gas chambers to the mass graves or later, when the bodies were being burned, to the fiery pit.

They described the Nazis in charge of Treblinka in brutal detail: Dr. Irmfried Eberl, the first Commandant who got fired for making a mess of things; Franz Stangl, the second Commandant; August Wilhelm Miete, the Angel of Death who took people to the *Lazaret* and shot them into a pit; Ivan the Terrible, who worked in the gas chambers; and Kurt Franz, the *Lalka*. When it came time to tell them about the *Lalka*, Sam had to explain how the *Lalka*, the cruelest of the Treblinka Nazis, saved him from death. He could not understand why, but it was true. He would not be alive if not for the *Lalka*.

"How many were killed there?" Esther asked with tears streaming down her cheeks.

"I can only guess," answered Sam, "but it must have been close to two million."*

This was much worse than all the terrible things Esther had imagined were happening in Treblinka. Her body trembled with silent sobs as she thought of all the people she knew from Stoczek who were taken to Treblinka. How they must have suffered. She could only hope that Moishe and Chaim's parents and sister had escaped this awful fate. She and Chaim hadn't heard from them at all this past year. But they continued to have hope that they were still alive, hiding somewhere.

Sam explained that he had left his parents back in the summer of 1941 and he had no idea whether they were still alive or not. But he knew that many of his siblings who had been living in Slonim were dead. Esther couldn't believe it.

"I lived in Slonim at the time of the massacre," Esther explained. "I didn't know your siblings, but my whole family was murdered, shot into pits outside of town. I survived because I was in the hospital recovering from typhus."

On the third night of hiding, the four of them opened the barn door, looked out and seeing no one in the yard, they crept across the grass to Helena's front door. They knocked and Helena answered. They thanked her with words and money and told her that they were heading out to the forest.

Sam had stuffed gold coins, *Złotys*, jewels, and whatever else of value he could fit into his pockets before he escaped from Treblinka. He had buried them where he hoped no would find them and then dug them up just before the uprising. He dreamed of escape and was sure the money and jewels would help him survive.

In the forest, Velvel Schneiderman thanked Esther for saving him but

---

* There are various estimates as to how many were murdered at Treblinka. Timothy Snyder in *Bloodlands*, puts the number at 780,863. *See* Snyder, *Bloodlands*, 273. Chris Webb and Michal Chocholatý put the number at 885,023. *See* Webb & Chocholatý, 193. Yitzhak Arad puts the number at 881,390. *See* Arad, 392-95 — Appendix A, Tables 3 & 4. Sam, however, believed that it must be at least two million.

decided not to stay with them. He wanted to move on as quickly as possible. He would travel at night and hide during the day. He hoped this plan would help him stay alive.[76] Sam, however, decided to stay and hide with Esther and Chaim. Though he desperately wanted to try to find his parents, he knew that it was not safe to travel through the Polish countryside now. The Nazis were in control of all of Poland and if they caught him, there would be no escape. Further, even where there were no Nazis, there were Poles who were happy to turn in a Jew for a reward.

This awful war would have to end sometime. Sam had heard from the Ukrainian guards in Treblinka that the Soviet Army was advancing. It felt safer to stay and hide here and hope that the Soviet Army would hurry. But in the meantime, they would take some additional precautions to stay alive.

"Let's dig a pit in the forest," Sam said. "We can stay in the pit until winter comes."

Esther and Chaim agreed. They took shovels from the Styś families and walked down a path that cut through the forest. The tall, stick-like trees seemed placed at random, but they were plentiful and the canopies of green rose high into the sky. There were tall grasses waving in the wind and low plants. Walking on this path for five-minutes led to a paved road. Esther later explained that this road was used by the Nazis to travel to and from Treblinka. On the other side of the road, they found a path that led deeper into a dense part of the forest. Here the trees were similar — thin and tall, with a high canopy — but there were many more of them and the lower growing plants were varied and plentiful, filling in the empty spaces between the trees. The forest floor was covered with dead leaves and scattered grasses. Mushrooms grew among the plants. The smell of the forest was fresh, especially after a good rain, when the clouds dissipated and the sun shone through the tree tops. If Sam, Esther, and Chaim didn't know how dangerous this forest was for Jews, it would have struck them as a beautiful, peaceful place.

They chose a spot that was far enough away from the road so that passers-by would not see or hear them. But it was only a ten or fifteen-minute walk back to the Styś homes, close enough to receive food or help in an emergency. They worked all day digging the hole. But they encountered a problem — what to do with all the dirt? If it looked like there were mounds of dirt in the forest, people would suspect that Jews had dug a hole and might be hiding somewhere and look for them. So, they spent hours spreading all the dirt around the forest so that no one would know that a pit had been dug.

Now they had to cover the pit. They took some wood, cut planks, and tied them together with thick black rope. The planks fit flush over the top of the pit. They used more rope to create a pulley system so that they could pull the wood planks over the top of the pit while they were inside. Then they took some prickle brush from the forest floor and bound them together with more rope so that they could pull the cluster of brush on top of the wood once they were inside the pit. They hoped this was enough to camouflage the hole.[77]

The pit was large enough for the three of them to stand, sit, or lie down, but they could do nothing else. It was small and cramped and smelled like a mixture of dank wet earth, moss, and urine. When it felt safe, Esther went to visit Helena and Janina. She and Janina cooked together. One day, Esther gathered different types of mushrooms in the forest and brought them over. She showed Janina how to make a soup out of these different kinds of mushrooms. Esther sometimes used the Styś' sewing machine to repair their clothing. Using the machine, Esther taught Janina how to sew brassieres. Over the two years she was in hiding from the Nazis, Esther and Janina became friends. They talked about the war, life, and religion, as they cooked and cleaned. Esther didn't bathe in their home. She, Sam, and Chaim bathed in the nearby river when the weather permitted. When it was too cold, they became encrusted with layers of dirt and lice, but Helena brought them a bucket of water once a week to wash their filthy bodies. Sam and Chaim were not invited into the house. They remained in the forest or the barns.

Władysława's nine-year-old son, Eugeniusz, often had the job of taking food to the pit. He was the youngest of all the Styś children and as such, he was the least likely to draw attention as he walked through the forest. He pretended to be playing, and as he played, he would go near the covered pit and leave food prepared by his mother, Helena, Edward, or Janina. Sometimes Eugeniusz and his 11-year-old brother, Jan, would go out to the pit just to see how Sam, Esther, and Chaim were doing. They would talk with them for a while and provide some needed diversion.

As the fall turned into winter, the fruit trees and berry bushes dried up and the temperature dropped into the 20's. Helena and Władysława told Sam, Esther, and Chaim to move back into the barns. Helena would manage their movement, telling them where to hide on any given day. When they were on Władysława's property, they hid in the fake haystack in the barn. In Helena's barn, they hid among the farm machinery and slept on the hay that was stored there. As he did out in the pit, Eugeniusz would come to visit in the barn and would sometimes play cards with them. He got along well with all of them, but he especially liked Chaim. He was the closest to his age.

The food provided by the Styś family was critical, but they were still hungry all the time. It was never enough. They rarely went out in the day time, but when they did it was to gather mushrooms. Food was always on their minds. At night, they dreamt about food and in the day they discussed all the food they would eat once they were free.

The days, weeks, and months crept by. They were scared all the time, fearing for their lives. In the winter, they were so cold, they wondered if they would survive. Frost and snow covered the ground and some days the wind blew so hard, it penetrated their bones. They took hay and covered themselves to sleep, but still, they shivered through the night. Helena's son, Polikarp, made moonshine vodka in the house. At night, he would sometimes visit Esther, Sam, and Chaim in the freezing cold barn, a bottle of moonshine in his hand. The vodka that they drank that winter warmed them, and, even if only for a few minutes, took the chill out of the night and lightened the darkness. They were grateful for this bit of artificial warmth.

Just as they thought they would never be warm again, the winter snow melted and the sun began to shine. Spring flowers bloomed and a sense of hope was renewed in their hearts. They heard from the Styś family that the Soviet army was getting closer. It was only a matter of time. They just had to hold on and stay out of sight.

Sometimes, Nazis came to Polish homes to ask for food or to search for hidden Jews. Władysława didn't want the Nazis coming into her yard when Sam, Esther, and Chaim were hidden in the barn. To keep them away, she tied headbands around her children's heads with large letters written in black: "**TYPHUS.**" With these headbands, the children were sent into the yard to play. When the Germans came by her house, they would see the signs on the children's heads and stay far away. Perfect.

Over these past ten months, Esther and Sam told each other their deepest secrets and shared their hopes and fears. Living in such a close, confined space, led to a deep emotional attachment. Then, one night in the spring, as Sam slept, his mother came to him in a dream. She appeared "as clear as day," Sam later said. She had one message for him.

"Shmulkele, you should marry her and she should be your wife," his mother said. "Don't look for another. This is the one."

He had not been thinking about marriage, only about survival. But after this dream, he realized that Esther had to be the one. She was strong, smart, kind-hearted, and resourceful. If they survived the war, she would be a good partner for life. They knew everything about each other after hiding together for these past months.

"Esther, I believe that we will be liberated soon," Sam may have said. "When that happens, will you marry me?"

Esther was caught off guard. They had never discussed marriage. But, she realized that if they survived, he would make a good husband. He was smart, funny, and hard-working. She would never have to explain how terrible the war years were. He knew.

"Yes, I will marry you," she responded. "I hope it will be soon."

SAM AND ESTHER

Freedom

1944-1945

Summer arrived. Sam, Esther, and Chaim moved back to the pit in the forest. They cleaned up the new level of winter dirt as best they could, but such was the life of a hidden Jew in the Polish woods. They knew the end of the war was coming. They heard German trucks rumble along the road nearby and they smelled fires that the Germans set as they fled the area. Then the sky began to roar and they knew the Red Army had arrived.

The Soviet tanks and infantrymen arrived in July of 1944.[78] The crossfire between the Soviets and the Germans was terrible, shots were flying everywhere. The ground was "jumping," Esther later said, from heavy artillery. Esther, Sam and Chaim lay down, making themselves as flat as they could, behind a big tree. They had survived this long, they didn't want to be killed by crossfire between the Germans and the Soviet armies now. They saw tanks and trucks on the road nearby and ran towards them, not knowing if they were Polish or Soviet soldiers. They heard them talking, Sam knew Russian and he yelled:

"They are Russian, Russian! We are saved."

The Soviet soldiers took one look at the three dirty and bedraggled humans and knew that they were Jews in hiding.

"*Yevalna* (you can go)," the soldiers said.

They couldn't believe it — they were free.[79] They ran to the Styś homes, but what they saw jolted them into a new reality. Władysława's home and barn were burnt to the ground — totally gone. Their fields, usually overflowing with tall golden summer wheat, were scorched, blackened and flat. There were traces of a burn smell still in the air. Helena's home was the only building standing. They went through the gate and knocked at the door. The door opened and they saw Helena. Esther and Helena fell into a long hug and began to cry.

"It's over," said Esther. "But what happened here? We smelled the fire from the woods."

"It was the Germans," Helena said. "As they fled, they threw flaming bundles of hay into our homes, barns, and fields."

The flames burned hot, like a furnace. But Helena had been watching as the Germans came and threw a flaming bundle into her house. She ran as fast as could into the house. She kicked the fiery hay down the stairs into the cellar and grabbed buckets of water and threw them down onto the fire and extinguished it, saving her house.

"Where is Władysława's family and Edward?" They asked.

"They are here, trying to figure out what to do. They lost everything. They will rebuild, but in the meantime, they will stay here. We have made our house into two apartments. So many have lost their homes. We have six families living with us."

"How are you managing with your wheat crop destroyed?" asked Esther.

"We are managing. One of the families living with us has some wheat left on their farm. They are making moonshine from their wheat with Polikarp's equipment and selling it at the Stoczek market on Mondays. Because of the fires, very few families have any wheat. So, moonshine is the best currency. With moonshine, you can buy anything. Władysława and I are using the smashed wheat that is left over after the moonshine to feed our cows. They love it and are producing lots of milk. We are making cheese and sour cream and selling it in Stoczek."

"Thank you for everything that you did for us," Esther said. "We will go to Stoczek. We don't have to hide any more. We want to see if anyone is still alive. Maybe we will find Chaim's parents and sister, Chana."

"I am sorry to tell you, but you know that Janina and Chana were friends from school. We heard that Faiga Leah and Chana fell into the hands of the devil," Helena replied. "You will not find them in Stoczek. I am sorry."

This was a hard blow. Both Faiga Lea and Chana were gone. Chaim's face was ashen and he could barely stand. They decided to go to Stoczek anyway. Maybe his father David or, at least some other Jews, would be there.

As they walked the four kilometers (2.4 miles) into town, they were silent, contemplating the news they had just heard. As they entered the town, they could feel the emptiness. There were so few people. As they walked the streets of Stoczek, they realized the magnitude of the tragedy. Stoczek was *Judenrein*. The houses and stores that had been standing twenty-two months ago when Esther, Moishe, and Chaim fled, were still there, but they recognized no one.

After a few hours of walking around town and asking people if any Jews survived, they found a few who had returned. They were living in abandoned homes. Sam and Esther followed their example and found a home to live in. Chaim may have stayed with them for a while, but his father had not returned, so he left Stoczek. They said their goodbyes, hoping to meet again.

The first thing to do was to bathe. They could not wait to get the layers of encrusted dirt off their bodies. They used some of the money Sam still had from Treblinka to buy new clothes. They began to feel human again. They also used Sam's money to buy food and supplies. There was still a market in Stoczek on Mondays and people, like the Styś family, came from the surrounding areas bringing their food and wares to sell. Sam and Esther made some money by buying wheat on the black market. Because of all the destroyed wheat fields, wheat and flour were highly valued commodities. They began *handlin* — buying wheat in nearby towns, transforming it into flour at a mill and selling it in Stoczek.

Sam and Esther decided to get married in December. The wedding took place in a small house in Stoczek. Ten survivors joined together to make it a festive affair. Among them were: a few survivors that they had met in Stoczek; Velvel Schneiderman; and Shmuel Rajzman, Sam's "best friend" and cell leader in Treblinka. Shmuel served as *Mesader Kedushin,* officiating at the ceremony. There were no Rabbis in Stoczek after the war; there were hardly any Jews at all.

1944 - Treblinka Survivors who survived the Uprising. Back Row, right to left: Velvel Schneiderman, Chaim Yankel Ciechanowski, Shmuel (Sam) Goldberg, Zigmand Brathandel, Shimon Rosenthal. Front Row: Lejzer Ciechanowski, Shimon Goldberg, Oscar Kudlik, Shmuel Rajzman, Oscar Strawczynski, Gutek (Gustav) Boraks, Yaakov (Jacob) Domb. Credit: Yad Vashem (names listed as they appear in Pinkas Stok – Stoczek Yizkor (Memorial) Book, 427, with additional information from Donat, 267.[80]

But after all the suffering, the hunger, the loss, they were happy to celebrate. They ate, smoked *Belomorkanal*[81] (fancy Russian cigarettes), and drank *schnapps*. The singing and dancing went on into the night.

"Shmulke," Shmuel Rajzman said to Sam before he left, "a group of us who survived the uprising are getting together to take a photo. Velvel Schneiderman will be there too. You should come and be in the photo."

"I will try my best to be there," Sam said.

Sam and Esther stayed in Stoczek until the spring, but they heard that it was safer to live in Ostrow. The Soviet army had a strong a presence there and they prevented the Poles from killing the returning Jews. They had heard stories of Jews being killed by the Poles when they returned to the towns and cities. Even without its 8,000 Jews, Ostrow was a large city with close to 10,000 residents. There were a few Jews living there, but it was a small group, not even enough for a *minyan*.*

Esther and Sam moved to Ostrow in the spring of 1945. Esther was pregnant and they rented a small one room apartment, with a kitchen attached. The bathroom was outside and there was no running water. But Ostrow had electricity, so electric lights shone in their small home.

Sam returned to a building in Ostrow where his father had run a *Yatzke* (a type of butcher shop) before the war. Sam reopened the *Yatzke*. He purchased livestock and killed them, selling the meat at the *Yatzke*. Sam needed some help, so he approached a non-Jewish pig farmer named Józef, whom he had known before the war. He asked if he wanted to go into business with him at the *Yatzke*. Józef agreed.

There was plenty of business. The Soviets took livestock as booty from Germany and would sell them to locals as they traveled back to the Soviet Union. Sam and Józef bought animals from the Russians, killed them, and sold the meat.

"We made money without limit," Sam later said.

In Ostrow, Esther gave birth to a beautiful baby girl. They named her Faiga Bracha, after their mothers: Sam's mother, Faiga and Esther's mother, Bracha. With her naming, Sam and Esther began to realize the depth of their loss. This child would never know her grandparents, uncles, aunts, or cousins. After growing up in such large, extended families, this was a hard reality. But, they had to move forward; they were starting their own family. They became close friends with the other survivors living in Ostrow, worked in the *Yatzke* and cared for baby Faiga.

It was not long after Faiga was born, maybe a few weeks, when some non-Jews came to Sam and offered to buy his family's estate and the *Yatzke*. But Sam didn't want to sell. They persisted. So, on a Friday, just after receiving a fresh shipment of cut meat to sell at the *Yatzke*, Sam paid a visit to his father's lawyer in Ostrow. He told him about the offer to buy the estate and wanted to discuss the best terms.

---

* Quorum of ten Jewish men needed to pray in community.

"Listen to me, Goldberg," the lawyer said to him, "run away today, not tomorrow. If you don't run away today, you won't be here tomorrow. They are going to kill you."

"Why," asked Sam.

"Because they want your property and they hate Jews" the lawyer replied.

Sam left the lawyer's office shaken and went straight home. Esther was home with baby Faiga, preparing for *Shabbes*. Sam told her what the lawyer had said and he told her that she should pack up their belongings. Sam ran to Józef, his business partner, and knocked on the door. His wife opened the door and seeing that Sam looked white, she quickly invited him inside. Józef came out to greet Sam and saw right away that something was wrong. Sam told them what his lawyer had said.

"Please, Józef, you have a car," Sam begged. "You must drive us out of town. I have a wife and a baby daughter. You can have my half of the business. I don't want a penny from you. Just take us out of here, tonight. Take us to Łódź."

"I am afraid," Joseph answered. "If they kill you, they will kill me too. I don't want to be killed."

"Józef," his wife said, giving him a stern look, "you must take them. They will be killed."

So, he agreed. He would come to their house that night at 10 o'clock to pick them up. That gave Sam a few hours to help Esther pack everything up. Sam ran back home.

"Józef will pick us up at 10 o'clock and take us to Łódź. I'll finish packing. You get the baby ready."

Sam and Esther packed the essentials for themselves and baby Faiga. Sam took all the money he had at home and any remaining jewels he had from Treblinka. Józef arrived and they got into the back seat of his *Samochód* (a type of Polish car). As they drove out of town, the Poles who wanted to kill Sam and Esther saw them leaving. They ran after the car and began to shoot. They kept shooting and shooting. But Józef drove so fast that they escaped. Finally, out of Ostrow, they drove southeast for 220 kilometers (136 miles), all the way to Łódź. Once they were out of danger, Józef slowed the car. Along the way, they discussed the future.

"What will you do in Łódź?" asked Józef.

"We know some people there," Sam replied. "We won't stay long. Now that the war is over,* we will move on to Germany. We will go to a camp for displaced persons in the American zone. We want to go to America. We have had enough of Poland. We have no future here."

They arrived in Łódź in the middle of the night. They couldn't find anyone they knew at this time of night, especially on *Shabbes*. Perhaps they found a small hotel that was open and got a room for the night. They said goodbye to Józef.

"We cannot thank you enough," Sam said to him. "You saved our lives. Good luck with the *Yatzke*. Please say goodbye and thank you to your wife."

*   Germany surrendered to the Allied Powers on May 7, 1945.

Group of Stokers in Lodz, Rosh Hashanah 1945. Back Row: Right to Left: Itze Althshuler, Chaim Kwiatek, Simcha Viergzbinski, Chaim Kwiatek's cousin from Walamen, unknown, Avraham Stalwitz, Chaim Kwiatek's other cousin, Velvel Schneiderman, Naomi (Norma) Pshpyorke, Velvel's wife. Middle Row: Shmulke Goldberg and three people not from Stok. Front Row: Eli Yankel Teitelbaum, Sara Teitelbaum, two children who were hidden during the entire Holocaust. Reprinted from Pinkas Stok – Stoczek Yizkor (Memorial) Book, 439.

"Good luck to you," Józef replied. "I will take care of the *Yatzke.*"

In the morning, they found some survivors. Dora Wapniak, who they knew from Ostrow, invited them to stay with her. They were elated when they discovered that both Velvel Schneiderman and Chaim Kwiatek were in Łódź. Velvel introduced them to his wife, Naomi. They met other survivors, including some Stokers. Just a few days after they arrived, it was *Rosh Hashanah.* The survivors gathered to pray together and mourn their loved ones.

After *Rosh Hashanah*, they were ready to set out for Germany. Their goal was to immigrate to America. They had heard that it might take a while, but they were determined to make it to the "*goldene medina*," "the golden country."

Displaced Persons Camps

OCTOBER 1945-MAY 1949.

The darkness of the night felt heavy. The October air in 1945 was crisp and cold. How many times had they moved to a new place in the past six years? Too many. This time, the journey was dangerous, but it paled in comparison to the others. Being smuggled, by bus, from Łódź to Munich, Germany held risks. Without passports or travel documents, they could be arrested or sent back to Poland. On May 7, 1945, the Nazis surrendered to the allies and the gas chambers were stilled for good.

Brichah,[*] the organization conducting the smuggling operation, assured them that the journey would be successful. They knew which roads to take and which border police could be bribed and were sympathetic to the Jewish refugees. They had three borders to cross: Poland to Czechoslovakia; Czechoslovakia to Austria; and Austria to Germany. They would enter directly into the American Zone[**] to Munich.

The leaders of *Brichah* had a second, more dangerous illegal journey on their minds, from Germany to British-controlled Palestine. Their goal was to get as many refugees smuggled from Germany to Palestine as possible. Sam and Esther

---

[*] *Brichah* is Hebrew, meaning flight or escape.
[**] The conquering allied powers divided Germany into four zones — Russian, French, British and American.

discussed whether to go to Palestine or America. Palestine — *Eretz Yisroel* — was the home of the Jews. Esther's years in *Hashomer Hatzair*, her Zionist youth group in Stoczek, had taught her a great deal about life in the Jewish homeland and created dreams of living and working hard to create a vital Jewish State. But, they had heard of the dangers of the journey, of the ships turned back by the British and of those sunk at sea. Even if they arrived safely to Palestine, life there would be filled with hardship. The lack of housing, malaria and other diseases, and the violent skirmishes with their Arab neighbors were alarming. There might be a full-blown war between the Arabs and the Jews and Sam would be drafted into the *Haganah*, the Jewish army in Palestine. They had enough war and hardship for one lifetime. No, from Munich, their dream was to immigrate to America.

Wrapped up in a warm blanket, baby Faiga was ready to go. They met the other travelers at the appointed place in Łódź. Dora Wapniak gave them a bag of food for the journey and said farewell. They were elated to have the food. After living through years of hunger and uncertainty about their next morsel, having food in a bag at their side calmed them and reassured them that the journey would be successful.

The bus was there waiting with its door open and lights off, not wanting to attract attention. They climbed the few stairs up into the bus, turned to make their way down the main aisle to find an empty seat. The bus was already half full. They caught sight of their new friends Chayke and Moishe Zablotsky. Chayke was easy to spot with her red hair. The Zablotskys had come to Łódź from Czechoslovakia with their infant son, Shevach. Relieved to see that they were on the bus, Sam and Esther settled into a seat just behind them.

It was the darkest part of the night when the bus rolled out of Łódź. The large tires turned and soon a rhythmic, soft mechanical sound permeated the cabin. The sound was frightening and calming all at once. They were leaving *finstere* (dark) Poland for good. They never wanted to come back. Their families had been murdered and the towns had been emptied of Jews who had made their life in Poland for over 1000 years. The community and the culture as they knew it was gone. A profound sadness swept over them. Sadness for all they had endured and for all they had lost these past six years. After their rescue from the murderous Poles in Ostrow and hearing about similar harrowing experiences, and even pogroms, they knew that there was no future for Jews in Poland. But, as they held their baby daughter in their arms, they felt the weight of their bodies press into the seat as their sadness mixed with hope for the future.

Before the sun rose in the sky, they had crossed into Czechoslovakia. A few hours later, they entered Austria. When the bus approached the German border, anger and hatred welled up inside both Esther and Sam. Hitler and the German people had started this war and murdered their families and millions more. They didn't want to breathe German air or touch the bottom of their shoes on its contaminated soil. It was a bittersweet moment because this was the only portal out, their escape route to a new world and a new life. The American military had set up Displaced Persons (DP) Camps where the refugees could find lodging, food, clothing, and protection from the antisemites. They were grateful for the protection. They hoped their stay in the DP Camp would be short, and that they would soon obtain visas and be on their way to America.

The bus stopped in Munich in front of a large hotel. Getting off the bus and looking around this Bavarian city, they saw full city blocks in ruin with rubble everywhere. The remnants of graceful arches and intricate building designs hinted at a glorious past. The hotel where they were dropped was intact, with running water and electricity. It was a gathering place for survivors.

Entering the hotel, they were immediately welcomed by workers with the American Joint Distribution Committee (the Joint). They were offered a hot drink and some food. They settled into a room where they could bathe and get some sleep. The next day, they would be assigned a DP Camp. It would most likely be Föhrenwald.

On that first day in Munich, Sam and Esther were told that the American Military, who ran the DP Camps in the American Zone, had been ordered to separate the Jewish refugees from the non-Jewish refugees. Föhrenwald, just southwest of Munich, near the town of Wolfratshuasen, was selected to be one of the Jewish camps. Non-Jewish refugees had been moved out and Jewish survivors from other camps were transferred to Föhrenwald. This change, made in October of 1945, was based on the Harrison Report which criticized the conditions in the camps for liberated Jews. The Harrison Report, ordered by President Truman to detail the conditions in the DP Camps, recommended that the Jewish survivors be separated into their own camps.[82] The day after their arrival in Munich, the Goldbergs and the Zablotkys boarded a bus to Föhrenwald.

Stepping off the bus at Föhrenwald, they saw right away that this was no paradise. The camp was fenced in with two-meter high mesh wire. The buildings were from a 1939 IG Farber work camp, intended to house 3,200 workers employed in the nearby munitions factories. During the war, IG Farber employees were joined by slave laborers, all of whom worked in the factories. The buildings were solid, made of concrete, but were not well-maintained. When Sam and Esther arrived, the American military was in control, working together with United Nations Relief and Rehabilitation Administration (UNRAA) and the Joint to care for the Jewish refugees flooding in. Three thousand Jews were housed at Föhrenwald; it was already near capacity.

As Sam and Esther explored their new home, they saw rows and rows of white cement barracks, built in a military style with tall, steep, slanted roofs. The street signs had American names like New Jersey, Massachusetts, and New York. The roads were unpaved, but there were concrete sidewalks with a few evergreen trees sticking out — a weak attempt at beautifying the drab place. But, the streets were filled with Jews speaking Yiddish. What a relief to hear Yiddish spoken in the street. After living in Stoczek and Ostrow for the past year, with so few Jews, this was wonderful. It felt like a *Shtetl*.

Esther and Sam were initially assigned to one of the barracks. They would share a room with the Zablotsky family. Maybe they walked down New Jersey Street and found their building. Opening the door, they saw a white sheet hanging from the ceiling of the small room. There were camp-style beds in the room and a table, but little else. The Zablotskys took one side of the small room and Sam, Esther and Faiga occupied the other. It was not much, but it was a sturdy, strong building, with running water and central heating. Most importantly they were safe and with ration cards in their pockets, they were assured of food.

Within weeks Sam and Esther were reassigned to another room. They still shared their space, but with a single man. They felt lucky to have a single roommate. As Jews from Eastern Europe and even from Siberia and Tashkent came flooding in, the population of Föhrenwald swelled from 3,000 to 4,847 by the end of 1945.[83]

Once they settled in, Sam and Esther asked around to see if Velvel and Naomi Schneiderman were at this DP Camp. They too had left Łódź, but it was unclear where they ended up. It didn't take long, they found them and were reunited yet again. Then, some weeks later, the door to their small room opened and in walked Sam's cousin, Shaya Schloss.

"Shaya, you're alive," Sam screamed running to throw his arms around him. "How did you make it? How did you find me?"

"I met Chaim Kwiatek in Munich," Shaya responded, "and he told me you were here. We came on the next bus. You must meet my wife, Faiga. She's from Łódź."

"Mazal tov," Sam cried. "This is my wife, Esther. She's from Stoczek, and this is our daughter, Faiga Bracha. She was born in Ostrow."

They stared at each other in happy disbelief. They sat for hours and told each other their stories, crying and together, remembering their parents, brothers, sisters, Aunts, Uncles, and cousins. As far as they both knew, they were all dead

Shmulke (Sam) Goldberg and Shaya Schloss at the DP Camp Föhrenwald approx. 1946. Credit: Shaya Schloss.

— gone forever. The pain and the sadness overwhelmed them, but they were focused on the future — they both hoped to get visas for America.

Esther and Sam learned how to get what they needed in the DP Camp. Esther went each day to the "kitchen." She stood in line for bread, milk, and some military rations. She would take her rations back to her room and carefully unpack them. The rations were a meager lot. They received three ounces of meat, fish, or cheese and some dry or canned goods. Sometimes she also stopped at the local German food office and received some potatoes or a few vegetables.

Each morning, Sam and Moishe Zablotsky would have breakfast and then head out of the camp. They went to *handl*. Before he ran from Ostrow, Sam managed to take his cash and the remaining Treblinka jewels. This cash was critical to sustaining their life in the DP Camp. He and Moishe bought whatever they could — gold, dollars, cigarettes, chocolate, coffee, anything that could be resold for a profit or bartered for the things they needed. In post-war Germany, the economy was not functioning. The black market was the place to get what you needed. They would find willing buyers for their goods and with the profits they bought food and their other necessities.

The U.S. Military tried to clamp down on the black market in the DP Camps, but it was a losing battle. The black market thrived and people smuggled things into the DP Camps, from buttons and thread to cows. Though Sam was not involved in the cow smuggling operation, he saw how they managed it. Children would distract the guards at the camp gate and a group of adults would surround the cow and walk with the animal in the middle, hoping the guards would not see it. Once the cow was inside the camp, they would take it to a designated basement. They would wait until dark and a *Shoichet* (ritual slaughterer) would *shecht* the cow. After the cow was dead, the *Shoichet* would inspect the animal and determine whether it was kosher. Butchers would work all night, cleaning and cutting the meat. In the morning, all the residents of the camp knew if the meat was kosher or not. Someone would walk through the camp calling:

"Meat available in such and such barracks."

If the call was for meat in Barracks A — it meant kosher meat. If the call was for meat in Barracks B — it meant the meat was not kosher. There was a market in the camp for both kinds of meat. None of it went to waste.[84]

One day, Sam heard that an American Rabbi employed by the Joint was in the *Shul* giving out *Talleisim* (prayer shawls) and *Tefillin* (phylacteries). Sam went right over; he had not worn *Tallis* and *Tefillin* since 1939, over six years. As he entered the *Shul*, the Rabbi was indeed there with a stack of *Talleisim* and many pairs of *Tefillin*.

"May I have *Tallis* and *Tefillin*," Sam asked.

"Yes, of course," the Rabbi answered. "What is your name, *Reb Yid*?"

"Shmulke Goldberg," Sam replied. "Rabbi, I have a problem," Sam continued. "My parents and my wife's parents were murdered by the Germans, *Yemach Shemum* [may their names be erased], and we don't know their day of death. When should we commemorate their *Yahrzeit*?"*

There were so many people who had lost loved one and didn't know the date of death. So, the Rabbi assigned *Yahrzeit* dates — one after the other. The next person who approached him would get the next date.

"For your parents, the *Yahrzeit* will be the 25th day of *Cheshvan*,"** the Rabbi said, "and for your wife's parents, the *Yahrzeit* will be the 26th day of *Cheshvan*."***

Sam and Esther felt a sense of comfort to have *Yahrzeit* dates, but it forced them to face the reality that their parents and siblings were all dead. With a date to say *Kaddish* (the mourner's prayer), they could process their new reality. Everyone they met at the DP Camp had lost family members. They would talk for hours about what they had lived through and about their lost loved ones. Some of the people they met had been in Concentration Camps, some, like Sam and Velvel, in Death Camps, some, like Esther, in hiding, while others were exiled to Siberia or Tashkent. Most had lost family; many had lost their entire family. The Joint's tracing system attempted to locate surviving family members. Esther and Sam checked, but found no one alive.

---

*   *Yahrzeit* is the anniversary of a person's death. On this day, each year, close relatives say the mourner's *Kaddish* and light a *Yahrzeit* candle.

**   *Cheshvan* is a month on the Jewish Calendar, that usually coincides with November.

***   In a twist of fate, Esther's Yahrzeit is the 27th of *Cheshvan*.

The hoped-for visas to America were not forthcoming. They were beginning to understand the United States quota system for refugees. It was stacked against them. Quotas were allocated by country, with no regard to their status as Holocaust survivors. They were told that the quota for citizens of all Eastern European countries was 13,000 per year. Under this system, they were considered Poles and Poles had a ten-year wait. This was upsetting enough, but then they learned that the quota for German citizens was 26,000 per year and that former Nazi and SS officers were obtaining entry visas.[85] They were enraged.

They made the best of life at Föhrenwald. Sam was busy *handlin* and bringing home the necessities of life while Esther was busy caring for Faiga. There were so many new mothers in the Camp, that Esther had lots of friends with whom to discuss her daughter. The birth rate at Föhrenwald during the years after the war was the highest in the world.[86] Shaya and Faiga Schloss were part of the baby boom as their son, Jack, was born at Föhrenwald.

Sam, Esther and Faiga at DP Camp Föhrenwald approx. 1947. Credit: Goldberg Family Archives.

Although the countries of the world were still turning a deaf ear to the plight of the survivors, at least they were free. They wanted to take control of their lives. The survivors created their own police force, court system, school system, including a nursery school for the young children, vocational training facilities, run by ORT — the Organization for Rehabilitation Through Training[87], administrative committees, *Shuls,* a *Mikve,* sports clubs, a newspaper (*Bamidbar*), a library and reading room, a kosher kitchen, theater groups, orchestras, and cinemas.[88] The Joint helped fund many of these endeavors.[89]

Baby Faiga began to walk and to speak. Sam and Esther were anxious to get their visas to American. A DP Camp was no place to raise a child. Velvel and Naomi Schneiderman had moved to another DP Camp in Stuttgart 233 kilometers (144 miles) away. They had moved there because Naomi had a sister there who had some connections. They hoped that this would speed up the visa process. Velvel wrote to Sam and Esther encouraging them to move to Stuttgart. His wife's sister could try to help them as well.

"Let's go," Sam said, "what do we have to lose? Here we are just waiting and waiting."

Esther agreed. They packed up their few belongings and bought train tickets to Stuttgart. Sam had saved some money and was doing well enough in his black-market trading that they decided not to live in the Stuttgart DP Camp barracks. They rented a room from a German woman who had lost her husband during the War. Having a whole room to themselves seemed like a luxury. The room had electricity and a small kitchen. They still received ration coupons from the DP Camp and obtained some food with them. One day, Sam took the bus from their apartment to the DP Camp to cash in his ration cards.

"I want a frozen kosher turkey — a whole turkey," Sam said.

"Ok, do you have enough ration cards for a whole turkey?" she asked.

"Yes, I do," Sam replied.

The worker left the counter and went to the huge freezer. Returning with a frozen turkey, Sam thanked him and headed out of the camp. He found the bus he needed to get back home and got on.

"*Jid* — Jew," a German man screamed at Sam, "go sit in the back of the bus."

Sam was shocked at this outburst. The war was over, the Germans had lost and surrendered. What did this German think he was doing? Sam looked the man in the eye, and appearing as if he were about to oblige, he took the frozen turkey and hit the German over the head. The man fell to the floor. Just at that moment, the bus stopped and Sam jumped off. No one stopped him or said a word. Catching the next bus, Sam returned to the apartment. He told Esther what happened and she was relieved that no one had chased him. Esther roasted the turkey and its meat lasted for several meals. Turkey never tasted so good.

Sam continued to *handl* on the black market in Stuttgart and "made some good money." Sam's business ventures were many and varied. One day, he heard of a unique opportunity. There was a diamond bracelet on the market. There was no way he could buy this bracelet himself. He didn't have enough cash. He reached out to some of his friends and fellow traders to partner with him. The cash was collected and the purchase completed. Now they were in possession of this beautiful, sparkling, bracelet. Then, the police arrived at his door.

"Mr. Goldberg, are you in possession of a diamond bracelet?" the police said.

"Yes," said Sam. "I bought it for cash."

"You are under arrest," the police told him. "This bracelet belongs to a wealthy woman, and she reported it stolen this morning."

"I didn't steal it," Sam said. "I bought it for cash, a lot of cash."

"Well, the owner wants her bracelet back. We will have to take you down to the police station."

Esther watched as they took Sam and the diamond bracelet away. She began to cry. What would happen to them now? If Sam went to prison, she and the baby would be alone. She couldn't imagine this. How would they manage?

Esther knew where the last of the Treblinka jewels were hidden. She went to the hiding place and found the largest remaining jewel. She placed it in her purse, bundled up Faiga, and headed out the door. She knew from friends that there was a lawyer in town who would help survivors when they got into legal trouble. She went to his office and told him about the diamond bracelet bought on the black market and how the police had come and arrested her husband.

"Do you have any money?" the lawyer asked.

"No," said Esther, "but I have this jewel. Will it help?"

"Yes," the lawyer said, "that is quite a jewel. Give it to me and I get your husband out of jail."

Esther had no choice but to trust this lawyer and give him the jewel. She went back home and waited. The lawyer went to the police station with lots of cash. Some money exchanged hands and the police agreed that if Sam would return the bracelet to the owner, he would go free.

"But a huge sum was paid for this bracelet," the lawyer insisted. "It was not all my client's money, he had partners. They need their money back."

"The owner told us she would refund most of the money. She just wants her bracelet back," the police said.

To Esther's relief, Sam walked into the apartment later that day unscathed. He told her what had happened and showed her the money. The wealthy woman had indeed given back most of the money. Sam split the money among his partners.

Esther was so relieved. They heard a few days later that the men who stole the bracelet were caught and sent to jail. Another disaster averted.

Meanwhile, they were following the political news in American. By the end of June 1947, the United States had only allowed 15,478 Jewish refugees living in the DP Camps in Germany to enter the country. But there was good news, the United States enacted a law in July of 1948 — The Displaced Persons Act — authorizing visas for 202,000 displaced persons and 3,000 displaced orphans. They were eligible as long as they had arrived in Germany by December 22, 1945. Sam and Esther were overjoyed because they had arrived in Germany in October of 1945. They were eligible for one of those visas. They also heard that the law required that thirty percent of the immigrants be "agriculturalists."[90] Very few of the Jewish refugees from Eastern Europe were farmers. But Sam was a farmer; he would get special consideration. He and Esther were hopeful for the first time in years.

Their joy was tempered with the knowledge that most Jewish refugees from Eastern Europe came after the cut-off date. It was clear that the United States was trying to exclude most Eastern European Holocaust survivors. This was unfair.

Sam and Esther went to the Stuttgart DP Camp and got an appointment with a representative of the Hebrew Immigrant Aid Society (HIAS), the organization that aided refugees in the process of immigration. They told the representative that they had arrived at Föhrenwald in October 1945, before the cutoff date. Also, Sam explained that he was a farmer, so they qualified under the "agriculturalist" category. Sam had received word from his mother's sister, *Tante* Shosha Mischler, in New York that her son, Phil, a successful businessman, would sponsor them. The HIAS official told them that she would put their name forward for

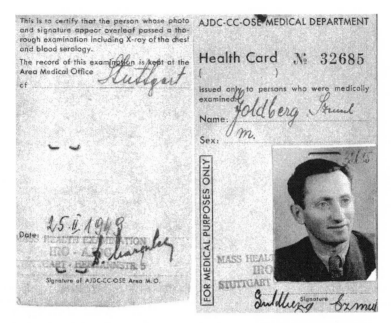

Sam Goldberg Health Card, Stuttgart, November 25, 1948. Credit: Goldberg Family Archives.

one of the new refugee visas, but that they must be patient.

As 1949 began, they had not yet had heard from HIAS. But then, a HIAS official sent them a notice to come to the office in the Stuttgart DP Camp. They hoped for good news.

"Your immigration has been approved — *Mazal tov*," the official said smiling.

"Thank you," Sam and Esther were elated.

"When do we leave?" they asked excitedly.

"In May," the official replied. "You are slotted to travel across the Atlantic on the USAT Marine Jumper. This is a naval ship that was chartered by the United States War Department Army Transportation Services to take refugees to America."

"Thank you," Esther and Sam said in unison. They were finally going to on their way to a new land and a new life!

Sam completed his business dealings and they began to sell or give away things that they were not going to take with them to America. They didn't sleep the night before they sailed, their nerves kept them up! What would they find in

International Refugee Organization, dated September 3, 1948. Credit: Goldberg Family Archives.

this new land they call the *goldene medina*? How would they manage with little money and no English skills and a baby to feed and care for?

Faiga, now almost four years old, had no idea that her family was going to move half-way around the world to live in a place where people spoke a language that she didn't understand. But there were people who would help them to make the transition. They would live with the *Tante* Shosha until Sam could find a job and make enough money to rent an apartment. Shaya and Faiga Schloss were already in New York, living in the Bronx. Velvel and Naomi (now Norma) Schneiderman were living there, too.

In the morning, they arrived at the dock and couldn't believe how big the ship was. They were told that it was a single propeller, steam turbine ship that was 523 feet long. As they boarded carrying their suitcases and holding Faiga's hand, the ship's officer greeted them. He explained that the men and the women would sleep in separate parts of the boat. Sam would sleep in the lower deck with the men and Esther and Faiga would sleep on one of the upper decks with the women and children. The ship could hold 3,451 people.[91]

Traveling at 18 knots or around 20 miles per hour, the boat took a week to cross the Atlantic Ocean to America. Neither Esther nor Sam had ever been on a boat. Sam didn't feel well at all. His stomach felt upside down and he wanted to vomit. Others told him this was normal on a boat and he would feel better in calm waters and once they reached New York. The boat was full of refugees, many of whom were survivors like them. Esther and Faiga's stomachs fared better than Sam, but after the novelty wore off, they were anxious to reach New York. There were other children Faiga's age, but the boat was a difficult place to entertain them.

Europe and its pain and heartache was behind them, an ocean away; America and a new life was before them. They had heard about the Statue of Liberty that greets the ships in New York harbor. So, when the day came that the boat's captain announced that they would reach New York, Esther, Sam, and Faiga joined the other passengers on the deck. Everyone was jostling for a spot on the boat's rail — hoping to be the first to spot Lady Liberty. It was May 28, 1949 when the green lady was spotted; a great cry went up from the passengers. Tears and hugs abounded. Clapping and whooping could be heard as they made their way into the dock.

They had made it to America, the *goldene medina*. A new life awaited them. They must live for those who would never have this opportunity, who had been lost.

"[I]n every human being, there is a spark of the divine. So you don't have a right as a human to abuse that spark of the divine . . . even the person beating you, spitting on you, you have to think of that person — years ago, that person was an innocent child, innocent little baby. . . . [We must] try to appeal to the goodness of every human being. And you don't give up. You never give up on anyone."
—Congressman John Lewis. January 26, 2017.

Part II

Treblinka — Return of the Ring

JUNE 22, 2016

I stood in this place of horror and pain and felt nothing. It was empty, antiseptic. The sun beat down and there was no shade to escape it or find relief. Bees were everywhere, buzzing with the sound of death. It was in the air. It was in the earth.

But where are the train tracks? They are gone. In their place stands some feeble cement markers. I am outraged. Those tracks brought thousands of *Kedoshim*, Holy Ones, each day to this place of death and torture. The tracks are themselves holy and should be enshrined. Why? To erase the last vestiges of the reality of Treblinka?

The space lay abandoned but for the thousands of gray, lifeless, memorial stones, clustered together, as if none of them want to be alone. Each stone represents, not a person, but an entire community — murdered here. Most of the space is covered with grass and dirt, but among the memorial stones, the earth is capped with concrete. If we could drill down, through the concrete and dig into the earth, we would find the ash and bone of 870,000 victims.

This is my task, I think to myself, to dig through the concrete, through the earth, through the ash and bone, through the pain. I dig deep into Sam and Esther's story. But as I dig, I find more. I find my story, connecting me to this family, to the Holocaust, to Jewish history, to the world, a narrative that allows me to confront my own soul.

Treblinka Memorial with Marcin Borucki and Shoshana Goldberg in foreground. Credit: Grzegorz Maleszewski.

I continue to walk through the memorial stones and out onto the grass. As I wander, I wonder where Sam's barrack was? Where was the laundry? Where were the gas chambers? I cannot tell in the Treblinka of today.

I glanced at my left hand and saw the ring — the Treblinka ring. It's a simple band of white gold with small, repeating triangle designs and asterisk-like markings that pock the ring like bullet holes. Nothing could protect the owner of this ring from her fate. Maybe she was a mother, maybe a grandmother, maybe an Aunt, maybe she went to her death in the gas chamber holding her baby. I'll never know. But her ring lives on, on my finger. This precious treasure was found here by Sam as he worked in the laundry.

Just before the uprising, Sam dug up this treasure along with other treasures and reburied them deep in his pockets. Escaping through a hole blown into the barbed wire fence, he ran to life and ultimately to Esther. After the liberation in the summer of 1944, Sam and Esther were married by Shmuel Rajzman, Sam's cell leader in the Treblinka uprising. Was this the ring that Sam placed on Esther's finger on that special day? I don't know. But I do know that Esther wore this ring, and after her death, Sam gave it me. It came across the continent to Seattle in my husband Shlomo's* pocket as it had been in his father's pocket before him. Since that day, almost 21 years ago, I have worn and treasured this ring. When I look at it, I remember Esther, but it also connects me to this place — Treblinka.

When Sam escaped, he ran to the thick cluster of trees that ring the perimeter. His first obstacle was the Bug River. It's close by — maybe two kilometers (1.2 miles) away from Treblinka. Sam told us the story of jumping into the Bug river as his personal *Kriat Yam Suf* — splitting of the Red Sea — like the ancient Hebrew slaves escaping their Egyptian masters. As Sam walked once again on dry land, he continued to run and kept going for another 20 kilometers (12.4 miles) until he reached the part of the forest where Esther was hiding with her brother-in-law, Chaim.

I wanted to run through the trees to reach the Bug River, as Sam had done. It was so hot. Our family, my husband, Shlomo, our future Israeli-son-in-law, Micha, all our children, Elisheva, Jack, Shoshana, Esther, and I, got into the van and drove to the Bug River. We changed into bathing suits and gathered together taking in the scene. The river was about fifty meters across and the water was a brownish, yellow color. Shlomo and our children said a blessing of thanksgiving for the miracle that happened to their father/grandfather here. Micha and I, not blood-related, did not join in the blessing, but gave the traditional Jewish response to a blessing *"Amen."* As the blessings were recited I thought of all the miracles that happened to Sam and to Esther and of the blessings of my life.

The warnings of the river's dangerous current did not deter us. We screamed "this is for you *Zeyde*"** and walked into the warmish water. Someone started to sing the Gospel song *Wade in the Water* and the rest of us joined in, laughing all the way. I felt guilty laughing after visiting Treblinka. There was nothing to laugh about there. But the laughter was therapeutic.

---

* Shlomo's full name is Shlomo Zelig Goldberg. His first name is after Esther's father — Shlomo Zalman and his middle name is after Sam's father — Zelig.
** A Yiddish word meaning Grandfather.

The drop off was sharp and the current was strong. We lay on our backs and floated down stream. It was easy to see how Sam drifted down the river. We were, however, conscious, in all the meanings of this word. We were wide awake and very aware. We were conscious of the miracle. We were conscious of our place in the flow of history and time. We were glad to be alive and together as a family — a part of Sam and Esther's legacy.

How it All Began

1984-1985

It was my wedding day. I was about to marry the man of my dreams, he was handsome, smart, funny, Jewish, a doctor with a beard. Wow — a package deal. I was in love with this trim man of average height, with light green-eyes and brown hair. His parents and sisters traveled to Seattle from the East Coast for our big day, with spouses and children in tow. The wedding came off without a hitch, complete with klezmer musicians (my doing), followed by a 16-piece orchestra (my mother's doing).

As a Seattle native, I thought I knew about east coasters, after all, I had gone to Barnard College in New York City and lived in Washington, D.C., working for a Senator. I met Shlomo's family over the course of the year. I knew that his parents were survivors of the Holocaust, but I had no idea what I was getting myself into. Growing up in a water-front home on Mercer Island, a suburb of Seattle, attending private Jewish day school until ninth grade and hurrying my way through high school to start university early, privilege was my middle name. My exposure to Holocaust survivors growing up was very limited. And my Holocaust knowledge consisted of those horrible educational movies with the footage of the liberation of the concentrations camps, with piles of emaciated, dead bodies along with the skeletal humans who were yet alive, but just barely.

I had some inkling that this family was different from mine the very first time I met my future in-laws. I traveled to Miami Beach in April of 1984, just after we got engaged. I was nervous as I said hello to them and exchanged small talk. With towels around our necks, Shlomo and I announced that we were heading to the beach and would be back by dinner. Esther, short and solid, with brown hair that was teased in the puffed-up style of the times, was wearing a print house coat with snaps down the front. She jumped at me from her small kitchen and thrust a package of food into my hands.

"Thank you so much," I said, "but we don't need any food at the beach. We're not hungry just now and we will be back by dinner."

I could feel this wasn't going to work. She insisted that we take the food with us to the beach. We went back and forth a few times, with Shlomo watching my first real interaction with his mother. Feeling uncomfortable, I agreed to take the package and we escaped out the door.

"That was weird," I said as I shoved the food into Shlomo's hands.

He looked embarrassed by his mother's behavior, but he gently explained:

"It's all because of the Holocaust. She went without food for so long that now, so many years later, she still cannot shake the fear of being without food. And God forbid something should happen to us on the way to the beach, at least we will have some food."

"Oh," I said feeling bad about making a fuss.

My first encounter with Sam did not go well either. He began speaking to me in Yiddish. I knew just a few Yiddish words, like *mentsch* (what my father hoped his children would be) and *schlepp* (what my mother asked us to do with the grocery bags). Upon realizing that I didn't understand "Jewish," Sam looked at Shlomo and asked if I was a *Shiksa* — a non-Jewish woman. I knew enough Yiddish to know that *Shiksa* is a negative label, especially for someone who was going to marry his only son.[92]

Here stood my future-father-in-law, three inches shorter than me, with wispy gray hair and a stomach that protruded over his belt, asking if I was a *Shiksa*. His implication, which offended and hurt me, was that I was a Jewish ignoramus because I didn't speak Yiddish. I had gone to Jewish Day School, belonged to an Orthodox Synagogue and as a teenager made the decision to observe the laws of *Shabbat*,* though my parents did not. I had chaired the Columbia/Barnard

---

*   I use the Israeli or Sephardic pronunciation of this word in Part II. A Yiddish or Ashkenazik pronunciation is *Shabbes*.

United Jewish Appeal campaign and spent my junior year of college studying at Hebrew University in Jerusalem. Hmmm.

I had jumped down the rabbit hole. Yiddish was flying everywhere as friends stopped by to meet Shlomo's "*Kallah*" (bride). I did a lot of smiling and nodding. Nothing in my suburban, Seattle Jewish life had prepared me for this. After that first short visit, I wondered whether this chasm between Sam, Esther, and me could ever be narrowed.

I realized that the Holocaust was the central event of their lives. The memory and trauma of it was integral to who they were and the pain was ever present. I watched as Esther took daily trips out to the small balcony to sneak a cigarette. She would smoke and cry. When she was done, she would wipe her tears, come back into the apartment and resume her kitchen activities. I had never seen my mother cry — ever. So, this routine was foreign to me. The Holocaust was not etched into the landscape of my family's history. I was an outsider to this life drama, but now I had a front row seat.

At our wedding, it hit me that Shlomo had no extended family. My large family showed up in force: my two living grandparents, my uncles and aunts, and my many cousins. Thanks to Hitler, Shlomo had no grandparents, no uncles, aunts, or first cousins. I could not imagine growing up without my wonderful, vibrant extended family, but this was the reality of Shlomo's family experience.

After the wedding, Shlomo and I lived in Washington, D.C. for a year and a half. It was during that time that he told me a story that made a crack in the impenetrable Holocaust wall for me. Shlomo worked in a research lab at the National Institutes of Health. As Christmas approached, one of the non-Jewish research technicians asked him:

"Dr. Goldberg, how do Jews celebrate Christmas?"

"Well, in my family, we celebrate Christmas in the ancient Polish tradition," Shlomo said with a straight face. "The family gathers around, we go down to the basement, we lock the doors, and hope there is no pogrom."

"Oh, what is a pogrom?" she asked not understanding his humor.

"I'm only joking," he said. "But a pogrom is a violent attack by non-Jews on Jews. Christmas was a favorite time for pogroms."

"Ok, thanks," she said, ending the conversation that she may have regretted initiating.

For me, this story spoke volumes about the Goldberg family. Christmas is a time for fear, not celebration.[93] Persecution of Jews is real and this message penetrated deep into Shlomo's consciousness. This opened my mind and my heart to the suffering and the fear that Sam and Esther had endured.

In 1985, we moved to New York City where I attended New York University Law School and Shlomo did a clinical fellowship in Hematology and Oncology at Columbia University Medical Center. For Shlomo, it was a homecoming, as he had grown up in Brooklyn and had gone to high school and medical school in Manhattan. For me, living in Greenwich Village was exciting and, though it was in the same city, it seemed a world away from Barnard College and the Columbia University campus.

We were happy to escape New York during the cold winters and head down to visit Sam and Esther in Miami. Our bathing suits were packed amidst our must-read books. In these early years, I kept a protective force-field up to shield me from further hurt. But, like butter left out of the fridge, I softened.

We usually visited over a long weekend. For *Shabbat* meals, Esther served chicken soup with *matza* balls, *gefilta* fish, chicken, potato *kugel,* and other eastern European foods. Every bite was delicious. Esther was one of the best cooks I had ever met and her kitchen smelled like something Joan Nathan[*] could have only dreamed of. If we were lucky, she would make *kreplach* — dumplings with chopped meat inside. With each bite, the powerful, but subtle flavors burst into my brain. For dessert, there was Esther's famous apple cake — dough filled with apples, cinnamon, and loads of sugar. I felt like I was tasting a bit of the sweetness of pre-war Poland. For Esther, food was love and I began to feel the love.

As we sat at the *Shabbat* table, Shlomo and I sang *Zmirot*, ancient multiverse songs written in honor of *Shabbat*. There was one song that Sam particularly loved, called *Shimru Shabtotai.* The song has a sweet, slow melody, with the notes of the chorus rising to heaven and then descending back to earth. After we

---

[*] Joan Nathan is a well-known author of Jewish cook books.

finished singing, Sam would tell us how much he loved it and thank us. He began to call me Darling — with that Yiddish accent of his it came out as "Daaaahling." The tenderness with which Sam said the word and his warm smile healed me. He would never again call me *Shiksa*.

I came to understand that for Sam and Esther, these *Shabbat Zmirot* brought back memories of their families before the war. Growing up in Stoczek or Bagatele, the Wisznia and Goldberg families sang many *Zmirot* at their Shabbat tables. But, the Nazis destroyed their families and ended their *Shabbat* tables. Sam and Esther were singing with me. Things were getting better.

This is My Chance

1986-2016

Ihad never known a Holocaust survivor well enough to sit with them and hear about their experiences first-hand. Now, as I grew closer to Sam and Esther, I wanted to know. Learning about their past was a key to further unlocking the door to our relationship.

Esther didn't want to talk about it with me ever. Sam was a willing accomplice to my interest in learning about those times. He would tell his stories around the dining room table or at the Passover *Seder*. On two occasions, he allowed Shlomo to video his story-telling. He told us of his escape from the German POW camp, his time in Treblinka, and how he met Esther and then lived with her and Chaim in the forest pit. Sometimes he would cry, especially when he spoke of his parents. I sat in rapt silence. My jaw would drop and my stomach would turn upside down. I was awash with grief for his loss and suffering.

In 1997, Sam agreed to be interviewed by the Shoah Foundation. So now, we had three separate interviews of Sam, one professional and two by Shlomo — all in Yiddish. I couldn't understand any of them. More importantly, thanks to Shlomo and his two sisters, Fay and Molly, there were now nine grandchildren. Since none of the grandchildren spoke Yiddish, it became apparent that the stories must be translated into English. These stories were their legacy of their grandparents' lives.

Shlomo spent hours translating his father's Yiddish interviews onto cassette tapes and then I spent hours transcribing the tapes into the computer. Not only did we spend hours working on the tapes, but there was also this new technology called the Internet. We used it to find as many books on Treblinka as we could. We amassed a Treblinka library and read each book. This "Treblinka phase" provided us with hours of discussions about what we learned. When we were done, the immensity of the evil hit us, and the world seemed like a darker place than I had ever imagined. I felt so angry — at the Germans, at the Poles, at the Ukrainians — at the world for letting this happen. Life's unfairness hit me hard. I spent my youth water skiing on Lake Washington and attending Barnard College. Sam spent his youth suffering in Treblinka and hiding in a pit deep in a forest in fear.

Although Esther still refused to discuss her experiences during the Holocaust with me and most others, my sister-in-law, Molly, persuaded her to speak on video. Esther spoke in English and I transcribed the interview onto the computer. She reminded Molly that she and Sam had a recurring fight over who saved whom. Esther insisted that if Sam had not entered her life in August of 1943, she would not have survived. Sam is equally insistent that it was Esther who saved him and without her he would surely be dead. Listening to Esther tell her story of survival to Molly, I was struck by the human capacity for evil. But hearing the stories of those who had helped Esther and her courage and sheer will to live, gave me a glimmer of hope for humanity. My moral imagination was rekindled.

After we translated and transcribed all the interviews, I thought, "this is a book waiting to be written." But, in 1997, we lived in Seattle and had three children, ages 9, 7 and 5. And, by the fall of 1997 I was pregnant with our fourth. No time to write a book.

After listening to Sam and Esther's stories, I embraced all their survivor craziness, from the food, to the Yiddish, to the crying, to the guilt. The stories, now rolling around in my head, brought me to a place, not of understanding, but of admiration. How did they survive? The chances of survival were infinitesimal. For Polish Jews, the chance of survival was 9%.[94] For a Treblinka survivor, chances plummet to .0073%.[95] I grew up with suburban privilege and entered this family with no understanding of their experiences and with some resistance to them. I was beginning to understand that my children were growing up with a different reality. They had the honor and burden of being the grandchildren of survivors, especially someone who had survived Treblinka.

Esther was diagnosed with a brain tumor and she died on Thanksgiving in 1997, which corresponds to the 27th day of the Hebrew month of *Cheshvan* — one day after the dates given to Sam at the DP Camp as *Yizkor* commemorations for his parents and for Esther's parents. Shlomo was present at her death, holding her hand and singing to her. I arranged childcare and flew to Miami Thursday evening. There would be a memorial on Friday and then Shlomo would travel on Sunday to Israel, to bury her in *Eretz Hachayim* — Land of the Living — a cemetery outside Beit Shemesh. Friday's memorial was filled with tears and words of love. Placing his hands on the casket, Shlomo asked his mother for forgiveness. The family spent a quiet *Shabbat* together. On Saturday afternoon, the condo was quiet — everyone else was napping.

Being four months pregnant, I was always tired. But I didn't want to sleep for fear that I would be wide awake all night. My emotions were raw; there was an open wound on my heart. After being a member of the Goldberg family for thirteen years, my love and admiration for Esther had grown roots. Her wisdom was not from books, but from real life. Just as the day she had met Sam and Velvel in the forest, she exuded strength and resilience. In the condo that afternoon, the light streamed through the glass door that led to a small balcony. Stepping out onto this 19th floor perch, the Atlantic Ocean appeared — a calming site. The sun was warm and the single chaise invited me to rest. As I lay there contemplating the shortness of human life, I felt the child in my womb move. This was the "quickening," that moment when the fetus is felt for the first time. I knew, at that moment, that this baby was a girl and her name would be Esther.

After Esther's death, Sam continued to live in Miami Beach. He missed Esther but enjoyed the steady stream of casseroles brought over by Yiddish-speaking women, his morning *schnapps* after *Shul*, and card games with friends. But, six years after Esther's death, Sam suffered a stroke. Fay, Shlomo, and Molly agreed that the best thing to do was to move Sam to Seattle where he could live in a skilled nursing facility near our home. Fay and Shlomo sat on either side of Sam on the Seattle-bound flight. As the plane was flying over Oklahoma City, Sam whispered:

"I can't do it anymore."

He stopped breathing. The plane made an emergency landing in Oklahoma City. Shlomo and Fay got off the plane with Sam's body.

Shlomo called me at home and told me that his dad had died on the plane. He explained how he had given him mouth to mouth resuscitation, but he couldn't bring him back. A Chabad* Rabbi had come to the rescue and would watch the body overnight. In the Jewish tradition, a dead body is not left alone between death and burial. The Chabad Rabbi arranged for a *Shomer* to stay with Sam all night.** Arrangements were made to get on a plane the next morning to New York. I would need to send his passport overnight to our good friends, Steve and Naomi, who would meet him at the airport and hand-off the passport. He would fly to Israel and bury his dad next to his mom, hopefully before the beginning of *Rosh Hashanah* (the Jewish New Year) just days away.

I put the phone down in a state of shock. My children gathered around staring at my face, wondering what was wrong. Bursting out in wails that I didn't even know were possible, tears erupted from my eyes and a mournful sound escaped my throat. When Esther died, I was sad, but not surprised. She had been ill for some time. But here, when that phone call came, my mind had been busy planning for Sam's arrival. I knew he had a stroke, but I felt good that he would be so close and we could help him and visit him daily. But it was not to be.

Since Sam's death, I felt the presence of the book. But again, my life got in the way. I had a busy law practice and four children to manage — homework, volleyball, basketball, baseball, birthdays, vacations, holidays — all the things that fill our lives.

In October of 2013, my father, Irwin Treiger, died at the age of 79. He was diagnosed with liver cancer and died two weeks later. His death caused an

---

* Chabad is short for Chabad-Lubavitch — which is an Orthodox, Hasidic group, based in New York. One of their primary missions is outreach to Jews living everywhere. Because of this mission, Chabad Rabbis and their families live in cities, small and large, throughout the world and strive to bring Orthodox Judaism to the Jews of the area. We are grateful to the Chabad Rabbi in Oklahoma City.
** In the Jewish tradition, a *Shomer* stays with the body between death and burial. In Hebrew, a *shomer* is a guard. A *Shomer* in this context is one who "guards" the body from harm or evil spirts.

earthquake in the solid ground beneath my feet. He was my *terra firma* — always there to provide support, advise, and love — always love. With his death, I lost a certain surety that I had about life. Things we want to do, but delay, may never get done. My dad always said that when he retired, he would write the family history. He never retired and he never wrote the family history. His death left a hole in my life and in my heart that will never be filled. After his death, I confronted the loss of Sam and Esther yet again but this time in a new light. I better understood the loss of a parent. Until you go through this yourself, you don't really know what it feels like or the emotions that arise from it.

I re-examined my life and my priorities, reminding myself that my core value is tradition — maintaining it and keeping it present and fresh. Tradition isn't history; it's not a dead, flat experience to be examined as one might examine a corpse during an autopsy. It is a living, breathing thing. It took me two years to come to terms with what I would do — I would retire from my law practice and dedicate myself to preserving Sam and Esther's history. Not as an autopsy of their experience, but as a way to preserve their lives and their traditions and bring that into the world of the living, into my world.

When I retired from my law practice, I didn't tell anyone the real reason. I took the summer off to enjoy my children who were home and to bask in the glorious Seattle summer. I was often asked what I would do now that I had retired from my law practice.

"You are too young to retire," I was told.

I knew what I wanted to do, but I was scared to say the words out loud. During the holiday of *Succoth*, Shlomo and I sat alone in our *Sukkah* (outdoor hut) on a warm fall day.

"I know what I want to do next," I told him.

"What is that?" he asked me curiously.

"I want to write a book about your parents," I said.

There, I had said it. But before he could respond, I added:

"Of course, I need your permission and the permission of your sisters. I would never do it if any of you object."

I got the OK from all the siblings and thus began my journey to tell the story of Esther and Sam. I re-read Lucy Dawidowicz's *The War Against the Jews* and all our Treblinka books. I consumed Timothy Snyder's *Bloodlands* and *Black Earth,* Peter Fritzsche's *Life and Death in the Third Reich,* and many more. My knowledge base went up a steep learning curve. It was exciting to engage with the scholarly works on the Holocaust as well as the many memoirs I read. I was hungry for the full picture and it felt great to begin to fulfill this dream.

Next, I signed up for a class at the University of Washington in non-fiction writing. I was hopeful that I could turn my legal writing style into something non-lawyers might enjoy. When I began, I had no idea that this Tuesday evening class would become so important to me. It opened my mind to new ideas and writing styles and my life to new friends. My fellow students were talented and smart. I am not sure what I enjoyed more, getting their feedback on my work or reading theirs. I learned about people's travels, their religious beliefs, animals of the Pacific Northwest, music, Buddhism and the human body, mountain climbing, and so much more.

One dark Tuesday night in December, I left my house a bit late and I will admit that I was speeding. We had a guest speaker and it would be rude to walk in late. Well, you can probably guess what happened — I saw those horrible red and blue flashing lights in my rear-view mirror. I pulled over and received my speeding ticket. But of course, the police stop made me 30 minutes late to class. Sitting in class, I tried to push the image of the flashing lights out of my mind and focus on the guest speaker. She was discussing her book and explaining that she was writing a blog connected to the book for a full year. A blog, what a great idea. A blog related to my book could provide an opportunity to write about Sam and Esther and about World War II and the Holocaust in general.

My blog "soyouwanttowriteaholocaustbook.wordpress.com" came to life, was linked to Facebook, LinkedIn, and Twitter. I began posting my written pieces. I was nourished by sending my words, thoughts, and emotions out into the world. This was a first step in bringing Sam and Esther's story to life.

My next step in creating a living, emotional story was to visit Poland. It was the day in the *Sukkah* when I told Shlomo that I wanted to write a book about his parents that I also told him that to do my best on the book, I would need to visit

Poland and retrace his parents' steps. I knew this was a touchy subject.

"I know," I said, "your mother told you never to step foot in *finstere* (dark) Poland. I'll understand if you can't go with me."

"I'll think about it," he told me.

It was at that moment that I began to scheme to take my then 17-year-old daughter, Esther, with me on this trip of discovery into the past. Who better to travel to Poland with than the young woman who had been named for Esther Breindl Wisznia Goldberg. If Shlomo decided not to go, she would be my travel partner. I told Esther about my plan to write the book about her grandparents and to visit Poland. I told her that she could have a choice to go to Poland on The March of the Living[96] with other teenagers or go with me, first to Minsk, Belarus — to visit my Grandmother's place of birth — and then on to Poland to explore *Bubbe* and *Zeyde's* stories. She did not hesitate:

"I want to go with you, mom."

Esther was to graduate from high school in early June, so the trip would be after graduation. By June Poland should be thawed out. The first thing I needed to do, was to locate a knowledgeable tour guide. I contacted friends at the Seattle Holocaust Center for the Humanity, and they recommended that I call Joanna Millick at MIR Corp., a travel agency. She told me that Joanna was Polish and had a master's degree in the history of the Jews of Poland. Joanna led tours organized by the Holocaust Center.

Joanna and I met and she wanted me to tell her more about Sam and Esther. I sent her their stories and she stayed up all night reading them. She was in. Since then no one has become more integral to my journey than Joanna. She is my "super hero travel agent." Esther and Sam's pain was her pain; their triumphs were her triumphs. No words can express my thanks. I am proud to now call her my friend.

After participating in the writing class and meeting Joanna, I began to grasp the enormity of what was happening. With each new person I encountered, my world changed for the better. I wondered who else I was destined to meet along the way.

I told Joanna that I wanted to visit Stoczek — Esther's home town, Bagatele — Sam's home town, the forest in which they hid, and Treblinka. I explained that I would also love to find the home of Helena Oleśkowa, the non-Jewish woman who Esther had spoken of as her savior. I just wanted to stand where they had stood, breathe the same air that they had all those years ago, feel the dirt, and take a picture to help me remember all of it. But I had no idea where it was, so I called my sister-in-law, Fay, to see if she could help me locate the house.

"I have no idea where Helena lived," Fay told me when I asked her. "But I know there were two sisters who helped my parents, Helena and her sister, whose name I don't know."

"Do you have an address or something that might help me find Helena's house?" I asked.

"No," she answered, "but I have these old letters from Poland I found after my father died. Maybe they can help. But there is one small problem — they are all in Polish."

"Send them over," I pleaded. "That is amazing." It was a stroke of luck!

Joanna translated the letters that had been written between the years of 1971 and 1991. A few of the letters were dictated by Helena because she did not know how to write. Many of them were written by Elżbieta Maleszewska (pronounced Maleshevska). Maybe she was Helena's daughter. But honestly, I couldn't figure out who was who. As I held the letters in my hand and read Joanna's translations, my heart raced. I was hearing the voices of people who had been part of Sam and Esther's life during those dark years.

For example, here is a letter from Helena to Esther, written on October 4, 1971.

Dear Krysia,[*]

I did not write to you for a long time because you know that I cannot write myself and each of my children have a lot of responsibility so I had to wait until one of them find time to write to you. Thank God I am health and the children are doing well. I already have a great grandson. Only Krysia's husband is very sick so no doctor is not trying to calm us down. They are all saying it is hopeless sickness. He has asthma and a sick heart. It all makes us upset because in the family he was very beloved and liked and a

---

[*] *Esther went by Krystyna (Christina) — it was the most Christian sounding name she could think of. She also went by the short versions: Krysia (Krisha) and Kryśka.*

good human being. He is only a young man, only 45 years old. As far as I am concerned, I am with my youngest son, Maniek, I am doing well with them. We live well together. We coexist fine. He is the best farmer and also the richest one because they work very hard and they know how to manage things. If you came to us you would not recognize our buildings. The grandchildren have everything. They graduated from middle school, technical school. Two of them are studying to be engineers. Maniek says when they finish school, he will send them to school some more. My beloved, in your last letter, you wrote about sending you a birth certificate for someone. But I lost the letter. So if the person needs it, please send affirmation to me to Zofia Styś who is Maniek's wife, because otherwise, they will not give it to me. On this condition, send $50 because every time I go somewhere, they want me to give them a few Złotys because they know it is a birth certificate to America of a Jew and every employee in city hall wants some Złotys. They all say Maniek would not be so rich if it wasn't for those Jews from American.

You know yourself that you send us something in the letter once every two years, that you send us something in the letter once every two years and nothing more. But I thank you for the letter you send and from time to time, my children when they come over, they remember you, and your memory. As long as they live, they will not forget you. As far as Edek and Stasiek, Edek has it worse problem with legs and cannot walk. Staskow, is very sick, she is "going stupid" poverty, dirt and complete poverty came to their house. None of the children take care of them. Edek will sometimes get some clothing or food from others who feel bad for him. What you sent to cover the finger of the child, they didn't ever leave that but they left it for themselves. Krysia — as far as that man, if he is ok with this condition, please send notary approval that I can represent him and I will send his birth certificate. We have to work hard to make it ok. Best regards to your family. All the best — Oleśkowa.[97]

❋ ❋ ❋

Here is a letter from Elżbieta to Esther, dated December 12, 1980.

Dear Krysia,

First I want to ask you about your health. How is your husband doing? And in general how are you all doing. As far as we are concerned everything is the same. Children are growing and studying well. Sometimes they bring us so much joys and sometimes a little worries. Our son, Grzsio* is now in the 4ᵗʰ grade. Our daughter Jola is in the 3ʳᵈ grade. They take the bus to Stoczek. Our youngest daughter, Ewa, goes to kindergarten in Lipka. I work in this kindergarten as a care provider/teacher. Me and my husband are both health, which we both wish you from the bottom of our heart. My father complains about his leg, but beyond that he is feeling quite well. This winter so far was very cold and lots of snow, now the temp went up and everything is melting. But maybe for Christmas everything will stabilize. I finish with this and I send best regards to you and to your whole family. I wish you lots of health good spirit and all God blessing for the upcoming Christmas for the year 1981. I sent kindest regards from my husband, my children and my dad, Janka and Genka,

Elżbieta

Whenever we go visit daddy,** we talk about you because he remembers you quite well.[98]

❄ ❄ ❄

Esther wrote back to the Styś family. One letter was written on June 6, 1990, just after she received the news that Helena had died:

Dear Zofia with your lovely family:

I read your letter and I am so sad that your lovely mommy died. She was very good to me, I am alive because of her. I will write you one example of her fantastic behavior during the war. She was baking bread for her

---

* This is Grzegorz Maleszewski. Maleszewski is the male form of the name Maleszewska.

** Her father was Stanisław Styś.

family and she hid a huge loaf of bread for us. After midnight I came to her house and she gave me this loaf even though it was very risky for her. I will never forget it. I am sorry that she felt pain in old age. I mean that she didn't have joy of her children and grandchildren. I imagine the worst was Marian's death. I was happy when I sent an invitation to him. I wanted him to come to America. I am thinking about him all the time. Zofia, . . . In Florida it is very warm like always. I am very old and my husband doesn't feel good but we raised our son to be a doctor. He helps us a lot. Even the best cures don't help when you are old. He always says that every person should take care of his health. I think that you have amazing children, so you must take care of yourself to enjoy time spent with them and their children. I end my letter with hope you will stay healthy. Greetings from my husband. Zofia, please send me an answer because I want to know how things are going in your family as long as I am alive.
Yours unforgettable Kryśka.[99]

* * *

One sleepless night, Joanna began googling some of the names. When she entered Maleszewski, a Facebook page came up. It was a Facebook page for Stare Lipki, a very small Polish town. On that page, she found someone named Jaroslaw (pronounced Yarolsav) Maleszewski. He was the Mayor of the town and his phone number was listed, which was very brave of him. Joanna bravely picked up the phone in the middle of the night and called him as it was daytime in Poland. She explained why she was calling and just like that we had a Skype call set up for the next day.

As I sat in Joanna's office in front of her large computer screen, she clicked a button and Jaroslaw appeared on the screen. He was sitting in his house, some 8,000 kilometers (5,000 miles) away. His 18-year-old son, Damian, had set up the Skype call for us and was hovering and waving in the background. I explained that I was writing a book about my in-laws' experiences in the Holocaust and that I was planning a trip to Poland to do research for the book. He told us that he was related to Elżbieta's husband, but both Elżbieta and her husband had died years before. However, their son Grzegorz (pronounced Jegorsh) Maleszewski, lived in a nearby town. Incredibly, Elżbieta's father-in-law was still alive at the age of 101! He promised to speak to her father-in-law and Elżbieta's son and get back to us. To top it all off, he told us that he lived just on the edge of the forest where some Jews hid during the war and many of the pits that they had dug were still there.

"Would you take us to see the pits when I come in June?" I asked.

"Certainly" was his reply.

Wow. Chills went up and down my spine. After we said goodbye, I let out a holler and Joanna and I hugged. This was amazing news. What a breakthrough, I felt that the book was becoming more real.

That was nothing compared to what happened next, a week later Joanna and I Facetimed with Grzegorz, Elżbieta's son. He stood, six feet tall, slim, and bald in the middle of a green, grassy field outside of a meditation center he was helping to build for his church. It was morning in Seattle and evening in Poland. We talked for about an hour and as we did, the sun set. The darkness fell around him, but his face lit up like the sun as we spoke. He had heard about Sam and Esther and also that his grandparents had hidden Jews, but he didn't know much of the story. He described how when he was a boy, his mother, Elżbieta, had received beautiful letters from America. He loved the envelopes and was enamored by the stamps. It was a big deal when a letter arrived.

Grzegorz explained that Elżbieta was not Helena's daughter but her niece. She was the daughter of Władysława and Stanisław Styś. Further, Władysława and Helena were not sisters, but sisters-in-law. Helena's husband was Aleksander Styś and the two Styś brothers lived next door to each other.

All this time I had thought that Helena's last name was Oleshkowa, but it wasn't, it was Styś. Oleshkowa means wife of Oles or Alexander. Apparently, Poles referred to a married woman by referencing her husband and Oles was diminutive for Aleksander.*

"Both houses, Władysława's and Helena's," Grzegorz said, "are still standing. They are next door to each other. I will take you there."

---

* See Styś family trees in Appendix B.

I told Grzegorz about the letters and how they were the key to meeting him. He asked me if I would scan his mother's letters and send them to him. His mother had died when he was young and it would be meaningful to have copies of the letters written by her. I assured him that I would do so. At the end of this hour-long conversation, he remained standing in the open field, but the sun had set and now darkness surrounded him. As he gazed into the iPhone, he said, "My heart is full and my soul is filled with joy."[100]

The next week, Grzegorz got together with his Uncle Eugeniusz (goes by Yugenyik) and his Aunt Alina (goes by Alizia) Styś. Eugeniusz was the son of Stanisław and Władysława and was about nine-years-old at the time of the war. On Facetime, Eugeniusz described how his nervous father had created a fake haystack in the barn, where the Jews could hide in the winter. As a boy, he would take food out to them and sometimes stay with them and play cards. He remembered them well.

"Esther," he said, "was a stunningly beautiful woman. But I liked Chaim best. He was closest to my age."

They lived right next door to his Uncle Alexander and Aunt Helena. There was a third brother, Edward. He lived with Eugeniusz's family. He explained that the Nazis didn't pay attention to Edward because of his disability.

"Edward," Eugeniusz said, "was disabled. He had polio. He was one of the heroes of the story."

Grzegorz sent me a letter written by Eugeniusz in 2010. The letter was addressed to the Polish Veteran's Administration. Those who could prove that they had helped Jews during the war were eligible to receive a Veteran's pension. Eugeniusz was awarded the pension. It reads, in part:

> *"During the winter, the members of this [Jewish] family stayed in our util-*
> *ity buildings, that is in a cowshed and a barn — in section of the barn*
> *where the hay was. The hay section was prepared for several people. In the*
> *hay a special hiding place was made — it was constructed of wood and cov-*
> *ered with hay with hidden entrance and few wholes "as windows" which*
> *were used for observation by the people in hiding. . . . [They were] joined by*
> *an escapee from the camp in Treblinka — Sam Goldberg. . . . My brother,*

mother, uncle Edward and myself took turns to take the food to the hide-out. We did everything in secret, so even our neighbors could not suspect anything. I, as the youngest member of the family, was not drawing atten-tion and could more easily than adults approach the hideout and leave food a couple of times during the day. The agreed area to leave food was the place near the dog's house where in a characteristic copper dish I left food, if it was not possible to take it directly to the hideout. Such form of delivering the food did not raise suspicion, as one could always explain it was for our dog."

I learned so many new things from that letter and my talk with Eugeniusz. Sam and Esther had never mentioned a fake haystack in the barn and I had never heard of Edward Styś. My trip was expanding my hoped-for visit to Helena's house. It had now become a visit to two houses and barns where Sam and Esther had hidden. There, we would meet three of the Styś children and their fami-lies. As these details and others became part of our journey to Poland, Shlomo made the difficult decision to join us. In the end, Shlomo and I had all four chil-dren, plus our future son-in-law, Micha Hacohen, on this important journey with us to confront and understand the past. We had no way of knowing what we would find or how we would feel, but I expected that we would feel anger, grief, and sadness. I was especially worried about how Shlomo would feel visiting *fin-stere* (dark) Poland and facing the demons of his parents' past. My exploration of Sam and Esther's story had already left me breathless and hopeful about learn-ing so much more on our journey. Amazingly, the children and grandchildren of Helena and Władysława Styś would meet a child and grandchildren of Sam and Esther Goldberg. We were going to become part of their story and bring their past into the present, into our lives. At that moment, my heart was full and my soul was filled with such joy.

Excitement,
Awe and Horror

JUNE 19, 2016

This was it — our incredible trip had begun. My daughter, Esther and I were thrilled and eager to get started. This first leg of the trip would be just the two of us visiting Belarus. We took a picture of ourselves on the airplane, posted it on Facebook and landed some 20 hours later in Minsk, Belarus. Our purpose was to visit Samke (also called Shamki), the *Shtetl* where my paternal grandmother, Rose Steinberg Treiger was born and lived until the age of seven when she immigrated to America. My father had always wanted to visit Samke — another dream delayed and now gone. As I visited his mother's birthplace, I felt his presence.

Samke is gone, the weeds and trees have overtaken the once serene *Shtetl*. There is still one resident of the place, Raisa, a short, wrinkled-faced woman with a head scarf. She was born there. She lived in a wooden house that looked like a bunch of Lego pieces put together — colors and all — with a dog, goats, chickens, and pigs. After our visit, as we drove out of town on the overgrown dirt road, gratitude surged through me, gratitude to my great-grandmother, Chaya Tzivia Steinberg, for whom I was named. It was she who had insisted in 1911 that their family leave the *Shtetl* and move to America. All Jews who stayed in Samke were shot into a pit by the Nazis in 1941.

My daughter, Shoshana, and her fiancé, Micha, were waiting for us at the hotel in Warsaw on Friday. That evening, we attended *Shabbat* services at the

Nozyk Synagogue. I felt as though we had just stepped into a novel. There were so many characters at the services: Rabbi Michael Schudrich, Poland's bearded, balding, and energetic New York-born Chief Rabbi; Holocaust survivors with walkers; young Jews who had only recently discovered their Jewish heritage, and visitors from all over the world.

The Nozyk Synagogue was built in 1902 and it is the only synagogue in Warsaw that survived the war. The Germans used it as stables and a depot. Its large edifice sat back from a busy commercial street and was surrounded by trees and a courtyard that wrapped around its base. The refurbished interior had high ceilings with a balcony for women on each side, about three-quarters of the way up. It was well-lit with both electric lights and the sunlight that streamed through its windows which lined both the lower and the upper sections. A chandelier hung from the high ceiling. The expanse of the synagogue's main floor was filled with wooden pews, set in straight rows, separated by a decorative carpet down the middle. The carpet led to the *Shulchan*, the table, where the *Torah* scroll was read. My eye was drawn further to the front where the Ark sat brooding with its dark wood, roman-style pillars and gold and blue onion-dome top.

As the group of 30 or so sang *Kabbalat Shabbat,* the prayers to welcome *Shabbat,* the room filled with music. The sound bounced off each vaulted section of the ceiling and back to my ears, sounding like a hundred voices. I sat and listen — in awe. *Shabbat* in Warsaw was a mystical combination of traditions from a world destroyed and one being reborn.

Sunday morning our Polish driver, Stanley, did a great job of getting us to the city of Lublin in two and a half hours. Just outside the city, on a hill, sat our destination, Majdanek. It felt like a Holocaust movie set, only it was the real thing. Wire fencing surrounded the camp. Foreboding wooden guard towers stood at the entrance and even more of them surrounded the perimeter. Most of the buildings were long, dark brown, wooden shacks with slanted roofs. They looked as though they might fall over during a good storm. It was hot and I had an uncontrollable urge to run far, far away.

The order to build this camp had been given on October 7, 1941, four months after the Germans expanded the war by attacking the Soviet Union. It was built to house the captured Soviet soldiers and use them as slave labor. I was appalled at the idea that prisoners looked down at Lublin, it was so close, yet such a different reality. I imagined people imprisoned here wondering why they were not free with those people just down the hill. So close, but unreachable through the barbed-wire fence and the machine-gun laden guards standing high in the wooden towers.

The original solution to the "Jewish Question" was to relocate the Jews of Europe to somewhere deep in Russian territory or to Madagascar, a French island colony in the Indian Ocean off the Southeast coast of Africa. But, by the end of 1941, Hitler and Himmler were convinced that it would be impossible to relocate the Jews of Poland. There was nowhere to put them and there were just too many of them. After the gas experiments at Auschwitz and Chelmno,[101] the Nazis knew they had a means of killing large numbers of Jews in a short amount of time and at little cost. Hitler and his evil conspirators were ready to "eliminate" the Jews.[102] Thus, began the transformation of Poland from a war zone to a sphere of genocidal murder. Building the Operation Reinhard camps — Belzec, Sobibor and Treblinka — was not sufficient. Himmler decided to repurpose Majdanek. It became a hybrid camp, a labor camp as well as an extermination camp. On March 25, 1942, the camp held only one hundred prisoners, none of whom were Jewish. Three months later, Majdanek imprisoned 10,600 men, almost all of whom were Jews. Women were added and the numbers grew. The camp continued to imprison both Jews and non-Jews inside its confines.

In the 1940's, there were seven gas chambers. Today, only two remain, standing side by side inside the same building, just on the right as you enter the camp. I was shocked at how small they were. One was smaller than my children's bedrooms at home, the other a bit larger than the first, but not much. The dull gray walls of the larger gas chamber were streaked with blue residue left by Zyklon B, which along with carbon monoxide was used to asphyxiate the victims. Standing motionless before these chambers, my body began to convulse with sobs. There were mothers holding their children, fathers clutching their sons, old people unable to stand. I saw Jews and non-Jews. I saw people gasping for breath. I saw them saying *Shma Yisroel*. How am I to understand what happened here? The

One of two remaining gas chambers at Majdanek. Credit: Karen I. Treiger

crimes committed here were done by humans of flesh and blood. I took a deep breath of fresh, non-toxic air, and appreciated being alive.

After being gassed, the dead bodies were placed on wooden wagons and pushed across the camp to the crematorium. The crematorium was also smaller than I imagined. The red brick building had a tall chimney reaching up to heaven — delivering the souls of the dead. Before being shoved into one of the ovens, lined up in a row, the corpses were searched one last time for gold teeth or other hidden valuables. The bodies were burned and the ash removed to be used as fertilizer.

After the uprisings at Treblinka and Sobibor, Heinrich Himmler, one of the most powerful men in Nazi Germany, got worried about further Jewish resistance in the camps. So, he issued an order that on one day, November 3, 1943, Operation Harvest Festival was to take place during which thousands of Jews, including all those at Majdanek, were to be shot. Eighteen thousand Jews were shot into pits dug at the edge of the camp. The Nazis blared music over the camp's loudspeakers to drown out their screams. The pits are still visible and look like

Oven used to burn bodies after gassing at Majdanek. Credit: Karen I. Treiger

scars in the earth that will never heal.

A massive concrete dome monument was erected just next to the scar pits. The monument is cold, gray, and impersonal. But under the dome lies an immense heap of ash and bone. The thousands of now silent screams penetrated my soul. I thought of the 50,000[103] people who had not survived this place. I recited the *Kaddish* — the traditional Jewish prayer for the dead.

"Yitgadal V'Yitkadash Shmei Rabbah."

How many times had this prayer been said at Majdanek? Too many to count. How many tears had been shed? Too many to count. But count we must. Each person, Jew and non-Jew that died here, must count. They counted during their lives — they were important to someone — a mother, a father, a brother, a sister, a husband, a wife, a *Talmid* (student), a teacher, a friend. They were turned to ash. It's here, standing as a silent testimony to the lives they lived and lost.

Warsaw

JUNE 20, 2016

At 7 a.m. the hotel's breakfast room opened and the espresso machine provided my elixir as I waited for Shoshana, Micha, and Esther to join me. Seated at the table next to me was a gray-haired man with a soft, kind face. He looked to be in his 80s and was having breakfast with two women, one looked to be of a similar age and the other woman was much younger. His accented English transported me back to Miami Beach, sitting around Sam and Esther's table. They and all their friends spoke heavily accented English. I wondered if he was a Holocaust survivor visiting Poland with his family. I felt an immediate connection to him.

Sliding closer to their table, I introduced myself and I learned that he was Yurik Sears with his Israeli-born wife and their daughter, Tamara, a professor of art history. With a soft, passionate voice, Yurik explained that he had been a child in the Warsaw ghetto. His mother had been murdered early in the war when she had gone to Warsaw's Pawiak prison to try to free her brother. After her death, he went with his father each day to the shoe factory where his father worked, hidden under his coat. After a year of this cloistering, his father arranged to have Yurik smuggled out of the ghetto and hidden with a family who lived on a farm outside of the city. Once there, Yurik hid for a year in the attic of the farmhouse. After the first year, he was allowed to live in the main part of the home. Yurik's father survived the war and they were reunited. Over 70 years later, Yurik was back in Warsaw to attend the wedding of one of the grandchildren of the family that saved him.

Being transported this way back to the Warsaw ghetto aroused a painful image of a father filled with grief and worry. The courageous story of hiding a boy in the ghetto and arranging for his safe escape would bring deeper meaning to the day as we walked the streets of the ghetto. The stones had stories to tell.

"My parents were married in the Nozyk Synagogue here in Warsaw," Yurik said. "I visited the *Shul* just yesterday. It's beautiful. I could see my parents standing there under the *Chuppah**.

"I was there for *Shabbat* services just two days ago," I said. "It is indeed beautiful."

I conjured up the image of Yurik's parents standing under a *Chuppah* in that magnificent space. Yurik and I discussed the beauty of the synagogue and then he and his family said their goodbyes as they headed out for some touring. We too would soon be walking the streets of Warsaw. Esther, Shoshana, Micha, and I lingered over our coffee as we waited for Jack and Elisheva to arrive from the airport. Shlomo would join us later in the day.

We were also joined for the day by Aleksander Czyzewksi (pronounced Sheshevky). Aleks, a young man of 27, who showed up in jeans and a blue collared tee-shirt with a full brown beard and the same sweet smile I remembered from Seattle. Standing at about 5 ft. 10 inches, he was the same height as my son Jack. Aleks was born and raised in Warsaw, but he lived in Seattle for three years to attend Seattle's Jewish high school. He and Jack were classmates and friends. I *kvelled*** as I watched their long, hard hug. During those years, Aleks was a welcomed guest in our home and at our *Shabbat* table. I generally knew his family's story and how he traveled from Warsaw to Seattle to attend a Jewish high school, but I was eager to hear more. Later we would meet his parents, Adam and Elżbieta, for a meal at one of Warsaw's kosher restaurants.

Marcin Borucki, our tour guide and translator for the next three days, arrived at our hotel to meet us. I liked Marcin right away. His easy-going manner, flexibility, and sense of humor would fit right in with our family. Boarding the spacious tourist van, with large windows, air conditioning, and comfortable

---

*   Jewish wedding canopy.
**   Yiddish word expressing a feeling of happiness and pride.

seats, we drove through the city to Warsaw's "Old Town." The old red-brick market square is surrounded by San Francisco style, pastel-colored, row houses. The square is filled with vendors selling flowers, scarves, and other tourist items. Marcin informed us that this area was destroyed by bombs during the war. The Soviet regime reconstructed Old Town based upon pre-war pictures. Compared to the Soviet-built, squat, gray, block buildings that peppered the rest of the city, these beautiful old wooden, row houses were an enchanting sight.

Old Town is a short walk from where the Warsaw ghetto stood. Approximately 460,000 people had been locked inside the ghetto, a space just under one square mile,[104] with seven people living in each room. The ghetto was in the heart of the city that now bustled with activity. I touched a remnant of the ghetto wall, trying to feel the stories embedded in the red bricks. Was this one of the spots where a tunnel was dug under the wall and a small child sent through to steal some food to bring back to the family?

There was a surreal sense of life where the ghetto once stood. It looked nothing like what was portrayed in Roman Polanski's 2002 movie, "The Pianist." The image of people in rags, lying on the streets of the ghetto, begging for food has been supplanted by the new city full of trams, buses, an underground metro, and hordes of people and cars filling the streets. Has all that happened here been forgotten?

Melancholy settled over me as Marcin led us to the *Umschlagplatz* — the place where Warsaw's Jews were gathered before being loaded onto the trains to Treblinka. It was depressing to stand there on a sunny June day knowing that between July 23 and the beginning of September, 1942, 265,000 Jews were taken from here to Treblinka, most of whom were dead shortly thereafter.[105] We stood inside the memorial, consisting of two simple gray brick walls about three meters tall with no roof and about four meters of open space between them, meant to symbolize an open freight car. This does not come close to representing what happened here. Recalling another scene from "The Pianist," I felt the shadows of thousands of people sitting on their suitcases, waiting to board the train. Leaving my family inside the memorial, I stepped to the other side of the wall where there was an open field with trees and grass. "Ah," I thought, "this is the place," it could fit hundreds. At Treblinka, Sam had washed the clothes of the Jews who had sat here, waiting. Who knows, maybe my ring was sown into a dress of a woman who boarded a cattle car here and now it had returned to yet another leg of its sojourn.

The sky turned dark and it started to rain which felt appropriate. The gloom of the sky matched the gloom in my soul. Our next stop was the old Jewish cemetery. This was bound to just add more sorrow to the day.

Our group was now complete, as Shlomo joined us at the gate of the cemetery. After hugs were exchanged, we were ready to enter this sacred place. Donning raincoats, we entered through the large, double black wrought iron gate. I was surprised to see that the enormous cemetery was filled with erect tombstones and clear pathways. During the war, the cemetery had been looted and destroyed and during the Soviet era, the Jewish cemetery had not been on their list of places to fix and maintain.

"It was not always so nice here," Aleks explained. "After the war, the *matze-vos** were piled on top of each other and in various states of ruin. As a student in Warsaw's Jewish middle school, I would come here each week with classmates. We cleaned the debris and wiped the dirt and the grime from the *matzevos*."

The statue of Dr. Janusz Korczak, the proprietor of the Warsaw ghetto orphanage, stood tall amongst the low tombstones. He had no grave; he was murdered at Treblinka. Janusz Korczak was his pen name. He wrote children's books in Polish. His birth name was Henryk Goldszmit. He is depicted walking with a young child in one arm and holding the hand of another child who is followed by yet more children. Legend has it that Korczak had the opportunity to leave the Warsaw ghetto and find freedom and safety outside of Poland. But he refused, boarding the train to Treblinka with his children.[106]

Then something happened to wipe away the gloom in my soul. We came upon a large tombstone with a domed top. The tombstone had three panels of red marble with writing, separated by roman-type columns. This was the grave of I.L. Peretz, one of the greatest Yiddish writers of the 20th Century,[107] whose stories I have read. We were delighted to learn that his tombstone was designed

---

*   Jewish tombstones.

by someone from Stoczek, Esther's home town. Peretz died in 1915 at the age of 63. He has a beautiful tomb where we and others can come and remember and honor him.

"Let's sing a Yiddish song," Shlomo said, "in front of Peretz's grave."

"Great idea," I agreed.

Aleks took the phone to video the moment and we stood before Peretz's grave, with our arms wrapped around each other. We swayed back and forth as we sang *"Roshin Kis Mit Mandlin,"* a Yiddish lullaby. The rain fell around us as we sang, but it did not dampen our spirits. Upon finishing the song, we broke into a wordless melody and began to dance, waiving our arms in the air. Fits of laughter followed and poof, the mood was changed. We walked out of the cemetery, smiling.

It was time to get out of the rain and go to Warsaw's Jewish museum, called the Polin Museum. The museum, which opened in April of 2013, sits in the ghetto and is an impressive structure made of glass, copper, and concrete. The museum shows the history of the Jewish community in Poland going back a thousand years. Our museum tour guide was a thin, black-haired woman who seemed to enjoy our many questions. At one point, someone asked a Holocaust-related question and during the conversation, Shlomo mentioned that his father had survived Treblinka. Our tour guide almost fell over. She was so excited to meet Shlomo, the son of a Treblinka survivor. It took her a few minutes to regain her composure and continue with the tour. The tour guide did not ask Shlomo for his autograph, but I thought that she might.

At the end of the tour, Shlomo, the celebrity, as well as the rest of us, were exhausted and hungry. Off we went to the restaurant to meet Alek's parents, Adam Czyzewski and Elżbieta Czyzewska.* Over a delicious meal, they told us their story.

Elżbieta, a short, bright-faced brunette, grew up Catholic. Her father was a Jew who survived the war hiding in a small village and fighting with the partisans. He never told her that he was a Jew. When she asked why he had no

---

* Female last name for Czyzewski.

relatives, he told her that he was an orphan and had been sent to a village to be cared for. When she was a child, kids in school would tease her that her father was "a stinky Jew."

"I asked my father," Elżbieta said, "what is a Jew and why are these children calling you a stinky Jew? He told me: 'It is nothing. They are just teasing. Don't pay any attention to them.'"

She felt something was different about her Catholic family. Her father was a dentist. He was a hard worker and never partied or drank much. The most important thing to him was studying and buying books. She knew that their neighbors gossiped that her father did well because people sent him money from Israel.

"This idea that my father got money from Israel was crazy," Elżbieta said. "My father had no relatives at all. I will say that he has all the values of a good Jewish husband and father. I subconsciously knew our family was different than our neighbors, but I didn't think we were Jews. In 1990, after Adam and I were married, we moved to Warsaw. I met one of my new neighbors.

'This new government is composed of all Jews,' the new neighbor said.

'That is not true,' Elżbieta replied, 'and even if it is true, so what?'

'No wonder it does not matter to you,' the neighbor replied.

"The neighbor was intimating that it does not matter because I am a Jew," Elżbieta continued. "I was shocked. We were in Warsaw — an entirely different place. Why does the neighbor think I am a Jew? I called my mother and said, 'tell me the truth.' So, my mother told me, 'yes, your father is a Jew.' That is how I finally learned of my Jewish roots," Elżbieta told us, finishing her story.

At about six feet tall, Adam wore jeans and a button-down light purple shirt. His Harry Potter round black glasses and gray trimmed beard made him look professorial. He had always known that his mother and grandmother were Jewish, but it was not discussed when he was growing up. It could be dangerous. His grandmother was hidden in a convent during the war, but she had never talked about being Jewish. His family had been agnostic; they didn't practice any religion.

"I was eight years old in 1968 when the government kicked the Jews out. Nobody got expelled, but they were forced out. Before 1968, my great uncle was a communist and kind of protected us. But after 1968, there was no more protection."

"How did you feel about being Jewish?" I asked.

"I was totally neutral to the idea," Adam said. "I knew that I was part Polish, part Ukrainian, part German, and part Jewish. It was just part of my background. I had a lot of Jewish friends. We would go to the Jewish cemetery in Bytom and smoke cigarettes. But we never talked about our Jewish past."

"Did you tell Elżbieta that you were Jewish before you got married?" I asked.

"No," he replied, "It didn't seem important at the time. But the night before I left for my wedding, my mother told me that she and her mother were Jewish and they had come from Gombin. She told me that my grandmother had been hidden in a convent near Auschwitz for two years. It was not until after Elżbieta learned that her father was Jewish, that we began to discuss the topic. But we had no knowledge of being Jewish and what it meant. The only things we knew were from stories by Isaac Bashevis Singer," Adam said completing his story.

Then, when their son Aleks was about ten years old, they saw a movie called "Sunshine" about a Hungarian Jewish family. It opened a dialogue about their Jewish identity.

"The movie is about the same type of story but in Hungary," explained Elżbieta. "It's about a family that was assimilated before the war and they abandoned their religion and then they abandoned their Jewish last name. Changing their religion and their name did not protect them from the Holocaust. And the only person who survived decided to take back his Jewish last name."

"We have a son," Adam said. "What about his future? What kind of identity will he have? Aleks saw the movie with us and on the way back home we discussed our identity."

"Yes," Elżbieta continued, "we felt the same kind of strangeness pictured in that movie. So, we asked Aleks — 'who do you want to be?' Then, we enrolled him in the Warsaw Jewish middle school. The first Jewish holiday we ever celebrated was *Chanukah* that year. Slowly we went to *Shul* and attended Rabbi Schudrich's lectures. He told us that you never stopped being Jewish and you can be Jewish even if you were not raised Jewish."

"Is that why you sent Aleks to Seattle for High School?" I asked.

"Yes, he wanted to continue his Jewish education past middle school," Adam said. "Rabbi Schudrich helped us make the arrangements."

Aleks graduated from the Northwest Yeshiva High School, went on to college at Yeshiva University in New York City and then did graduate work at the Interdisciplinary Center in Herzilya, Israel, graduating with a master's degree in Homeland Security. The choice of the Czyzewski family to identify as Jewish was stark and powerful. It took courage and guts. They had to do some repair work on their families' Jewish chain. Because Elżbieta's Jewish roots are through her father and traditional Jewish law determines Jewishness through one's mother, both she and Aleks went through a conversion.

"Judaism has many layers," Adam concluded, "and we still have much to learn."

The Czyzewski family defied Hitler by taking back their Jewish identity. Sam and Esther defied Hitler by living through the war, remaining Jewish, and bringing new, Jewish life into the world. I too am defying Hitler by telling Sam and Esther's story. Most important, I am the proud mother of four Jewish Goldberg children who after this day of touring Warsaw were ready for the main event — visiting Bagatele and meeting the Styś family. We would need a good night's sleep.

Bagatele — Scam or No Scam

JUNE 21, 2016

There was a nervous buzz as we finished breakfast. No one complained about having to get up early and everyone was ready to leave for Bagatele on time. We were well-acquainted with our tour guide and translator, Marcin, since we had spent the previous day with him touring Warsaw. New to our group was Gawel Jozefczuk, a videographer we hired to join us for the day. He was a quiet, thirty-something man with a hipster beard. He climbed aboard the van with his camera. I sensed that this was going to be a life-changing day for all of us.

Not long into the hour and a half ride, Shlomo passed out Hebrew printed copies of Psalm 30. He had composed music to a few of its verses to sing for the Styś family later in the day. For the next half hour, Shlomo taught us the song, while Gawel filmed the experience. The melody infused the words with passion and brought new meaning to this ancient text. After singing it in Hebrew, we tried singing it in Polish, but that did not go well. After falling into fits of laughter, we gave up hope on the Polish version. Each of us settled into our own thoughts. On the way out of Warsaw, we drove through a town called Ossow, the home of Julek (Idul) Wilk. Mr. Wilk was a Goldberg cousin from Bagatele, who, at the time, we didn't know existed. Shlomo and I were sitting next to each other in the van and we discussed what we might see in Bagatele.

"Your sister Fay visited Bagatele," I said. "When she was there, she learned that the Goldberg home is no longer standing, but you can see where it was.

When we get close to the end of the town, there will be a field with no building, but a tree in the middle of the field. That's it. Your other sister, Molly, also met someone when she was here a few years ago who knew of the Goldberg family and pointed out where the farm was."

"I don't believe any of it," said Shlomo. "I think Polish tour guides pay people to claim they knew their relatives during or after the war. For a bit of money, they will tell tourists that this was where your family lived."

"Ok," I said, "we shall see."

Before I knew it, the van turned off the main road and I saw a sign with bold white lettering spelling "Bagatele." We had arrived. This was my first chance to feel the place of Sam's birth and bring his story to life.

Our driver took a left at the sign, turning off the main highway onto a smaller, two-lane road lined with houses and trees heavy with green leaves. The houses were next to fields bursting with crops. The homes were two stories, mostly brick with slanted roofs and gardens with flowers of yellow and purple. After a kilometer or so, the road narrowed to one-lane and turned from pavement to dirt. Through the big front window of the van, I saw that the road stopped a few blocks down. We were nearly at the end of the village.

A wrinkled-faced woman stood at the side of the road, in front of a long, white wooden structure. Not five feet tall, she wore a patterned-brown hat with lines and dots that covered her head, enclosing all her hair inside; only the bottom of her ears stuck out. She wore a long blue housecoat open at the front to reveal an orange shirt tucked into black work pants, which were stuffed into some serious gray rain boots with fake fur on the top section. Until she spoke, I was unsure whether she had teeth. Marcin suggested we stop the van and talk to her. Shlomo and I looked at each other, raising our eyebrows and I thought — if she says she knew the Goldberg family, it would be too tidy, too contrived to believe.

Five Goldbergs, one Treiger, one Hacohen, Marcin, and Gawel filed out of the van. As I exited the van, I realized that I was holding my breath because I was so nervous. I took a few deep breaths. Marcin translated our questions to this old woman, who stood alone on this empty street.

"Hi, do you live here? Did you ever know a family named Goldberg? We are looking for the place they lived."

She looked at us. We were a large group (one with a video camera) huddled around her as if for warmth, though it was not cold. With the help of a few *Złotys* was this woman here to create a "Polish roots experience" for our family? I waited for her to say:

"Yes, I have lived here my whole life— and yes, of course I remember the Goldberg family. They lived just over here — such a tragedy."

Instead she spoke in a quiet, weak old voice:

"No, I was not born here and I don't live here. I don't remember any Goldberg family. My son lives here and I am visiting him."

Then, as if out of nowhere, a man, about six feet tall, with unkempt gray hair, a gray mustache, and day-old stubble on his face joined our group. He must have come from the large white house, just next to the barn of the same color. The man appeared to be about fifty with a generous paunch, wearing blue jeans, a gray tee-shirt with a blue zip-up sweat jacket. He was missing four front teeth on the top and when he spoke he looked like the woman. He addressed his mother and asked, in Polish:

"Who are these people?"

With Marcin's help, we introduced ourselves. "We are the Goldberg family from Seattle, Washington. We are visiting to try to find the house and farm that used to belong to Zelig Goldberg."

"Tac, Tac (yes, yes), my grandmother told me stories about Zelig Goldberg," he responded. "They used to live just over here — just next door. They had a prayer house there too. They prayed on Fridays."

Surprised, we continued to listen. The farmer told us what he knew from his grandmother. There were many Jews here before the war.

"All these farms were Jewish farms," the man said. "The Goldbergs lived here," waving his arm in the direction towards the end of the town. "And the house was over there — near that tree. Someone came here a few years ago and asked me about the Goldberg farm."

"Maybe one of your sisters," I whispered to Shlomo.

"After the war," the farmer continued, "people said that one Goldberg survived. That he survived Treblinka."

"Yes, that's my father," Shlomo said nodding.

All of a sudden this became real. This man was not prompted by Marcin to say these things. He seemed genuine. My heart beat through my chest as we walked over to the property the farmer had pointed to. My four children walked together. It was quite a sight: Jack, towering over the girls, with his light-red, short-cropped hair, wearing a green REI rain coat; Elisheva, with her long, golden hair in a tight braid down her back, wearing a black North Face fleece; Esther wearing a baseball cap and a maroon sweatshirt from her High School basketball team with — Goldberg 24 — on the back; and Shoshana, with her bright blue sunglasses sitting atop her thick head of black hair, wearing Micha's plaid button-down shirt over her own tee-shirt. At that moment, the contradictions were glaring. On the one hand, what were we doing here? How out of place could we be? Sam had never come back here after the war, why had we come? On the other hand, this was amazing. The four Goldberg children were walking down the street of Bagatele together, toward their *Zeyde's* home.

As we walked, there was only one house — a brick one — on the left side of the road. Was this Sam's older brother Hersh Meyer's house? Had his five children play here in the street? On the right side of the road, there were no houses, just tall grass, followed by fields of crops stretching far into the distance. The crops were green and healthy looking. Some were tall and stalk-like while others were low to the ground and had large leaves.

Then, there was the tree. I had the urge to run to it and touch it, but I held back, afraid of looking silly. It stood out in an otherwise flat area, covered with wild grasses with vivid purple flowers mixed in. This section of land was surrounded by neat rows of potatoes and wheat. The tree stood tall with a solid brown trunk and branches that spread out wide, full of verdant leaves. I could have put my arms around the trunk to give it a hug, but I didn't because there were armies of ants crawling on the bark.

After a few pictures were taken under the tree, we were uncertain what to do. This tree was the remnant of *Zeyde's* farm. My heart felt heavy that after

Under the tree on the Goldberg farm in Bagatele. Back row, from left to right: Jack Goldberg, Esther Goldberg. Front row, from left to right: Shlomo Goldberg, Elisheva Goldberg, Shoshana Goldberg. Credit: Karen I. Treiger

generations of Goldbergs living here, all that was left was this tree.

"Let's run around the tree," Elisheva declared.

"Yes," Shlomo agreed, "let's run around the tree."

"Let's sing the song," Esther said, "while we run around the tree."

Esther began to move around the tree, swinging her arms and singing the song that we had learned on the way. We all followed. We did not hold hands; we just walked or skipped around the tree in a circle. Within seconds of beginning the song, the words fell away, leaving the melody as our voices gathered strength.

"I hope they all thought this was a religious act," Jack said, after we stopped, as we all laughed.

Jack was joking but singing the song while running around the tree transformed it into a sacred space and brought Sam's spirit back. It was a redemptive act. A feeling of confidence that I was meant to write this book and bring my family to Poland surged through me.

A younger man, wearing army pants and a plaid button-down shirt showed up to find out who we were. At first, he looked at us with narrow eyes and his slow body movements showed distrust. He was the current owner of the Goldberg property and wanted to know what we were doing on his land. As we explained that we were not here to reclaim the land, he softened, his body relaxed and his smile evidenced his relief. He showed us the old concrete foundation which was overgrown with yellow-green weeds and grass. The Goldberg farm had extended all the way to the road — far in the distance — bordered on the other side by trees. It was huge. We marveled at the estate that belonged to Zelig of Bagatele. Sam had said that their farm was 25 Hectares, almost 62 acres.

The house that stood on this foundation was a wooden structure with an inviting kitchen, sleeping rooms for Zelig and Faiga and their five children, a *Cheder*, and a *Shul*. On Friday, the smell of roasted chicken and fresh baked *Challah* would fill the house and seep out into the street. This small dirt road was where Sam, his father, and brothers walked on those same Friday afternoons to the *Mikve*. There they would bathe and immerse to prepare, both body and soul, for the coming *Shabbat*.

Just as we were ready to leave, the gray-haired, toothless farmer ran inside his home. When he re-emerged, he was carrying a glass jar filled with honey. He gave it to us as a gift. We took the honey and thanked him for his generosity. Shlomo shook hands with the gray-haired farmer.

"God sent you to meet us, so you could show us my family's farm," Shlomo said. "Thank you."

That was all I needed to hear to know that my skeptical husband believed that this was the place where his father was born and lived until 1939 when he was kicked out by the Nazis. Seated inside the van, Jack opened the jar and took a finger-full of honey and let the sweetness fill his mouth. No one else wanted to get sticky. I hope Sam would have been delighted that his grandson had a taste of honey that came from the land of his birth. If Sam's family had not been murdered, would they still be living in this one-road village?

But, where were the Goldbergs murdered? The fact that we don't know leaves me feeling empty. Not knowing must have been torture for Sam. There is some closure that comes with knowing what happened to your loved one. We know that in 1939, Henya and her husband went to Russia and were never heard from again and most of Sam's other siblings went east to Slonim, to the Soviet-controlled territory where they were murdered in August of 1941.*

The last time Sam saw his parents was in the summer of 1941. Sam left them and went to Stoczek and from there was captured and taken to Treblinka. After Sam left, his parents moved to Ciechanowiec where they had a cousin. Sam never learned how they died. But because Ciechanowiec is only 38 kilometers (23.6 miles) from Treblinka, it's possible that they were murdered there.

Sam was the sole survivor of his immediate family and, he thought, the only Bagatele Jew to survive the war. He survived 13 months at Treblinka and a full year hiding in the Styś family barns and in the woods around their home. As our van made its way out of Bagatele, we began a nerve-wracking forty-minute drive to meet the Styś family.

---

* It is possible that the Goldberg children were murdered at the same time and place as the Wisznia family, who were also living in Slonim. Esther survived the Slonim massacre because she was in the hospital.

The Styś-Goldberg Reunion

JUNE 21, 2016

Anxiety levels were climbing as we drove to Stare Lipki. This was the culmination of months of planning by Joanna, Grzegorz, and me. What would my family see and learn in the next few hours about Sam, Esther, and ultimately ourselves? How would our story be told after today? What secrets would be uncovered? I was wired and worried.

Our van pulled into a grassy area just in front of a wooden house so old it looked like it might fall down. As we exited the van, Grzegorz was waiting for us. I nearly fell down the stairs of the van I had so much nervous energy. Grzegorz was wearing blue jeans and a gray tee shirt with a simple silver cross around his neck. He looked just like he had on Facetime, tall, slim, and bald with a wide, welcoming smile. We had both worked to make this day a reality and the excitement was palpable. As Grzegorz and I embraced, Marcin jumped into his role as translator and Gawel ran the video camera. Introductions were made to Shlomo and all the kids.

"This is my grandparent's home," Grzegorz explained. "My mother, Elżbieta, moved here after she married my father. I grew up in this house and the letters were written from here."

"Was it Grzegorz who said his heart is full?" Shlomo asked me.

"Yes," I said.

Turning to Grzegorz I explained:

"I told my family what you said at the end of our Facetime conversation and that it had a deep impact on me. You said that your heart was full and your soul was filled with joy."

"Tac, tac (yes, yes)," Grzegorz said. "It was very meaningful. Joanna Millick read the blog post you wrote after our phone call to me and my family. I cried."

Wow, I thought to myself, my blog post made him cry. A fleeting moment of satisfaction swept over me. I refocused and moved on.

Grzegorz is unusual. When speaking through a translator, most people look at the translator when they are speaking and then turn to the person as the translator retells their word. Not Grzegorz. As his lyrical voice spoke Polish, he looked straight at me, as if I understood him. He did this with everyone. It was one of the many ways he connects. I felt connected to him.

Stepping over the threshold of the home, we entered a tiny room with two small beds pushed up against the walls. Between the beds stood a small table covered with a lace cloth like my grandmother used to have. But there was a flat screen TV on the small table. It seemed out of place. It was the scene from Charlie and the Chocolate Factory where Charlie's grandparents are so old that they never get out of bed. Grzegorz's grandmother, a short, 92-year-old woman with gray hair and whiskers on her chin, was eager to share her memories with us. There was nowhere to sit in the small room, so I sat on the bed next to her.

"I went to school in Stoczek with Jewish children," she began. "The Poles would pray and the Jews would just stand there."

I was taken aback at this opening statement. No small talk; she just jumped into Jews standing on the side while the Christian children prayed. This must have been an impactful daily event for her. I jumped in with her.

"Did you know Estera Wisznia from school?" I asked.

"No," she said.

His 102-year-old grandfather pulled himself to a sitting position in his bed with a bar that hung above his head. I don't think he had teeth, but his hair still had some color. Someone asked him which Jewish families he remembers from Stoczek. Straining to lift his head upright, he spoke in a whispered, strained voice.

"Moshku Kwiatek used to live here," he said.

"What did he do here?" Shlomo asked in a quiet voice, sitting just next to his bed.

"They were doing the sparkling water," he responded.

He said the name — Kwiatek. Shlomo's face belied his emotion, but his eyes glistened. It was the beginning of the next part of our family's journey.

We took a break from the intensity of the moment and Grzegorz showed us around the small house, where he slept as a boy. Jaroslaw Maleszewski, the Mayor of Stare Lipki, came to meet us. It was that middle of the night call by Joanna to Jaroslaw that began this cascading snowball.

"Thank you for helping me connect with Grzegorz," I said shaking his hand. "This would never have happened without your help."

"No problem," he said. "It is my pleasure."

"Please say hello to your son, Damian," I said to him as I got into the van.

Grzegorz rode with us in the van as we drove for maybe ten minutes to the home of Eugeniusz and Alina Styś. We passed Stoczek but did not stop; we would go there tomorrow. We traveled on a paved, two-lane road that was lined with trees and low growing bushes.

"Just ahead of us is the forest where Sam and Estera hid," Grzegorz said pointing to an area thick with pine and deciduous trees.

"This is it," I said, clutching the sides of my seat.

"Wow," Shlomo said, as his voice dropped an octave, trying to get the word to come out of his throat. He told me later that at this moment, and for the rest of the day, he felt numb. Maybe it was his mind's way of setting up a protective shield as he walked through his parents' lives.

As we pulled into the Styś' yard, my heart beat fast. There was a patchy, balding grass area, surrounded by wood buildings. One was a home and the others looked like garages or barns, but I couldn't tell. Did Esther and Sam hide in those buildings? A chill went through me, making me feel cold, though it was a sunny, 80-degree day.

As we spilled out of the van to meet Jan and Eugeniusz Styś, Gawel turned on his video camera. Shaking hands with Jan, I liked him right away. In his mid-eighties, he was everyone's favorite grandpa with his sweet face, protruding

Jan Styś. Credit: Karen I. Treiger

stomach, mustache, hearing aid, and suspenders over his light blue button-down shirt.

Turning to Eugeniusz, we hugged and it felt like I was seeing an old friend. Eugeniusz is the youngest of the Styś children and is shorter than Jan with more gray hair left on his head. His moustache made him look like a 1970's movie star. He wore a blue shirt under a gray sweater, though it was a warm day. Each of our children was introduced and shook hands. But when Shlomo met him his face lit up as my husband bowed low and

Shlomo meeting Eugeniusz Styś. Credit: Grzegorz Maleszewski.

kissed Eugeniusz's hand. All the ambivalence about what was true or not true in his parents' stories or what was true or not true about what the Styś family tells us, was swept aside for a moment. This was the man who as a child took food to his parents hiding in the forest.

Then a woman on forearm-crutches came to join our group out on the grass. After a few seconds, I recognized her as Eugeniusz's wife — Alina. I had met her on Facetime too. Alina, a confident, energetic, and talkative woman, was dressed in a simple, long gray tee-shirt and a patterned, long black skirt. She had just gotten out of the hospital the day before and seemed a bit unsteady on her feet, even with the crutches.

They invited us inside. The front door led into the kitchen, which, after four steps opened into a small living room decorated with peeling wallpaper and a few pictures of Jesus and Mary. Chairs covered every inch of space against the walls, except where there was a table laden with food and drink. We had told them that we keep kosher and could only eat fresh fruits and vegetables. The presentation was beautiful with plates of cut fruit and vegetables and bowls brimming with almonds.

The room was filled with three generations of the Styś family. Eugeniusz and Jan's children and grandchildren were all here to meet the Goldbergs. There were so many people in the room that a grandchild sat on her mother's lap and a few people, including Marcin, had no chairs and stood in the doorway. Before the rest of us settled in our chairs, Shlomo and Eugeniusz shook hands again.

"Do I look like my father?" Shlomo asked him.

"Yes, you look like his son," Eugeniusz answered.

"I am your son, too," Shlomo said with just the beginnings of a tear in his eye.

Eugeniusz looked like he might cry too, but before that happened, we settled in chairs and Gawel perched himself in the corner with his camera. Sitting on the edge of my seat, I took a moment to look around. This was happening. My original idea of going to Poland and *maybe* seeing the house where Helena lived during the war had blossomed into something beyond my dreams. Here we were in the place where Władysława and Stanisław Styś had lived with their children, Jan, Elżbieta and Eugeniusz, just next door to Helena's house. Grzegorz brought two large green posters, backed with thick cardboard and covered with glass, into the living room and propped them against the wall. He had made detailed family trees, complete with pictures, as a gift for us. Feelings of gratitude flooded through me. Gratitude to Grzegorz for all his help in putting this day together, gratitude to Shlomo and my children for joining me on this amazing trip, and gratitude for being alive in 2016 — an era of telephones, airplanes, and the Internet that had made all this possible. I was merging the past with the present — just what I had hoped for.

Our kids sat next to each other, Shlomo and I sat in the center of the room, with the food table at our backs. Jan sat with his daughter to the left of us and Eugeniusz and Alina sat opposite us, just in front of the family trees. The small room was hot as there was no air conditioning and so many people crowded into it. Shlomo, dressed in slacks and a jacket in honor of the Styś family, did not remove his jacket. He stood in the center of the room.

"There is no way to thank you for what you did," Shlomo said. "What you did was very unusual and we recognize that you and your parents risked your lives. If you had not done that, none of us would be here. It says in our books that if a person saves one life, he saves a whole world. You and your parents saved many worlds. My father is buried in Israel and on his tombstone there is a verse — 'You brought me up from hell, gave me life from the depths of the pit.' As I was preparing for this trip, I read further in the Psalm and the next verse includes a word that we use to describe people like you and your parents, who go far beyond what most people do — 'righteous people.' I thought that it is appropriate to sing this to you. So, I wrote music to accompany the verse. We would like to sing it to you."

Then we stood — all of us — Elisheva, Jack, Shoshana, Esther, Micha, and me. We joined Shlomo and sang the Hebrew verses from Psalm 30 to the music Shlomo had composed on our piano at home:

יְ-ה-וָ-ה--הֶעֱלִיתָ מִן-שְׁאוֹל נַפְשִׁי;
חִיִּיתַנִי, מיורדי- (מִיָּרְדִי-) בוֹר.
זַמְּרוּ לַי-ה-וָ-ה חֲסִידָיו;
וְהוֹדוּ, לְזֵכֶר קָדְשׁוֹ.

כִּי רֶגַע, בְּאַפּוֹ;

חַיִּים בִּרְצוֹנוֹ:

בָּעֶרֶב, יָלִין בֶּכִי;

וְלַבֹּקֶר רִנָּה.

You, Lord, brought me up from hell;

gave me life from the depths of the pit.

Sing to the Lord, you his righteous ones;

and give thanks to his holy name.

For his anger lasts only a moment,

but his favor lasts a lifetime;

Weeping may stay for the night,

but rejoicing comes in the morning.

Our voices rose together in a sweet melody and the passion reverberated through the room. With the song done, no one moved or spoke. The air in the room was heavy with emotion — pride, sadness, thankfulness, honor, joy, delight. Almost everyone had tears in their eyes. So did I.

After Shlomo's speech, we gave out gifts. We had brought boxes of smoked salmon from Washington State and copies of a picture of the entire Goldberg family from Jack and Emma's wedding. I wanted them to see the family they had helped save.

"Do you remember my parents?" Shlomo asked.

"Yes," said Jan with a single tear still drying on his face from hearing our song. "Later we will go to see the pit where your parents were hiding. This is where we children were going to see how they were doing there, how they were surviving there."

When Jan said this, my heart stopped. This was the first I had heard that we might see the pit where Sam and Esther had hidden all those years ago. I had no idea that the pit was still there.

"Did you know my mother before the Nazis came?" Shlomo asked.

"We knew your grandfather," Jan said.

"My grandfather?" Shlomo asked surprised.

"He was producing the water," Jan said. "Kwiatek. Whenever we were going to the Church on Sunday for prayer, we were saying — 'now we are going for the *kwas* water to Kwiatek,' and we were drinking the sparkling '*kwas* water.' This relationship revolved around going on Sunday for the water. Your grandfather realized he was in touch with good people, so when the Nazis came here, they came to my family to save their lives."

As Jan was speaking, I had to restrain myself from correcting him. Shlomo's grandfathers were Shlomo Zalman Wisznia and Zelig Goldberg, not Kwiatek. He was talking about Moishe's father.

I glanced at Shlomo. His facial expression was muddied by his warring emotions. Later, Shlomo told me that when he heard Jan say that his grandfather was Kwiatek, he felt as if he had the wind knocked out of him. He had to catch his breath. For so long the fact that his mother had been married to Moishe Kwiatek had been a family secret, Shlomo didn't even speak the name, and here Jan was saying Kwiatek was Shlomo's grandfather. But Shlomo held back and did not correct or interrupt Jan.

Jan continued to speak with tears running down his cheek. He described how as a boy of eleven, he went to school in Stoczek. From the schoolhouse window, he watched as the Nazis marched Jews to the Jewish cemetery. First, the Jews were forced to dig a pit and then they were shot one by one. This was a traumatic memory; still present grief spilled out in his words and on his face.

Eugeniusz stepped in and reminded Jan that Shlomo's father was Goldberg, not Kwiatek. Then Eugeniusz continued speaking and described how the Nazis forced all the Jews living in the district to move to the Stoczek ghetto. We knew from Sam, that the ghetto was an "open ghetto;" it had no walls and he and the other Jews living in Sadowne were forced to move there. The remaining Stoczek Jews who were not shot into the pit were transported to Treblinka in September of 1942.

Since the Kwiatek name had already been spoken, I took a deep breath, held it for a minute, and asked if they knew what happened to Moishe Kwiatek. We waited as they talked amongst themselves in Polish for what seemed a long time, but it was about sixty seconds.

"People say different things," Alina said, "but we want to tell you facts, not gossip. We don't really know."

"What's the gossip?" Shoshana asked, "we want to hear anything."

"There is one older, Janina," Alina said. "She is Helena's daughter. She will come later and may be able to tell you more."

I took a moment to look over at my children. They were listening to each word. What does this feel like for them? How will this change them? How will it change me? None of us will walk out of this room the same person as when we walked in and we will never forget this day. It was all bittersweet. I felt resentment and anger that the Nazis' obsession with murdering the Jews had forced Sam and Esther to hide like animals, in barns and pits. But meeting Jan and Eugeniusz and hearing what they had done to keep them alive created feelings of kinship and renewed hope for humanity.

Eugeniusz invited us outside. He wanted to show us the barn, Helena's house, and the pit in the forest where Sam and Esther had hidden. But before we went out, he insisted that we have something to eat. Knowing how important feeding guests is in Poland, I nodded to all my kids giving the signal that they should eat something. I took some fruit and some juice and the others did the same.

After the refreshments, we walked outside, over the scraggly, weed-filled grass and entered a wooden barn. This barn was rebuilt after the war, after the Germans had burned it down as they left in defeat in the summer of 1944. But it had the same footprint and style as the one that had sheltered first, Moishe, Esther, and Chaim and later Sam during the cold winter months. We entered the barn. We were all quiet as our eyes adjusted to the bits of light filtering through the cracks in the wood and our minds adjusted to the idea that Sam and Esther had hidden from the Nazis in this barn. One side of the barn was filled with old farm machinery. The other side was an empty space with hay covering the ground. It smelled like the barns I used to visit as a child for horseback riding lessons.

"This is where my father built a fake haystack," Eugeniusz said. "It was over here on the left side. It was about four meters by four meters. It had a wooden frame and was covered with hay. There were ropes attached to move part of it as

Outside Styś Barn where Fake Haystack was Built. From left to right: Grzgorz Maleszweski; Jolanta Lipka; Karen Treiger; Eugeniusz Styś; Maryla Wieczorek; Alina Styś; Esther Goldberg, Elisheva Goldberg; Maria Bugno; Shoshana Goldberg; Shlomo Goldberg; Agnieszko Dobosz and her daughter, Anna Dobosz; Danuta Dobosz; Jack Goldberg; Jan Styś; Micha Hacohen. Credit: Karen I. Treiger.

needed. Small slits were cut into the wood, allowing them to see outside a bit. The only access to the hiding place was through the main door of the barn. There was no secret entrance. The floor was covered with hay, but my father put some soft grasses over the hay, so it was nicer."

This hiding place served to protect both the hidden Jews and the Styś family. The harder it was to detect the hiding place, the safer it was for everyone. Shlomo and I lay down on the hay to see how it felt. Not too bad, but a bit scratchy. Soft grass was a good idea.

When we left the barn, Eugeniusz showed us where the dog's food pail stood, just outside the door. When it was too dangerous to deliver food to the hideout, he explained, it was left in the dog's pail. It would be retrieved late at night, when the darkness was thickest.

As he was growing up, Shlomo heard his mother say that she was so hungry during the war that she stole food from a dog. Shlomo believed that this meant she stole and ate dog food. But after hearing Eugeniusz tell us about food left in the dog's pail, Shlomo understood that perhaps their food was placed in the dog's dish. Later, Shlomo shared his attempt to reconcile this story. Why would his mother say she ate dog food if it was human food left in a dog's pail? Was the food leftover scraps that might have been fed to a dog? The truth of what the food was and how it was delivered will remain unknown. We are left with the story remembered and retold in different ways.

Even when personal food deliveries were possible, it was still carefully concealed. Eugeniusz described how his mother would wear a large Polish hooded poncho. She covered her head with the hood and placed food items behind her neck and under her arm pits, held there by the cloth. Once inside the barn, or deep in the woods, away from prying eyes, the food was delivered. Seeing the elaborate deception made a deep impression on Eugeniusz and his siblings. They internalized the fear of their parents and the need for secrecy about the hidden Jews.

When I got back to Seattle, I called Shaya Schloss, Sam's cousin, and asked if knew about the fake haystack in the barn. He confirmed that Sam told him about this winter hiding place. I imagined Sam, Esther, and Chaim sitting in a cold, unheated barn, looking at the world through small knife slits day after day. I know they had a deck of cards, but I had no idea what they did all day. All the while, they lived with the knowledge or worry about what had happened to their families. Esther knew that her parents, siblings, and husband were dead. Chaim recognized that his brother was dead, but he was in the dark about what had happened to his parents his sister or his two brothers. Sam had been in Treblinka for 13 months and had no information regarding his parents' whereabouts. Living with such fear and uncertainty and with no idea when this nightmare might end, must have made for tortured thoughts and long nights. Thinking about this led me to an even greater appreciation of my own parents and my good fortune of growing up in Seattle.

Next, we walked out of Eugeniusz's and Alina's yard, past the dog barking in its fenced-in pen and took a sharp left turn onto the dirt road in front of their home. Walking for not more than two minutes, we arrived at the small, old house of Helena (Oleshkowa) and Alexander Styś. Before us stood the house where Esther arrived a few days after the terrifying Nazi round-up. I could hardly

Outside War-time Home of Helena and Aleksander Styś. From left to right: Jack Goldberg, Karen Treiger, Shoshana Goldberg, Elisheva Goldberg, Esther Goldberg, Shlomo Goldberg. Credit: Grzegorz Maleszewski

believe it. My dream of finding Helena's house came true. I stood just staring at the house for some time, reflecting that this is the door that Esther, Moishe and Chaim knocked on that terrifying day in September of 1942. While the rest of the Stokers were running down the "Road to Heaven" at Treblinka, Esther, Moishe and Chaim found refuge here.

Later in the day, we met Helena's daughter, Janina Gołębiewska, who grew up in this house. Her wrinkled face, well-coifed gray hair and the gentle way she looked at me, hinted that she had seen much in her 90 years. She came to meet us dressed in an elegant rose-colored skirt and jacket that covered a delicate white blouse with pearl-like buttons. She recounted how in the early fall of 1942,* Moishe, Esther, Chaim, and their father, David, had avoided the round-up by hiding in the tiny attic of their house, finally climbing out of the window after three days and Chaim, Moishe, and Esther ran to her mother, Helena. [108] And

---

* Esther said that the round-up was just after Yom Kippur, which was September 21, 1942.

Janina Gołębiewska and Shlomo Goldberg. Credit: Grzegorz Maleszewski

now, we stood here at this home and were welcomed by Danuta Dobosh, Helena's granddaughter and current resident of the home. From the outside, I could see that the house was made of wood, but it was covered in a kind of gray plaster, with white blotches here and there.

"This was the original, pre-war house," Eugeniusz explained. "Most houses and fields were burnt by the Germans as they left in the summer of 1944. But Helena saved her home."

Entering through a low, small doorway, we stepped into the rooms where the family lived. We saw the room where Helena's son Polikarp (Danuta's father — now deceased) made moonshine that he shared with the hidden Jews in the cold winters to warm their souls. Danuta explained that Esther and Sam told her years later that Polikarp's moonshine saved their lives on those cold winter nights. We saw the small kitchen where Esther cooked with Janina. Janina described how they would cook together and talk about all sorts of things, from Hitler to Christianity.

"Krysia was very open-minded," Janina said. "This is one of the reasons I liked her so much. Krysia was very good on the sewing machine. She taught me to sew a brassiere. A bigger problem than their torn clothing was their old and broken shoes. They had no way to repair them. They were in terrible condition. Krysia was very hard working. God gave her help. Times were hard."

"Did they bathe in the home?" Shlomo asked.

"No, they never bathed in the home," Janina said. "They washed in the nearby stream. I am not sure what they did in the winter."

"Did Sam or Chaim ever come into the home," I asked.

"No, never," Janina replied.

It is not clear, even after talking with the family members for over five hours, where Moishe, Esther, and Chaim hid at first — in September of 1942. It seemed that they had hidden in the barns and the utility buildings on both families' properties, in barns of other neighbors, and out in the nearby forest. I am still unclear exactly when Stanisław built the fake haystack in his barn, was it in the fall of 1942 or sometime later? Janina clarified that it was her mother, Helena, who orchestrated where Esther, Sam, and Chaim would sleep each night. She had them switch buildings to draw as little attention to one place as possible.

When we brought up Moishe's death with Janina, she could not confirm how he was killed. But Janina told us that within a few months of their arrival, Moishe went by himself out to the Toporski forest to look for food and was murdered there. She believed that a Jew Catcher — a Polish man who scoured the forest looking for Jews — was the murderer. Hunting Jews was a profitable endeavor.

"Krysia came to our home when she heard that Moishe was killed," Janina said, "she cried and cried."

When Moishe died, Esther revealed to Helena and Janina that she was pregnant with her first child. She gave birth to the child in Helena's home, where we stood. Helena and Janina helped her with the birth, but the baby died shortly after birth. This was a tragedy beyond words and no one spoke. Now we knew. They all confirmed that Esther and Moishe had been married when they came to the Styś' home. All three of the Styś children knew that Moishe was murdered and Janina clarified that Moishe was alone, out in the forest, when he died. The mystery of the child was answered.

No one could speak, the stark reality of what had happened engulfed us. What words can be spoken after hearing such a thing. It was no wonder that Esther went out to her patio every day and cried. It was a marvel that she did not cry all day and night. I looked around and saw that there were tears in the eyes of all my children. Gawel, our videographer, was wiping tears away too.

Almost a year after Esther arrived on Helena's doorstep, Sam and Velvel escaped from Treblinka and found themselves in these same woods. Helena must have liked Sam right away. After all she allowed him to stay and hide with Esther and Chaim. Janina reported that her mother told Esther:

"Krysia, you should stick with Shmulik. You'll be happier and better."

Sam had the idea to dig a pit in the forest to hide. This is where they lived in the summer and early fall of 1943 and then again in the spring and summer of 1944. Janina described the pit as "very clever."

Walking from Helena's house down a path lined with tall grass blowing in the breeze, we reached an area with thin trees and low-lying brush on either side of the path. Within five minutes, a paved road with no sidewalks appeared and we turned right onto it for about a half of a kilometer (.3 mile). My kids commented that these trees looked just like the forests in all the Holocaust movies. But we were not in a movie — this was real life — we were walking through the forest where Esther, Sam, and Chaim had hidden. Their story was coming to life before our very eyes and we were now part of it.

We met Eugeniusz at a spot where there was a path into the forest. The stick-like trees of the forest stood sentinel — testifying to what had happened here. The forest was a lush green, with deciduous and pine trees mixed together. It was so quiet walking down the path that we heard the wind blow through the branches. Fallen leaves carpeted the forest floor and with each step there was a crunching sound that would have terrified Sam, Esther, and Chaim as they hid. That sound would mean that people were near. I saw the mushrooms that Esther might have picked, growing here and there and inhaled the fresh, crisp air. Plenty of light entered the forest, as the canopies of the trees shot up high, not wide. The birds were singing, as if they were trying to tell us something.

Shlomo, Jack and Elisheva Goldberg walking through forest where Esther, Sam, and Chaim hid. Credit: Grzegorz Maleszewski

We followed Eugeniusz, who walked down this path with confidence, like he had so many times before, carrying food to the hidden Jews. I was focused on following that 9-year old boy — just 74 years later. All of a sudden, Eugeniusz stopped. I had been looking down at the ground, so as not to trip on a branch or tree stump. I looked up and my mouth dropped open and a gasp escaped my throat. There before me was a hole in the ground partially filled with leaves where my mother-in-law and father in-law had been buried alive to hide from the Nazis.

"This was the pit that they lived in," Eugeniusz said. "It was big enough for all three of them; it was quite deep."

"Who dug the pit?" I asked. "Did you and your family help?"

"No," Eugeniusz responded. "Just Sam, Esther, and Chaim."

Janina referred to the pit as "so clever" because it was camouflaged well. She recalled that they used juniper branches on top. They were prickly, adding to the genius.

Shlomo did not hesitate, he went right down into the pit. He was the only

Eugeniusz Styś pointing to pit where Sam, Esther and Chaim hid. Credit: Grzegorz Maleszewski.

one who dared enter this holy space. Shlomo disturbed the dead leaves that filled the bottom of the pit and the scent reminded me of late fall. At that moment, I could not feel, I could not think — I just stood there looking at Shlomo and watching our children with yet more tears in their eyes. I knew that later, when I crawled, exhausted into my hotel bed, I would dream of what it might be like to live with bugs crawling over you, in a pit in the forest: no roof, no bed, no chairs, no water, no toilet, no bath, no refrigerator, no stove, no food, no lights. Sleeping would never be the same.

As we walked back out of the forest and back onto the paved road, I recalled what Eugeniusz had mentioned. He told us that the Nazis traveled this road all the time. It was one of the roads to Treblinka. Nazis would search these forests for escaped or hidden Jews. Nazi soldiers also showed up at Polish homes, demanding to search the property or insisting on confiscating something. Jan told us that one day a German soldier came to his home. Only he and his grandmother were home at the time. They did not speak German. The soldier wanted something, but neither Jan nor his grandmother could understand him. Exasperated, the German drew a picture in the dirt of a chicken egg. He wanted an egg. Well, they did not have chickens, only geese. The grandmother tried her best to convey in her broken German that they only had geese eggs, but what came out in German was: "we have cat's eggs." As this family story was retold by Jan in Polish, raucous laughter erupted from the whole Styś clan. It was not nearly as funny in translation, but we laughed too.

It was not just the Germans that they were afraid of. Shlomo said that his mother had told him of a Jew Catcher, who used to search the forest outside of Stoczek looking for Jews and turning them in to the Germans for a kilo of sugar. Before we came to Poland, we had thought that the Jew Catcher may have been someone in the Styś family. We learned, however, that this was not true. Every member of the Styś family helped the Jews and kept the secret of their presence.

"We were only children," Eugeniusz said, "but we knew that we could not tell a soul about the hidden Jews. It was our family secret."

It was after the visit to the barn and the forest pit that Janina came to meet us at Eugeniusz and Alina's home. Our family stood and sang the song of thanks a second time. When we finished, the room was again quiet and heavy with emotion. Breaking the silence, Janina said she wanted to sing us a song. She remained sitting in the middle of the room and began to sing — slowly, with her old, weak voice. The song was a Christian song about the goodness of God. While she sang, no one from the Styś family joined in and there was not a sound in the room. The air barely moved. What a moment. This 90-year-old woman who, as a teenager, had helped Esther and Sam and been part of their struggle, a true friend to Esther, was singing a religious song of thanks to us. Remarkable. What a way to end a life-changing visit with this unique family.

It was later that night, in a kosher restaurant in Warsaw that we learned of the identity of the Jew Catcher. We had dinner with another member of the Styś family who lived in Warsaw. She told us that the Jew Catcher's last name was Andrzejczuk.[109]

Andrzejczuk was not alone. There was plenty of incentive to hunt Jews. Poles were given a reward of sugar, money, or vodka, if they turned in a Jew. Even more incentive was the fact that the Germans would kill random residents of a village if they found a Jew hiding in the area. Upstanding members of the community, from doctors to policemen, would go out on "Jew Hunts" to find the Jews hiding in the area. If they found some Jews, the Poles not only got the stated reward, but the local community leaders were permitted to divide up the Jew's clothing or any possessions he or she had amongst their townsfolks.[110]

The question remained: why did the Styś family help? Knowing Jews before the war did not lead to mass numbers of people helping, feeding, and hiding them. Most Poles were bystanders, afraid for their lives and the lives of their children. There were some people during the war who did not succumb to the antisemetic propaganda and whose moral compasses did not go haywire. They knew what was right and wrong and they had to help.[111] The Styś family was comprised of such moral people. The next day, though, Shlomo came face to face with the Jew Catcher.

Stoczek Revisited

JUNE 22, 2016

"It is time," Grzegorz said from the front row of our van, "to visit Stoczek." It was the afternoon of our sixth day in Poland and we had spent the morning at Treblinka and the Bug River. I was tired, but this was one of the places I was most looking forward to, visiting Esther's home town, Stoczek, one hundred kilometers (62 miles) northeast of Warsaw.

We were now a group of twelve. Our videographer was not with us on this part of the trip, but Grzegorz had a video camera and he was busy documenting the experience. Grzegorz's two teenage children, plus a friend, were with us as well. He wanted them to understand what had happened in their back yard and that their great-grandparents had not been bystanders.

We drove into Stoczek and stopped on a non-descript street, lined with houses that were small but well-kept. Grzegorz led us down a short path between two houses which opened into a vacant, grass-covered lot. The lot was approximately 15 by 30 meters and was surrounded by homes on all sides. A large stork sat in an even larger nest on top of an electric pole. Thousands of storks make their summer home in Poland.

"This," Grzegorz announced, "is where the Kwiatek soda factory was."

This was a shock. I had no idea that we would visit the place of the soda factory. Kwiatek was a name almost forbidden to speak in our family because Esther's first marriage to Moishe Kwiatek and their baby were dark secrets not spoken. But here we were standing in the place where the soda water had been bottled and sold. Before we left for Poland, I had found a small picture of Moishe

Kwiatek in *Pinkas Stok*, the Stoczek *Yizkor* (memorial) book. He was short and broad, dressed in a suit and tie, with dark hair and his face reflected a look of determination and strength. He would have stood here before a two-story building, with a door big enough to fit a horse and buggy. He and Esther may have loaded a buggy with soda bottles and climbed up onto the flat board across the front of the cart. Moishe may have taken the reins of the two horses, given them a quick shake to get going and headed out of town. Among their loyal customers were the Styś families.

This was the spot where Jan, Eugeniusz, and Janina had come each Sunday after church for their "*kwas* water." The church was a five-minute walk, just on the other side of the town square. The church still stands today. It looks like a miniature Notre Dame, minus the flying buttresses. Its red brick façade is wide and long with a circular stained glass window between the two steeples. I could almost see the Styś children and hear their feet skipping down the block to the Kwiatek soda factory. Dressed in their Church clothes, they would order a sweet, cold, bubbly soda.

But the modern town of Stoczek holds little resemblance to the pre-war *Shtetl*. The town square, where the market was held twice a week, is now a small park with deciduous trees and grass with bald spots and cigarette butts strewn about. Its rectangular shape made me think of a football field, but it's about half the length. Esther Wisznia sat here on market days, selling shirts and blouses she sewed at home. Jewish men and women, some dressed in the latest fashions, others in Hasidic garb, would walk these streets.

Though there were poor families in pre-war Stoczek, there were some families, including Esther's, who could afford to buy an occasional hot roll with butter at Chana's bakery. The Wisznias lived just down the street from the bakery. In visualizing Esther's home, I had help from two sources. The first source was some photos of wood models carved by Chaim Kuper, born in Stoczek, who had survived the war. He had carved two home models, one in the likeness of his one-story home and a second in the likeness of his wife's two-story home. The homes were made of wood and had a brick chimney and two windows. The windows were positioned on either side of the door or, in some homes, just to the left of it.

Pre-war House in Stoczek. Credit: Karen I. Treiger.

A steep slanted roof made of wood or metal created a small triangular attic space. Esther's family lived in a one-story home on a quiet block down the street from Chana's bakery.

The other source of what a pre-war Stoczek home looked like came from standing in the empty Kwiatek soda factory lot. Just to one side of the lot stood the remains of a pre-war home. Now it's weather-beaten with pieces falling off the side and an overgrown, weed-filled yard. The slanted roof remains a prominent feature and the chimney sticks out like a stick of Wrigley's gum from its pack. Who knows, maybe this was the Kwiatek's home, it was after all just next door to the factory. I let my mind wander and tried to visualize the house as it may have been in September of 1942, with the Kwiatek family hiding in the attic, waiting breathlessly for the Nazis to leave.

Grzegorz announced that it was time to move on. We obeyed, taking some last pictures of the empty lot and the decrepit house. We settled back into the van, everyone predictably taking the same seats. But not for long. We drove just a few blocks. We exited the van and found ourselves outside a Christian cemetery. There, we paid our respects to the graves of Styś family members. The tombstones had pictures of the deceased. To see their faces was to get a glimpse of the past. Had I known we were going to visit their graves, I would have brought some flowers, as is the Christian tradition to honor the dead. But since I didn't have any flowers, I picked up a stone and in the Jewish tradition, placed it upon Helena's tombstone. I bowed my head in silence and thanked her. Would I have had the courage to help? I hope so, but I am blessed to never have been put to this test.

As Shlomo walked out of the cemetery, he stopped cold. He saw the name Andrzecjczuk engraved on a tombstone. This was the Jew Catcher! He was sure that was the name. He had just heard it the night before. Shocked, he snapped a picture. As soon as we sat down in the van, he showed me the picture and told me what he had seen. His face was white; he was shaken. He had heard stories about the Jew Catcher growing up, and now there was a name attached to the mythical figure and knowledge of his burial place. Seeing that grave and looking into the faces of his parents' rescuers in the same cemetery was a lot to take in.

As I exited the Christian cemetery, I noticed how well-manicured the grounds were. Colorful flowers adorned the graves. The tombstones were clean and the writing clear. The small red brick chapel in the center stood cheery and solid, with a steeple reaching up to the heaven. The Christian dead told me that they were honored and respected and have been well cared for.

Then we visited the Jewish dead. This was an altogether different experience. The Stoczek Jewish cemetery is no more — no tombstones, no flowers, no chapel. It is overgrown with weeds and littered with garbage. Under the earth — in this place — are the Jews of Stoczek who died before September 1939, who had the *zechus* (merit) to be properly buried. It was here that Jan Styś saw the Jews shot into a pit. Who knows why some were murdered here and others taken the twenty-two kilometers (13.7 miles) to Treblinka. Perhaps it was the old and disabled who would have had trouble making the trek to the gas chambers. Perhaps it was Nazi sport. No way to know.

In 1984, some people of the town gathered the remaining fragments of broken and faded tombstones and placed them, soldier-like in a row, in a fenced in area next to where the cemetery was. A memorial to the murdered Jews was erected. Shaped like a tombstone, the memorial stands on top of a three-tiered granite platform, announcing to visitors that the Jews of Stoczek were murdered here by the Nazis. But what had happened to all the other Jewish tombstones? There were hundreds of them here before the war. After the war the Polish economy was in the tank. Recovery was slow and difficult, especially under Soviet control. The Jews were all dead anyway and the tombstones were good building material. So, the Poles helped themselves and used them for walls and roads. This was not unique to Stoczek, it happened all over Poland.

Standing in this small rectangular space, I didn't give much thought to the fact that the memorial was clean and the grass surrounding the tombstone fragments was cut. Someone was taking care of this place. Good. It's the least they can do.

A few weeks after returning to Seattle, Joanna Millick, my superhero travel agent, told me something that silenced me. She told me that during her visit to Poland, two weeks after our visit, Grzegorz had taken her to the memorial in Stoczek. He told her that before we had arrived, he had visited the site and encountered a memorial covered in dirt and tombstone fragments covered in overgrown grass. Not wanting us to see it in this state of disrepair, Grzegorz had hired some locals to clean up the memorial and to cut the grass. So, when I got there and thought — "Oh, it's the least they can do" — it was really all Grzegorz.

When I first met Grzegorz on Facetime, I knew that I had met someone special. He explained that he had just finished spending the day volunteering his time with his Church to build a meditation center in his town of Wengrow. His generous personality was on full display over the course of our two days together as he guided us to all the places we visited and provided us with strawberries, tee shirts, stories, photos, videos, and many laughs. I may have been silent when I heard what Grzegorz had done at the Stoczek memorial, but I was not surprised. In a world filled with evildoers and depressing news reports, there are people like Grzegorz who volunteer to build a meditation center, spend time and money to clean up a Jewish memorial, and put their energy into making our visit perfect.

As we left the Jewish cemetery and got back in the van, I took a last look out the window. I heard the Jewish dead tell me that they had been dishonored and abused. Their ghosts were not at peace. They were crying for themselves and for their murdered children and grandchildren. I cried with them.

Auschwitz-Birkenau

JUNE 24, 2016

"Poland is one big Jewish cemetery. Jewish blood is everywhere."

I had heard this mantra before I went to Poland. However, there are some places where the concentration of Jewish dead is particularly intense. Treblinka, for example, holds the blood and ash of some 870,000 Jews. Sam escaped during the uprising on August 2, 1943, but the killing continued there until November of 1943. Once Treblinka was closed for business, the epicenter of the Final Solution shifted to Auschwitz,[112] where one million people were murdered.[113]

Neither Sam nor Esther spent any time at Auschwitz, but a pilgrimage there felt obligatory. With over 100,000 people surviving,[114] Auschwitz is the most well-known of the camps. "Today," Timothy Snyder states in *Bloodlands*, "Auschwitz stands for the Holocaust, and the Holocaust for the evil of a century."[115] Our group was now just four, Shlomo, Esther, Micha, and me. We had traveled by train from Warsaw to Krakow while Elisheva and Shoshana returned to Jerusalem and Jack flew home to Boston.

We drove from Krakow to Auschwitz with our tour guide and translator, Aliza. Even though Aliza was with us, we were required to hire one of the Auschwitz-licensed guides. Our assigned guide was an unsmiling, middle-aged man, with short-cropped hair, translucent white skin, and a round face. He was carrying a closed, black umbrella on a clear summer day. He only spoke Polish, so Aliza translated. As we stood at the entrance, I looked up at the black iron gate inscribed with the terrifying phrase:

"Arbeit Macht Frei" — "Work Makes You Free."

This phrase was made famous here at Auschwitz, but it was a copy. It was first imprinted on the wrought-iron gate at Dachau in 1936. It looked so nice that these same words were added to the gates of Sachsenhausen (1936), Flossenburg (1938), and here at Auschwitz (1940).[116]

Walking under the famous Auschwitz gate into the camp was surreal. Long lines of people waited to enter the austere buildings. The two-story, light-red brick buildings were organized in neat, clean rows, with green, well-cut grass in between the buildings with trees lining the paths. Were it not for the double-barbed wire fence and the many wooden watchtowers, it could have been a college campus somewhere in New England. These solid brick buildings, built in 1940, were originally built to house slave workers.[117] Prisoners arrived and filled the barracks. Like farm mules, Poles and some Jews were first brought here as slaves whose labor was harnessed in the name of the Third Reich.

We waited, along with the others, to enter some of the barracks. Inside one of the barracks, we walked in a long row, single file, past the glass walls. Behind the glass sat piles of shoes, luggage, and hair, as well as a small mountain of empty canisters of Zyklon B. How many cans of Zyklon B does it take to kill one million humans? Evidently, it took a lot. I had seen so many pictures of these piles of hair, shoes, and luggage that viewing them in person was unsettling. It was hard to process the connection to the human beings to whom they had belonged. My heart ached for the enormity of the loss and I listened with my heart as they told me their story.

The hair told me that the act of cutting a women's hair before her death was the ultimate act of dehumanization. The use of the hair for commercial and military purposes showed that her life was worth nothing — that only her hair was worth saving. The mountain of old, ripped, and dirty shoes showed that the victims had been forced to walk into the gas chamber on their own — an extreme insult — forcing each person to precipitate his or her own murder. The luggage revealed each person's individuality. Though they were murdered as if they were all the same, no two people were identical. Each packed their own bag and carefully chose what to take — necessities, family photos, personal documents, a favorite dress or shirt. Many did not know that they were heading to their deaths; they believed that they were being "relocated." These suitcases proved that each person had lived, had cherished belongings, and had very real hopes and fears. As we exited the barracks, I thought of my own hair, shoes, and luggage and how I take them all for granted. No more.

We entered the dreaded Barrack 11. "Of all the places in Auschwitz," writes Nikolaus Wachsmann in his history of the Nazi Concentration Camps, "this was the most feared: it was the bunker, the SS center for torture and murder. Prisoners called it the 'death block.'"[118]

As I stared into cement spaces that were barely big enough for one person to stand, a feeling of dread came over me. At first prisoners were forced to stay in these spaces with no food or water, just long enough to make them go crazy. Then they were taken outside to the adjacent yard and hung by their feet or simply shot as they stood against the tall gray concrete "shooting wall."

Block 11 grew in historical stature. It was the first place that gas was used to kill large numbers of human beings at once. The gas was a pesticide — prussic acid — known as Zyklon B. It had been tried on a few Soviet prisoners, but now, the Commandant of Auschwitz, Rudolf Höss, had given the green light to try it on a larger group. The experiment took place in September of 1941.[119] All cracks in the wall were sealed with cement before the two hundred and fifty patients from the Auschwitz hospital and 600 Soviet POWs from Neuhammer POW camp in Lower Silesia, were forced into the room.

"On contact with the warm air and the captives' bodies," Wachsmann writes, "highly toxic prussic acid was released and desperate screaming started, carrying all the way to the adjacent barracks. The gas quickly destroyed the victims' mucous membranes and entered their bloodstream, asphyxiating them from within. Some dying men stuffed bits of clothing in their mouths to block the gas. But none survived."[120]

The experiment proved to be a great success. For large scale killing, gassing would be much less stressful than shooting thousands in one day. This was the answer to the "Jewish Question."

"Now I was relieved indeed," Höss noted, 'that all of us would be spared these bloodbaths."[121]

The next step was to move the killing to the Auschwitz morgue, which was just outside the camp. It was large, equipped with a good ventilation system and had a crematorium in the adjacent room. Perfect. Now all they needed was more Soviet prisoners to kill.

The first test came in mid-September 1941, three months after the Germans attacked the Soviet Union. Some nine hundred Soviet POWs were gassed and cremated in Auschwitz's new killing center.[122]

This worked great. Himmler was pleased. He wanted more so on September 26, 1941, he ordered a second camp to be built near Auschwitz. It was to be called Birkenau and it would be equipped with four gas chambers and adjacent crematoria plus two converted Polish farmhouses that were tuned into gas chambers. Construction began on October 15, 1941.[123] Like Majdanek, Birkenau was built to "handle" the millions of Soviet POWs captured by the German army. Like Majdanek, Sam might have been sent here had he not escaped the POW Camp.

The entrance to Birkenau, just one mile down the road from Auschwitz, was as terrifying in real life as it was in pictures and movies. It was a long, squat, red brick building with an opening for the trains and cars to pass through. Unlike Treblinka, the train tracks that brought the desperate victims remained. On top of the opening, sits a face-like guard tower joining the two sides of the long building. The top resembles a crown on a head with hair. The two small windows just below are positioned like eyes and the opening for the train looks like a wide-open mouth. I was scared to walk through. I thought I might get swallowed like so many before me.

Inside the guard tower, there is a clear view of the vast expanse of the camp. The camp went on forever and though many of the barracks were destroyed after the war, enough are left to give a sense of what it looked like. Barbed wire still surrounds the perimeter and those ominous guard towers still pocked the landscape, just outside of the fence. We walked the length and breadth of the camp. Our tour guide finally opened his umbrella and he and Aliza walked under its protective shade. I was glad I had no protection from the hot sun so I could experience, even in the smallest way, exposure to the elements at Birkenau. The crushed, broken remains of the gas chambers and crematoria remained to help tell the story of this place. They scream out with the pain and suffering that occurred inside. Next to one of the gas chambers/crematoriums sit open pits where human ash was deposited. The "Kanada" building where the Jews' valuables were sorted, packed, and shipped off, is at the edge of the camp. It was called "Kanada" because Canada was viewed as a wealthy nation and this was the building where all the wealth was stored and sorted. We also stopped by the "toilet," with three long stone benches, running the length of the barracks, with holes in them for some hundreds of people to do their personal business at the same time.

Finally, we arrived at the Birkenau memorial. It was a large abstract memorial made of gray blocks of concrete. I didn't understand it. But I was having trouble understanding anything that I was seeing. Micha said he wanted to play us a song. Using his phone, he played a song in Hebrew, called *Father and Sons*, by Israeli artist, Evyatar Banai:

Soon I'd like you to leave,
So I can fall peacefully,
So you won't see the wounds open wide,
So we'll left alone and brake slowly.
Give up already, and leave,
So I can scream quietly,
Without your teared wide-open eyes,
So we'll left alone and brake slowly.
Fathers and sons,
Grandmothers and grandchildren,
Your mother's heart is blowing up,
Who's to be blame for her, who's to be blame for me,
Who will be separated from who
Father cries for his son, cries for his father.
Soon I'd like you to leave.
I won't afraid to fall down, won't afraid to grow up.
To drown or to glide,
To live or to die.

Fathers and sons,
Grandmothers and grandchildren,
Your mother's heart is blowing up,
Who's to be blame for her, who's to be blame for me,
Who will bury who
Father cries for his son, cries for his father.
Father cries for his son, cries for his father.

We stood for a while in silence. It was hot and I felt drained. My body and soul needed a rest. We walked back through the camp to the main gate, exiting to the parking lot. The pain and suffering here was on a very large scale. My mind had to work overtime to process it. We were told that over a million-people come here each year to visit the place that represents the lowest point of the 20th century. Ninety percent of the visitors are non-Jews. All of humanity should come to see what we can do to each other.

Before we left, Aliza told us an intriguing piece of trivia. During the filming of *Schindler's List*, Steven Spielberg had a cinematic problem. The Polish government would not allow him to film inside the Birkenau camp. So, when it appears that the train comes into the camp through the iconic Birkenau gate and the passengers disembark, they are not inside the camp. They disembark in the parking lot outside the camp. Spielberg filmed an empty train heading out of the camp, but in the movie, it looked like the train was going into the camp. The passengers unload in the parking lot, but a movie viewer would believe that they were inside. Very clever. Now you must watch the movie again, right? That's what I did.

Schindler, Krakow and Jewrassic Park

JUNE 23, 2016

Schindler's List, the 1993 Holocaust movie directed by Steven Spielberg, was filmed in and around Kazimierz, the former Jewish area of Krakow. It tells the story of Krakow's Jews during the war. An ethnic German businessman, Oskar Schindler, became wealthy off the cheap labor of the Jews in his factory. As the war progressed, Schindler began to care about his Jewish workers. He cared so much that when the Plashow Labor Camp, outside of Krakow, was to be liquidated and all remaining Jews were to be sent to Auschwitz-Birkenau, Schindler "bought" his Jews and saved their lives. In the end, he saved approximately 1,100 Jews by placing them on his "List."

Esther and Sam lived over 375 kilometers (230 miles) from Krakow, but when the war began Krakow was home to 56,000 Jews. During the war, the Germans made Krakow the center of their administration in Poland and Hans Frank took over the ancient and magnificent Wawel Palace at the top of the hill. The palace was built over the course of 600 years but saw its most stunning changes during the reign of King Casimir the Great (1333-1370). It is a campus, including a church with two steeples — one a clock tower and the other a bell tower — a grand residence that overlooks the Vistula River, and enormous guest quarters with grand courtyards. The buildings surround a garden with walkways and manicured grass. When the Germans arrived in 1939, they declared Krakow off limits to bombing and thus, it retains its ancient city charm.

The Jews were not among the charmed of the city, however. At least not between 1939 and 1945 when thousands of Jews were kicked out of the city during the first two years of the war. Then in early March, 1941, Hans Frank ordered the remaining 15,000 Jews to move to a ghetto about 10 kilometers (6.2 miles) from Kazimierz. Perhaps Frank thought Kazimierz was just too close to the Palace. The walk from Kazimierz to the Palace took twenty minutes.

Before the expulsion of the Jews, Kazimierz was the bustling, thriving home of the Jewish community. It was bursting with Synagogues, *Yeshivot* (Jewish schools), *Mikvaot* (ritual baths) and Jews — some wealthy, some not — some assimilated, some not. The Nazis may not have bombed Kazimierz, but they destroyed it. When Spielberg filmed his movie in the early 1990's, Kazimierz remained as it had been since the war, a decrepit, dilapidated, mess. The buildings were peeling and cracked. The population was poor.

However, *Schindler's List* created so much interest in Kazimierz that people took a new interest in the neighborhood and it was gentrified. It is now a hip place with restaurants, cafés, outdoor food trucks and concerts. It looks and feels nothing like the town I saw in the movie. The same street shown in the movie as a destroyed mess is today a beautiful lane with cafes and flower pots hanging on the outside of expensive apartments.

As I re-watched Spielberg's depiction of the expulsion of the Jews from Kazimierz to the ghetto, my heart broke. I had walked on those stones and I felt each sad and painful step they took, carrying their few belongings and holding the hands of their precious children. When the Jews moved into the ghetto, all 15,000 of them, they were forced to live in a space that had previously housed 3,000. The ghetto was surrounded by barbed wire and a tombstone-shaped cement wall. Part of that ghetto wall still stands today.

The only open space in the ghetto was a square piece of pavement that stands next to the tram line. This square is now a memorial, Ghetto Hero's Square, which was erected in 2005 and consists of a series of 33 large chairs facing in all directions. These chairs symbolize the household items that the Jews were forced to leave behind. There are also 37 smaller chairs set up on the edge of the memorial, near the tram stops symbolizing that anyone can be a victim. The emptiness of the chairs reflects Krakow's emptiness of its Jews.

Just at the corner of the plaza stands a landmark that is shown in *Schindler's List* — the Pharmacy that was owned by Tadeusz Pankiewicz. Mr. Pankiewicz provided life-saving medication to Jews in the ghetto. One such Jew was my friend Steve Baral's father, Martin Baral. He was a boy of ten living in the ghetto and was very ill. He went to Pankiewicz and asked for help and the pharmacist gave him the antibiotics at no charge, thus saving his life.

Steve's grandfather, Samuel Baral, worked in Schindler's factory and was number 41 on the "List." When I visited the Schindler Museum, I saw his picture on the wall. I stared at his face trying to see my friend in him.

In the final scene of the movie, the real-life Schindler Jews stand together with their descendants. This is an uplifting way to end the film, but it depressed me. Look what one man did by saving some 1,100 Jews, he insured that families would live on into future generations. But, what if there had been 10,000 Oskar Schindlers? What if there had been a million Styś families? How would our world be different?

Watching *Schindler's List* was an intense experience because I had walked the streets of Krakow, Kazimierz, and the ghetto just a week earlier. Spielberg made the war years come alive. But the Krakow of today is an entirely different place.

❋ ❋ ❋

JUNE 23, 2016

The narrow, curved, cobblestone streets of Kazimierz, the old Jewish quarter of Krakow, wind their way past old synagogues including the Synagogue of the Rama, most famous for Rabbi Moshe Isserles who was one of the most important Rabbis in all of Ashkenazik Jewry. He lived in the 1500's and is buried in the cemetery just behind the synagogue's walls. His tombstone has *kvitlach* (small pieces of paper with prayers or requests written on them) stuffed between every crack, like the *Kotel* (Western Wall) in Jerusalem.

We attended *Shabbat* services at another synagogue, the Old Izaac's

Synagogue, built in 1644. It is a towering building with gothic arched ceilings and a balcony for the women upstairs in the back. Today, in the Izaac's *Shul* there is a space for the women on the main floor, so the upstairs balcony sits empty, somehow lonely. The tall walls of the Synagogue have prayers written on them in large Hebrew letters. But the letters were faded, some have even disappeared.

We hit the jackpot of *Shabbatot** to be in Krakow. The Krakow Jewish Festival would start on Saturday night and the kickoff event was a *Melav'malka*, a traditional Saturday night get together, whose purpose is to hold onto the holiness of *Shabbat,* even though the sun has set. The *Melav'malka* advertised a line-up of world famous *Chazanim* (Cantors). Because these *Chazanim* do not travel on *Shabbat,* they had to be in Krakow by Friday evening. They led the services in Old Izaac's Synagogue. The powerful voices of the *Chazanim,* accompanied by the ethereal harmonies of Jerusalem's Great Synagogue choir, created a moving and spiritual experience.

"I felt the ghosts of the past sitting next to me," Shlomo said to me later. "Could you feel them?"

"Yes, I felt them and I heard them singing," I said.

During the Saturday morning service, there was one tune that made Shlomo cry. It was a slow, mournful tune. When he returned to Seattle, he sat down at the piano and figured out how to play the melody. Now, when he leads *Shabbat* morning services in our Synagogue in Seattle, he uses this tune.

These ghosts stayed with us as we continued to tour Kazimierz. We reached Szeroka street, the central road of the crowded Jewish Quarter. Jonathan Ornstein, the Director of the Krakow Jewish Community Center (JCC) calls it "Jewrassic Park" — in honor of Steven Spielberg, director of *Jurassic Park*. He so dubbed it because it was only after *Schindler's List* that Kazimierz was gentrified and became hip and cool. Imagine the Disneyland ride "It's a Small World" which depicts stereotypes from the cultures around the world. But here, every room you move through has a Jewish *Shtetl* theme. It is a grotesque bastardization of the rich Jewish life that once pulsed through these streets.

---

*   Plural of Shabbat.

Our first stop on Szeroka street was the *Klezmer Hois* (Klezmer House). The large sign outside explains that it's a hotel and restaurant. It has *Klezmer Hois* in English lettering and Yiddish lettering. It has three separate small dining rooms, each packed with patrons having dinner. The "*Hois*" is decorated as a pre-war Jewish home. There are low ceilings and arched walls, lined with a picture of *Hasidic*-looking Jews with long coats playing musical instruments and framed maps of Poland and Galicia.* Another poster shows an idyllic scene of ancient Israel with *Yam Kinneret* (the Sea of Galilee) in the background and a tall palm tree that dominates the foreground. Two figures appear in the picture, dressed in long, flowing robes of ancient times, resting next to a baby lamb under a white flowering tree. The bottom of the poster reads "COME TO PALESTINE." If only. If only the Jews of Poland had been allowed to "COME TO PALESTINE," they would have been saved. I burned with anger at the thought.

Each dining room of the *Klezmer Hois* had klezmer musicians. In one room, there was a small, dark wood table next the musicians with a *Chanukah* menorah in the center. They played to audiences of gray-haired non-Jews who sat in silence, eating dinner. Shlomo, Esther, Micha, and I stood in the back and sang along, dancing with our hands up high–*Chasidic*-style. The patrons stared at us as if we were aliens. The menu offered such Jewish delicacies as *gefilta* fish, Herb Herring, Litvak** style salad, Yankiel the Innkeeper of Berdytchov's Soup, broth with M*atza* balls, vegetarian Sabbath soup, three kinds of "beetroot soup,"*** and on and on.

Just a stone's throw from *Klezmer Hois* is a row of other restaurants with Jewish themes and klezmer music playing. It was a warm night and the tables lining the streets were filled. There was a café called Ariel, over the entrance there was a sign in Hebrew, "*Beit Café Yehudit Misada*" and in also English "Jewish Restaurant Café." Under the signage there was a framed *Hamsa****** with

---

* Galicia is a historical and geographic region that straddled the modern-day border between Poland and Ukraine.
** Litvak is a term used to refer to Jews from Lithuania. It is also a short-hand reference for a northern, intellectual, Jew.
*** Borscht.
****The *Hamsa*, is a palm-shaped amulet popular throughout the Middle East and North Africa. Some believe it has the power to keep away the evil eye.

the traditional *"Birkat Habayit,"* "Blessing of the House" in Hebrew. * The menu included the ever popular Berdyczowska soup, Karp Fish Jewish style, Roast Goose, *Czulent (Chulent)*, Passover cheese, and kosher wine. A klezmer group with an accordion, base, flute, and violin stood outside and played songs from Fiddler on the Roof. It was a warm evening and the tables were full there as well.

Further down the row there was a restaurant called Ester. We didn't go inside, but I took a picture of my daughter, Esther, under the "Ester" sign. I wondered if she should drop the "h" in her name to make it more Polish.

At the very end of the street, "the Old Synagogue," the oldest *Shul* in Poland (1407), loomed large. It's now a museum. Throughout Kazimierz, there were Jewish style tea shops, gift shops, book shops, and murals covering full sides of buildings with Yiddish words and Jewish themes. This portrayal of *Fiddler on the Roof* culture reaches a crescendo for one week of June with the Krakow Jewish Cultural Festival. The Festival draws thousands of non-Jews to the streets of Krakow. I was so happy that I got to see this portrait of Jewish culture. It was even stranger than I imagined when I had read about it as I planned my trip.

"Before you go, you should really read this book, *Return of the Jew,"* my friend Barbara had told me at Synagogue. "It will help you understand Poland better."

"Ok, thanks," I responded. "I'll see if I can get it."

I bought the 2013 book by Katka Reszke, *Return of the Jew: Identity Narratives of the Third Post-Holocaust Generation of Jews in Poland.* I began to read the book and could not put it down. The book details the story of the Jewish revival in Poland, both among Jews and non-Jews. It seems that it is now "cool" to be Jewish in Poland.

---

* The Blessing of the House reads:
Through this gate
Strife will not permeate
Though opening this
A curse will not kiss
Through this door
Horror will be no more
In this family
There will be no calamity
In this place
There will be blessing and peace
(translated by Shoshana Goldberg)

But then a crazy thing happened. I was speaking by phone to my daughter, Elisheva, about the trip. She stopped me as I was discussing the itinerary.

"Mom, stop," Elisheva said. "That's all good, but you should consider what is happening now with the Jewish community of Poland. Lots of things are going on. I met a woman from Poland at a conference here in Israel. I want to introduce the two of you, but I can't remember her exact name. It's Katya or something like that."

"Wait a minute," I replied going with a hunch. "Is it Katka Reszke?"

"Yes, that's her name," she said.

"I can't believe it. I just finished reading her book — *Return of the Jew* — it's amazing," I said. "I would so love to meet her."

"OK, I'll get in touch with her and let you know," Elisheva replied.

Elisheva connected us and we spoke on Skype. I had written two blog posts on what I learned from her book. We discussed her book, my blog posts, and what I should do in Poland to get a good sense of the current Jewish reality there.

In her book, Katka describes this strange marriage of *Fiddler on the Roof* and Disneyland. She explains that non-Jews in Poland are trying to come to terms with their brutal history and the mystique of the murdered Jews. For example, there is a project created by the Polish artist Rafal Betlejewski, called "I miss you, Jew." Betlejewski compiled a list of cities and towns where Jews used to live. He then visited these places and took "photos of individuals and groups standing beside an empty chair with a skull cap on it as a sign of Jewish absence."[124]

Betlejewski is not alone, Jewish art has become very popular in Poland. There are many Jewish festivals, with the Krakow Jewish Festival leading the way. In Warsaw, there is a Jewish Theater where non-Jewish actors perform in Yiddish for other non-Jews. Here actors can be seen "moaning and swaying" trying to "ape Hasidism . . . transmitting anti-Semitic stereotypes."[125] This theater group performs at the annual Singer's Warsaw Festival. Katka explains that "there isn't a week or perhaps a day in Poland without a 'Jewish event' happening somewhere."[126] All these events seem to create a virtual Jewish reality. Imagine — thousands of non-Jews doing Jewish circle dancing to klezmer music and eating "kosher-style" food in the streets of Krakow.[127]

The interest in things Jewish is not restricted only to the Kazimierz district, it extends to other parts of Krakow. The old town of Krakow is filled with beautiful, decorated old buildings and ornate old Churches. Next to the market square is a covered pedestrian lane, lined with tourist shops. Many sell identical wares — Polish pottery, purses, hats, jewelry, and small crystal glassware. But every other shop carries the Jewish figurines that I first learned about in Katka's book. They are wood carvings of Jews wearing long black coats, black hats, *Tziztit**, beards and *Peyes* (sidelocks). They come in various sizes and they hold different objects — a violin, an accordion, a book, or a staff. But the most common ones hold a coin and a money bag.

"These are Jews," the shopkeepers told me. "You see, Jews used to live here in Krakow and there was much Jewish culture here. These Jewish figurines are good luck charms. If you buy one and keep it in your home, you will have good luck, especially with money."

I asked three different shopkeepers and I got pretty much the same answer from all of them. I couldn't resist, I bought three of them, one from each shopkeeper. I don't think that they had any idea how offensive this was. I could also have bought a painting of a Jew counting coins, but I resisted. I was told that these paintings can be found hanging in the homes of Poles who live in the countryside. Even more absurd, the paintings and the wooden figurines are turned upside down on *Shabbat*. So, from Friday night at sunset until Saturday night at sunset, Poles turn their "good luck Jew" upside down.

While some non-Jews are turning their Jewish figurine upside down on Friday night, other non-Jewish Poles are volunteering at the Krakow JCC's *Shabbat* dinner. The JCC has 50 regular non-Jewish volunteers who assist with *Shabbat* dinner each week, as well as other JCC programs. Their group is called the "Volunteer *Mishugoyim*."

---

* *Tzitzit* are a group of specially knotted ritual fringes that attach to either a *Tallit* (prayer shawl) or a *Tallit Katan* (a four-cornered undergarment that is usually worn under one's shirt.) Some wear *Tzitzit* with the fringes sticking out of their clothing, hanging down their sides, while others wear the fringes tucked in and out of sight. In Numbers 15:38, the *Torah* commands that *Tzitzit* be placed on any four-cornered garment.

Jewish Figurines Author Bought in Krakow. Credit: Karen I. Treiger.

"People ask me, why are non-Jewish people involved in Jewish culture?" Magdalena Arabas, who was the JCC Coordinator of the Volunteer *Mishugoyim*, told me. "You are crazy. *Meshuga* in Yiddish means crazy. *Goyim* is the Yiddish word for non-Jews. So, we put it together and call ourselves *Mishugoyim*."

This is a brilliant name. I love it. Extra *Mishugoyim* come on board for the week of the Krakow Jewish festival. At the JCC, these non-Jews see Jewish traditions that they have heard or read about, come alive.

"People are missing culture and history that was in the past and are trying to do something better for the Jewish community," said Magdalena. "We are pioneers, doing things that no one else is doing."

If most non-Jewish Poles see Judaism as an extension of Tevya's town of Anatevka, the real live Jews of Poland, do not resemble Tevya or Golda at all. They are young, modern, and trying to figure out what it means to be a Jew in Poland. While the Gentiles attend Yiddish theater, the Jews attend a Limmud conference and the *Simcha* Jewish Culture Festival organized annually in Wroclaw since 1999. While the Krakow Jewish festival is going on out in the streets, the Jews go inside the JCC where there are alternative activities, such as lectures on Jewish topics and *Shabbat* meals.[128]

Before I read Katka's book and visited Poland, I never would have believed any of this. I thought that Polish Jews were either murdered during the Holocaust or got the hell out of there. Sam and Esther's story of being chased out of Ostrow by the non-Jews who wanted to kill them to take their property repeated itself all over Poland between 1944 and 1946. How is it that any Jews stayed at all?

Well, some Jews who survived the war did stay in Poland. They tried their best to assimilate. It was not safe to be a Jew in Poland. In the late 1950's Polish citizens were unhappy with the ruling elite and the dissatisfaction led to a resurgence of antisemitism. Between 1956 and 1959, some 50,000 Jews left Poland, mostly for Israel.[129] Of the Holocaust survivors who stayed, some "decided to disguise their Jewish identification and similarly made no mention of it to their children."[130] This was the story we heard from Adam Czyzewski and Elżbieta Czyzewska at the Warsaw restaurant.

Antisemitism grew in Poland in the 1960s, reaching a new post-war high after Israel's victory in the 1967, Six Days War. In 1968 the Minister of Internal Affairs waged an anti-Zionist/antisemitic campaign. The internal political wrangling blamed Zionists for crimes of the Stalinist era and more than 20,000 Jews left or were forced to leave the country. The Communist government's 1968 anti-Jewish actions seemed to make being Jewish or being pro-Jewish synonymous with "defying the authorities." A semi-clandestine study group, called the Jewish Flying University, was established. It had 60 to 80 participants and provided a way for Jews and non-Jews to study Judaism, Jewish history, and Jewish culture. It was forced to disband under martial law in 1981. Those Jews who remained after 1968 formed their Jewish identity in early adulthood, as they had no previous knowledge of their Jewish ancestry.[131]

In 1989, the fall of the Communist regime shook the Polish Jews. Now there was a third post-Holocaust generation, the grandchildren of survivors. Some discovered their Jewish ancestry in their teens or twenties, while others had always had some awareness of it. Nonetheless, it was not until the 1990s, after the fall of Communism, that these third-generation Polish Jews explored what it meant to have Jewish roots.[132]

"Over the last 21 years, thousands of Poles have discovered that they have Jewish roots and nobody knows how many thousands they are," Rabbi Michael Schudrich, the Chief Rabbi of Poland said. When asked, "[h]ow many Jews are there in Poland?" Rabbi Schudrich replied: "Pick a number, double it. It is too small. I don't know, but tomorrow there will be more."[133]

Reszke, who herself discovered her Jewish roots as a teenager, interviewed 50 young Polish Jews between 2001 and 2011 about how they had discovered that they had Jewish roots and what this new identity meant to them. These young Jews had a sense of mission that ran deep. After so many Jews were murdered in the Holocaust, they had a duty to stay in Poland and rebuild the Jewish community. One of Reszke's quotes tells the story:

"To be a Jew," said Max, "to be a Jew from here, yes, from Warsaw, from this city where you walk on corpses, where you walk on human skulls, yes. . . . This is no ordinary city, this is the New Jerusalem. . . . It's not an ordinary city; it's a very important city, and a very important country. . . . It is that feeling that this is your legacy that you cannot forget, that it is important and that nobody will remember it for you. I have a part in the legacy of the Holocaust and my part in it is to try to understand. I ought to, I feel that I should, I feel this responsibility, this duty . . . to remember, to think about it, to understand, and to somehow transmit that memory. It is some kind of absurd reaffirmation of the covenant."[134]

But it gets complicated quickly. Under Orthodox Jewish law, one is considered a Jew if one is born of a Jewish mother or converts according to *Halacha* (Jewish law). So, those whose Jewish roots stem from their father's side may be Jewish enough for Hitler to murder, but they are not Jewish enough for Israeli Rabbinical authorities and some diaspora Jews. The first thing they hear when they explain that their father is Jewish, but not their mother, is "But you're not really Jewish!" This is devastating to them.

"As a Polish Jew," Brozena stated, "I didn't feel recognized or respected enough by American institutions and of course not by Israeli institutions . . . it was as if we were second-quality Jews."[135]

These young people identify themselves as Jews. They are involved in different aspects of the ever more vibrant Polish Jewish community. When I asked them about antisemitism, they didn't seem bothered by it. This surprised me because studies show that in Poland, the belief that Jews around the world conspire to control the world's finances and media, referred to in shorthand as "the Jewish conspiracy" remains high, 63% in 2013. This number was similar to a poll taken in 2009 which showed that 65% of respondents held this belief. The study also found an eight percent increase in more traditional forms of antisemitism, including blaming Jews for the murder of Jesus Christ and the belief that Christian blood is used in Jewish rituals.[136]

These are antisemitic mantras that have been hurled at Jews with much destructive force over the centuries. But the Jew that has returned to Poland is moving forward into the 21st century. Some of them are choosing to convert, some are not. Some men are choosing to have a circumcision, some are not. It's all about the Jewish blood running through their veins. When Holocaust tourists like me meet these young Polish Jews, we are confronted with the past we know with the future that we did not know was possible. It is up to these young people to shape the future and make it their own. As the Jew returns to Poland, she will be cheered on by some of the non-Jews who think being Jewish is cool.[137]

The non-Jews who think being Jewish is cool were out in force for the beginning of the 26th annual Krakow Jewish Festival. The *Melav'malka* was held in the Temple Synagogue which was originally built in the 1860's as a Reform Temple. It was built in the style of the Leopoldstadter Temple in Vienna. Its gold ornate decorations and high, vaulted ceilings create a surreal setting for orthodox Cantors and the choir that we heard on *Shabbat*. Some were dressed in the long black coats of *Hasidim* and others in slacks and white shirts of a non-*Hasidic* Orthodox Jew. For over an hour, traditional Jewish melodies and prayers — mostly in Hebrew, a few in Yiddish — were sung — all to a packed house and great applause. This free event was just a teaser — the main Cantorial concert was to be the following night at 7 p.m. At that time, I would be on a plane to Israel.

On Sunday, before I left for the airport, I attended two events, one at the Galicia Jewish Museum and the second at the JCC. The Galicia Jewish Museum is run by non-Jews and had a photographic exhibit showing scenes of Polish Jewish life. The ceremony is an annual event. It honors Polish non-Jews who work to preserve Jewish culture and heritage. For example, Krzysztof Ostrowski received an award for his work in the Jewish cemetery in Pułtusk. It was destroyed during WWII and was abandoned until 2012. Mr. Ostrowski worked to gather the tombstones and make them into a memorial. Another was Krzysztof Godlewski, who received an honor for organizing a ceremony in memory of the pogrom that occurred in Jedwabne on July 10, 1941.[138] Non-Jewish Poles are trying to make sense of what happened during the war. A huge piece of their country's life and culture — the Jewish communities of Poland — was erased in six short years. They were each creating their own "I miss you, Jew" offerings.

The final event I attended was a concert by the JCC choir in the courtyard. I had spent time in the JCC building on Friday and for *Shabbat* meals. On Friday, I had the opportunity to speak with Jonathan Ornstein, the director of the JCC. When you walk in the building the first thing you notice are the bright colors — green and orange. This is not your grandmother's JCC. Upon entering the glass doors, one of the *Mishugoyim* volunteers greets you at the reception desk. She is there to answer any questions you might have about the JCC and to direct you to the proper office. I was ushered upstairs to Jonathan's office. He is a passionate believer in the mission of the JCC.

"The mission of the JCC," Jonathan told me, "is two-fold. First, to take people who were cut off from Judaism because of the Holocaust and welcome them back. Second, to take care of our survivors."

"Are your survivors dying off?" I asked.

"Well, some are dying," Jonathan responded, "but new ones walk through the door all the time. We have about 75 survivors here at the JCC. They are reconnecting Jewishly. Our latest is an 80-year-old survivor who walked into the building who had not had any contact with Judaism for 70 years. We are rebuilding Jewish life in Krakow the best we can. We want to give people the opportunity that was denied them."

He explained that to be a member of the JCC, you need to have some Jewish roots, but many programs are open to all. Some people come and sign up for classes about Judaism and then once they feel more comfortable, they open up and reveal that they have a Jewish grandparent. Jonathan referred to the "twin horrors" of the Holocaust and Communism that pushed the surviving Jews of Poland into a deep freeze. After the fall of Communism in 1989, Polish society began to thaw. Both Jews and non-Jews began to tiptoe around this thing called "being Jewish." Jonathan believes that there is a miracle of Jewish revival happening in Krakow and he is watching it unfold, all in the shadow of Auschwitz.

"We are Jewish despite Auschwitz, not because of it," Jonathan said. "We should not let ourselves be defined by tragedy. In Judaism, we let ourselves move beyond tragedy. At a wedding we break a glass, to remember the sadness, but that is in the context of hours of joy."

Sitting in the courtyard of the JCC, sipping a glass of Israeli wine, I looked up and saw Jonathan sitting on the roof of the building, looking down. He watched as the choir sang Hebrew and Yiddish songs to an adoring crowd of about fifty people. The choir singers ranged in age from about 25 to 80 as their harmonious music filled the air. One of the songs they sang was *Mizmor L'Dovid* — Psalm 23. Shlomo and I sing this tune each *Shabbat* at our table in Seattle. Hearing it sung by Krakow's Jews with such beautiful tones and harmonies, led me to recall the meaning of some of these ancient Hebrew words:

Though I walk through a valley of death,
I fear no harm,
For You are with me.
Your rod and Your staff —
They comfort me.
You spread out before me a table
In full view of my enemies.
You anoint my head with oil,
My cup overflows.
May only goodness and steadfast love
Pursue me all the days of my life,
And I shall dwell in the house of the Lord
For many long years.

The Jews of Krakow and of all of Poland walked through the valley of death. But now, there is a new table spread out before them, "in full view of my enemies" at Krakow's JCC and Warsaw's Nozyk Synagogue. I hope that the cup of the Jews of Poland overflows with goodness and love. I hope to return to Krakow and engage with this growing community in a meaningful way. I looked at Esther sitting next to me on a box that served as a makeshift seat in the JCC courtyard. I whispered:

"My heart is full and my soul is filled with joy. Let's go."

A *Talmid**, a Priest and a Cousin

SEPTEMBER 2016 — SEATTLE

The Poland trip was a roller coaster ride — from the horror of Majdanek to the joy of finding the Goldberg farm in Bagatele, from the darkness of Treblinka to the goodness of the Styś family, from the disgust of Auschwitz/Birkenau to the promise of Poles reconnecting with their Judaism. The entire time, Sam and Esther hovered, whispering in my ear that they knew the truth, that humans have the capacity for the greatest evil — to torture and kill — to shoot people into a pit, to gas them to death, to burn their bodies and extract the gold from their teeth, to hunt them down in the forest for a kilo of sugar. But, there was another truth that they also knew, that humans had the highest capacity for kindness — to give a fellow prisoner a cube of sugar, to hide and feed people as they are being hunted like animals, to cook food in a wash pot at Treblinka and bring it to the dying in the "hospital," to stand up for someone else, even in a death camp, to save others when it puts your own children in danger.

I opened up to holding these contradictory thoughts in my mind at the same time and living with the tension that it creates.[139] Before this trip I knew that I would discover new facts and meet new people, but what I didn't know was that I would reach the dark matter of the human soul. I now accept that humans are, at once, both evil and good. My work on Sam and Esther's story and my visit to

---

*   Student.

Poland taught me that I can choose which side of my nature to express. This is my new reality.[140]

I committed to express my kinder side. With this in mind, my first order of business upon returning to Seattle was to nominate the Styś families for the Yad Vashem honor of Righteous Among the Nations. Yad Vashem, the World Holocaust Remembrance Center in Jerusalem, created this title for those who aided Jews during the war. It was another way to thank them for what they did and to enshrine their family's name in *Yad Vashem's* holy list for all future generations to know who stood up to the hatred and murder that was all around them. Those who are so honored receive a medal and a hand-calligraphied certificate at an award ceremony. They also have the right to immigrate to Israel, become citizens and receive a government pension. I prepared an extensive file including copies of the letters, video of Sam and Esther, video of the Styś family from our trip, and a statement signed by Shlomo. The package was delivered to Yad Vashem in September.

With that important work done, I began to write. Then one day at dinner, Shlomo mentioned that he had recently spoken with a man named Fievel Goldfarb, who was born in Stoczek and now lives in Miami Beach. This was big news.

"How did you find out about him?" I asked surprised.

"My sister Fay told me about him," Shlomo replied. "He lives in the same building as my parent's condo."

"Can I call him?" I asked. "I would love to talk with him about Stoczek."

"Sure, you can call," he said, "you should ask him about my grandfather. He was a student of my grandfather in his *Cheder*."

"You're kidding — that's even better," I said jumping up to get a pen to write down the number.

I called Fievel the next morning. He was happy to talk with me and remembered Sam and Esther fondly. Within minutes of our hello, Fievel recounted, in his heavily accented English, the horror of the beginning of the war. The Nazis arrived in Stoczek within a few days of the September 1, 1939 attack on Poland. They had ordered all the Jews they could find to stand in the market square. Fievel, a boy of eight, was with his Uncle, holding his hand, as he stood in the square with other Stoczek Jews. The Nazis screamed at them as they began burning down shops and homes. Then, the Nazi screamed *"raus"* — "get out." Everyone began running at once. As they ran, the Nazis began to shoot.

"Half of them were shot dead," Fievel said. "I saw one man I knew on the ground and I shook him and said, 'get up, they are shooting people.' But then I saw that his eyes were turned up in his head. He couldn't get up. I ran back home and found my parents."

Fievel's home was burned to the ground. With nothing left, his family fled to the Soviet-controlled part of Poland, to Bialystok. But soon, Fievel's family was sent east by the Soviets to Siberia. There they suffered from freezing temperatures, down to forty below zero and had little food. Fievel's mother headed the Jewish burial society in their Siberian town, and in the winter, she had to hack through ice to get to the body to wash it and prepare it for burial. Despite all the hardships that they encountered, the whole family survived.

Before the war, as a seven- or eight-year-old boy, Fievel walked each day to *Cheder* from his home on the other side of the town square. He turned the corner at Chana's bakery and walked down the small street, counting eight houses to the Wisznia's. Fievel told me (more than once) that he was only eight-years-old when the war began and does not remember much. But he proceeded to describe the town, his *Rebbe* — Shlomo Zalman Wisznia, the *Cheder,* Chana's bakery, the Church, the Kwiatek soda factory, and Neiman's market, just next door to the soda factory.

As he began describing Chana's bakery, his voice changed. He sounded younger, like a boy. His family was poor and he could not afford to buy what Chana sold. He was friends with Chana's son — Moishele — he called him Moynik. In that little boy voice, he told me that one day, Moynik was eating a roll with butter. Fievel looked at the roll — he had never in his life had a roll with butter. Moynik had his fill of the roll and offered the rest to Fievel. Fievel's father taught him never to take charity. So, he turned down the offer. Shrugging, Moynik threw the remainder of the roll over the fence. Fievel told Moynik that he had to go home. They parted and Fievel ran to the other side of the fence to retrieve the precious roll. It was gone, maybe it was eaten by a dog.

"I will never forget that roll," Fievel lamented 80 years later.

Hearing this story from Fievel disturbed me. My mind jumped to the Jewish folktale made famous by I.L. Peretz, whose tomb we had danced at in Warsaw — Bontshe Szweig (pronounced Shvayg) — Bontshe the Silent. The story is about a poor Jew who dies. The heavens are astir with the news.

"Bontshe Szweig has passed away! Bontshe has been summoned to his Maker!" the angels declare. "A joyous din broke out in Paradise."[141]

He arrives at the gates of heaven and is greeted by the angels with a golden throne and a jeweled crown. Father Abraham himself welcomes Bontshe. Seeing the welcome he received, Bontshe was again silent. He was terrified that a mistake had been made. The heavenly court opens with the case of Bontshe Szweig before it. The defending angel begins:

"Not once in his whole life, . . . did he complain to God or to man. Not once did he feel a drop of anger or cast an accusing glare at heaven."[142]

The defending angel continues that Bontshe was silent when his mother died; he was silent when his stepmother was cruel to him; he was silent when his father threw him out of the house as a child; he was silent when he suffered terrible hunger; he was silent when people spat on him as he worked as a porter; he was silent when his wife ran off leaving him with an infant; he was silent when the child grew up and threw him into the street; he was silent.

The defending angel recounts the many horrible things that happened to Bontshe and how through it all "not one word against God. Not one word against man. The defense rests."[143]

The prosecuting angel steps up to make the case against Bontshe, but all the angel says is: "Gentlemen, . . . [h]e kept silent. I will do the same."[144]

The judge offers a heavenly reward beyond any human's dream:

"All heaven belongs to you. Ask for anything you wish; you can choose what you like," the Judge declares. [145]

"'Well, then,' smiled Bontshe, 'What I'd like most of all is a warm roll with fresh butter every morning.'"[146]

This request is met by silence. The Judge and angels "hung their heads in shame. The prosecutor laughed."[147]

The story of Bontshe Szweig is hard to hear in the context of the Holocaust. Bontshe's silence on earth did not serve him well while he was alive. He had a terrible life. But in heaven, he was a prince. His silence and acceptance of his lot was viewed as the ultimate saintliness. Yet, when all he asked for was a hot roll with butter, the Judge and angels bent their heads in shame.

Chana Holcman, a survivor of numerous concentration camps, lamented that Bontshe could have asked for the Jewish people to be redeemed, but instead he asked for a roll with butter. But, Chana understood Bontshe's request. She had spent hours in the concentration camps dreaming of food.

"Several times I took comfort in Peretz's 'Boncze Szweig,'" Chana wrote. "I thought to myself, what if Boncze, who went to heaven as one of the *'Lamed Vavniks'*" had dreamed all day about a roll with butter? Even when he was borne to eternity and when stood before God's judgment he was asked: 'Boncze, tell us what you desire, what you want, and it will instantly be granted.' Instead of a resounding scream, 'I want the Jewish people to be redeemed' and perhaps we would be redeemed, he had answered 'I want a roll with butter.' Still the simple truth is that the sword of hunger is mightier than the sword of death."[148]

This phone call reminded me how each Holocaust survivor's story is a universe unto itself and conjured up feelings of tenderness, and yes, pity, towards Fievel and towards the mythical character of Bontshe Szweig. After this call, I got back to work. As I sat in front of my computer screen, typing away, I saw that a comment on my blog was waiting for me. I love receiving comments — so I clicked. Here is what I found:

Dear Karen

I found and I read on your Blog the relation from the visit of the family Goldberg in Bagatele. It is very unpleasant that does not have traces after Jewish inhabitants Wąsewo and Bagatele. I want a little to repair

---

* *Lamed Vavnik* is a person who is among the 36 people in each generation that are so righteous that if it were not for them, the world would come to an end. *Lamed* is a Hebrew letter that corresponds numerically to the number 30. *Vav* is a Hebrew letter that corresponds numerically to the number 6. Together *Lamed-Vav* equals 36. These 36 hidden *Tzadikim* (righteous ones) are also known as *Tzadikim Nistarim* — hidden righteous ones. *See* Tractate *Sanhedrin* 97b; Tractate *Sukkah* 45b.

*this, to remind who lived in these places. I am Catholic priest which
works in Wąsewo and I want to write the book about Jews with Wąsewo
and Bagatele. For the time being I collect materials — recollections, photos, documents, all what can be found. This very important what I read,
because I managed to find the family related with Goldberg. Rejza born
Goldberg, was a wife of Erszek. Idul (Julek),* the son of Erszek lives cur-
rently in the town Ossow close Warsaw. Therefore very I would like to find
out about this as simulated to be saved the family of Zelig. Today I talked
with the inhabitant of Bagatele which is called Załęski. He remembered
that when at them had been the fire, the family of Zelig helped him. Please
for the message.*

Best regards

Father Rafał Figiel

What a world we live in! I couldn't wait for Shlomo to get home and tell him
this. That evening, I sat him down, and read the comment to him. His mouth
dropped, his eyes grew large, and his face flushed.

"My father told me," he said, "that one of his sisters, Henya, married a man
named Idul. After the war broke out, they went to Russia. No one ever knew what
happened to them. Maybe this is Henya's family. Maybe this is my Aunt's son!"

Well, my first call was to Joanna Millick. I told her about this and she was
amazed. When I told her that Idul (Julek) Wilk lived in Ossow, she told me that
on our way out of Warsaw to visit Bagatele, we had passed right through Ossow.
She remembered seeing a sign for Ossow in the video of our trip. We drove
through Ossow not knowing we had a cousin who lived there.

"Do you have time for a Skype call tomorrow?" I asked.

"Yes!" she responded.

We spoke to Father Figiel the next day and he told us that Julek was the son
of Rejza (pronounced Raisa) Goldberg who was born in Bagatele. Rejza's father
was Mottle Goldberg. Well, that was strange, because Sam's father was Zelig, not

---

* Idul is the name his parents gave him. It is a nickname for Yehuda. Julek is the
name he adopted after the war to blend in with his Christian neighbors.

Mottle. Hmmm. Maybe not *Tante* Henya's family.

Father Figiel had gathered his information from Yad Vashem's on-line database as well as from Mr. Załęski, the oldest living person in Bagatele. Father Figiel reported that Mr. Załęski remembered both Mottle and Zelig.

Father Figiel also told us about the Jews from the area before the war. The Jews founded Bagatele as a farming village in 1847. Initially, there were fifteen farms with 120 people. The Goldbergs must have settled in Bagatele after 1847, as the original list of families does not include any Goldbergs. In 1850, the Jews of Bagatele and Wąsewo petitioned their "*kahal*" — the Jewish administration for the region — to have their own *kahal* in Wąsewo. At the time, the closest *kahal* was in Wengrow, 68 kilometers (42 miles) away. This request was granted and it was recorded that there were 151 Jews in the new "*kahal*".

Father Figiel gave me Julek's daughter Magda's contact information. We promised to share research and stay in touch. I told him that I hoped to be back in Poland soon and would love to meet him. I thanked him for reaching out to me.

On Sunday, I sent an e-mail to Magda Wilk who lived in Warsaw. It bounced. I contacted Father Figiel to see if he had a different email address. He messaged me back and gave me a different e-mail. It was getting late and I decided to try tomorrow.

I know, I should not look at screens before I go to sleep. But I checked my e-mail Sunday evening, just as my eyes were closing. Well, I woke right up and my eyes popped right out of my head. I had an e-mail from Ola, who had gotten my e-mail address from her sister. She lived in Boston! She asked if we could Skype the next day! The next day, Monday, happened to be Labor Day. We set up the call for 4 p.m. This was *meshuga*.

Shlomo and I spoke to Ola and her husband, Marty, for an hour. We were delighted to meet each other. Her grandmother was Rejza, not Henya, and her great, grandfather's name was Mottle Goldberg, not Zelig. Mottle had seven children and had lived in Bagatele. He had been a farmer and an animal trader, like Zelig. We all agreed that Mottle and Zelig Goldberg must be related.

Ola described how her grandmother, Rejza Goldberg, had married a man named Erszek (Herszel) who came from a small town about eight kilometers (4.9

miles) away. After their marriage, they settled in Bagatele and had children, one of whom was her father, Julek Wilk. Upon hearing this, Shlomo became confused because his father had told him about *Tante* Henya marrying a man with the same name. This would need further clarification.

Julek Wilk was six years old when the war broke out. His parents and siblings were murdered by the Nazis. He survived by hiding in the woods and people's barns. After the war, he stayed in Poland. He was baptized a Christian and kept his Jewish identity a secret.

"I live just outside of Boston," Ola said. "I am a professor of at Tufts University."

"You live in the city with the largest concentration of Goldberg descendants," I said. "There are six blood relatives living within an hour and a half drive of you."

Ola was shocked. She believed that her father had no surviving relatives from Bagatele and now she discovered that she had cousins in Boston! Until last Friday, Shlomo and I had also believed that no one from Bagatele, besides Sam, survived the war. A family reunion was in order.

＊ ＊ ＊

FEBRUARY 21, 2017

My sister-in-law, Molly, was skeptical. She was not sure that the Wilk family was related to us. Her father had never told her about any other Goldbergs from Bagatele. But, here we were sitting around Molly's table in Newton, Massachusetts, just outside of Boston. Huge steaming bowls of home-made vegetarian Chinese food were placed on the table and a bottle of wine was uncorked. Also at the table sat Ola and her husband, Marty, my brother-in-law, Fred, my niece, Brittany, and her husband, Brandon, and their baby, Will, the first of the next generation. Julia, Ola's niece, joined us by Skype from Minneapolis for part of the meal.

"My father was traumatized by the war," Ola told us. "He was so young, six years old. He was left on his own to find a way to survive. He got some help from Polish farmers, but it was very hard."

"I am looking forward to meeting him," I said. "I will be in Poland after Passover, in April."

"He will be happy to meet you," Ola said. "My sister, Magda, is looking forward to your visit as well."

After the meal, we said goodbye to Ola and Marty. They walked out the door and I wanted to jump up and down and hug everyone I was so excited! My blog had helped us locate some Goldberg relatives from Bagatele that we never dreamed existed, one of whom lived in Boston! I restrained myself because I could tell from Molly's quizzical facial expression and slow gait as she carried dishes back to the kitchen that she remained skeptical.

"My father would have told me if we had Goldberg cousins in Bagatele," Molly said. "He never said a word about cousins. What does Shaya say?"*

"Shaya says he remembers the Mottle Goldberg family in Bagatele and that Mottle and your grandfather were cousins," I said.

"Well, if Shaya remembers them, then maybe they are cousins," she said.

We left it at that. I flew back to Seattle the next morning. My next task was to prepare for my trip to Poland in April. This would be my second trip to Poland and I was really looking forward to exploring more of this story and meeting Julek and Magda Wilk and Father Figiel.

---

*   Shays Schloss is Sam's cousin.

Yad Vashem Decision — too Late for Janina

O n February 28, 2017 I received the following e-mail from Irena Steinfeldt, the Director of the Righteous Among the Nations Department of Yad Vashem:

> *Dear Karen,*
>
> *The Commission bestowed the title on Helena & Aleksander Styś as well as Janina, Leokadia and Antoni.*
>
> *The formal letters will hopefully reach you soon. It takes about 2-3 months to prepare the awards, and it will be the embassy that will contact the Styś family and you to coordinate the ceremony. As for the date, it depends on the embassy and the other Righteous ceremonies they have to organize.*
>
> *Just to give you an idea, in 2016 Yad Vashem honored close to 400 new Righteous from the different European countries.*
>
> *The names of Styś will go online in the Righteous database when it is next updated in the beginning of April.*
>
> *All the best,*
>
> *Irena*

That was it — the decision had been made — The Styś name would be listed among the Yad Vashem's Righteous. But this decision had come too late for Janina.

Janina Gołębiewska, the daughter of Helena and Aleksander Styś — their last living child — left this world on Saturday, November 12, 2016. She was buried in the Stoczek Christian cemetery on November 16. She was 90 years old.

I was, however, confused by the e-mail as it seemed that only Helena's family was to receive the honor. What about Władysława's family and Edward? They had all helped Sam, Esther, and Chaim as they hid from the Nazis. Irena explained that the Commission for the Designation of the Righteous relies primarily on the testimony of the survivors. In Sam's and Esther's interviews, Helena was the only member of the Styś family mentioned. So, even though Shlomo testified that his parents spoke of two families that helped them while they were in hiding and Eugeniusz and Jan had described some of what their family had done for Sam and Esther, Władysława's family and Edward would not receive the honor.

On Monday, I called Grzegorz Maleszewski, the grandson of Władysława and Stanisław, and told him about Yad Vashem's decision.

"That's OK," he responded, "our family's reward is in meeting your family and in the book you are writing."

"When I come to Poland in April, I will visit with Jan and Eugeniusz and try to explain this to them," I said. "I feel awful. But, please know that to the Goldberg family, you are all righteous."

This trip to Warsaw was getting complicated. How would I explain the Yad Vashem decision to Eugeniusz and Jan? I don't understand it myself. My heart dropped in my chest when I thought about how I would have to look them in the eye and tell them that their family had not received the honor.

Poland — Round Two

"Hi Karen," a Facebook note from Joanna Millick read, "I just got a message from Grzegorz. His Uncle, Jan Styś, passed away. His funeral is tomorrow at 2 p.m. Grzegorz asked me to let you know."

I had to sit down. Here I was looking forward to my trip and knowing that I would soon see Jan. But this was not to be. I would now be arriving the same day as Jan's funeral, but not until 5 p.m., missing his funeral by a few hours. The sadness I felt and still feel is not just for the loss of Jan — which is enough — but it's for a generation that is leaving us.

My travel partner, Esther and I boarded a plane in Bologna, Italy, where we had been for ten days celebrating Passover with the Treiger family. We crossed into Polish airspace and landed at the Wroclaw airport to change planes. As we browsed the airport shops, I realized that we needed a gift for Eugeniusz and Alina. I found a beautiful candle shop and bought a large yellow candle encased in metal, cut as a flower motif. Candles are important in the Catholic religion, but I was unaware of their exact symbolic meaning. In the Jewish tradition when a person dies, the close family members light a tall *Yahrzeit* candle that burns for *Shiva*, the seven days of mourning. With this gift, this ancient tradition would traverse religions and centuries. I hoped that this candle would bring the Styś family some comfort.

✳ ✳ ✳

APRIL 20, 2017

The candle was the perfect gift. Esther and I gave it to Alina and Eugeniusz Styś at the end of a two-hour visit in their small living room. With the skillful translating of our friend, Aleksander Czyzewski, who had accompanied us from Warsaw, I explained that in a Jewish home a candle burns during the seven days of mourning. They nodded, understanding the power of a candle. It was strange to be back in this house. It felt comfortable, but I was sad and nervous. Sad because Jan had just died and nervous because I knew the *Yad Vashem* conversation was about to happen.

Just a few hours earlier, we had visited Jan's freshly dug grave, covered with beautiful flowers. Grzegorz was with us and he had popped open a special cylindrical container and lit a large, white candle. He put the metal top back on the cylinder and placed it next to the grave. This was his *Yahrzeit* candle.

Watching Grzegorz light the candle and place it next to Jan's grave made me wonder why religious traditions related to death include candles. Candles are unique. They bring light to the darkness. They light other candles while not diminishing their own light and beauty. They are extinguished with a simple puff of air. They can start a fire — which can be beneficial — like cooking or heat — or they can destroy — burning down a house, a forest, or even a whole town. Fire can kill; a reminder of the fragility of life and the power we hold as humans.

On our way to Eugeniusz's and Alina's home we stopped at Janina's grave in Stoczek. While her grave was not as fresh as Jan's, it hit me that less than a year ago, I met Janina, Jan, and Eugeniusz and now, only Eugeniusz remained. I grieved the losses but was grateful that we had met Jan and Janina last June and been able to talk with them. Then, the "what ifs" floated through my mind... What if we had waited a year to make that first trip to Poland? What if we had never met Jan and Janina? I was happy that I had not delayed this dream and was not confronted with those regrets.

Sitting with Eugeniusz and his wife, Alina, in their living room, the subject of *Yad Vashem* could no longer be avoided. Alina produced the letter they had received.

"Why is this honor just for Helena's family?" Alina asked in her straight forward manner. "What about Władysława?"

"I am so sorry that this was their decision," I said. "Shlomo and I nominated Helena's family, Władysława's family, and Edward. I am upset, too. It seems that they relied on Esther and Sam's interviews, in which they only mentioned Helena."

Alina did most of the talking. She explained that this decision was causing tension among the family. Doesn't the Polish government's award to Eugeniusz prove that his family also helped Sam, Esther and Chaim? She brought out the award letter, saved in a special plastic sleeve, to show me.

"This special pension," Alina stated, "is only awarded to people who helped Jews during the war."

Well, I thought to myself, I had sent Eugeniusz's letter describing his family's actions during the war to Yad Vashem. That hadn't worked. Maybe this letter would help because it provided proof that the Polish government believed that his family had assisted Jews during the war. Perhaps it would change *Yad Vashem's* decision.

"I will send the government award letter to *Yad Vashem* and see if it helps to change their mind. No promises, but I will give it a try."

Grzegorz promised to scan the letter and send it to me. Aleks agreed to translate it. I was not hopeful, but I would send it to *Yad Vashem* and request that they reconsider their decision regarding Władysława's family. There was an uncomfortable feeling hanging in the air. The *Yad Vashem* decision was unfair and we were all sad. I was the one who made the request and now I had hurt them and caused problems. I took some solace in the fact that the Styś family name would be forever enshrined in the register of *Yad Vashem's* Righteous, but at this moment, it didn't make me feel any better.

"By the way," I said changing the subject, "how was the group of young men that came to visit at the end of March? One of them was from Seattle. He's a good friend of Esther. They really appreciated coming and meeting you."

"Not good," Alina said with her body going stiff and her eyes growing wide. "After the visit my neighbors came over and said, 'what were those Jews doing here? What benefit are you getting from them?' It's very hard for us to have our neighbors feeling jealous. I don't think we will have more groups."

"I understand that this must have been so hard for you," I said as I processed this surprising and sad news, "but please know that the young men in the group and their tour guide, Tzvi, said that the visit with you was the highlight of their trip."

"I am sorry, but we cannot have more groups," Alina reiterated.

My hope and dream to have more groups come to visit the Styś family and the pit in the forest was shared by Grzegorz who, at this point, jumped into the conversation. He explained that it was important to keep the history alive and to have more people come and see what happened during the war and see what the Styś family did to help. This argument didn't change their minds, but Grzegorz told me that he would keep trying.*

Grzegorz had to leave, so Aleks, Esther and I also said our goodbyes and headed back to Warsaw. I left with a wistful feeling. I was happy to have seen them, but I was worried that I may never see Eugeniusz or Alina again. Given their age, there was no way to know. I hoped to come back for the *Yad Vashem* ceremony, but as of this time, we have no date for when it would take place. Patience is a virtue I must work on. I learned a great deal about this virtue from our newfound Goldberg cousin Idul Wilk.

---

* One more group did visit Eugeniusz and Alina — a group from Seattle, led by Joanna Millick, in June of 2017. Their trip to Poland was organized by the Seattle Holocaust Center for Humanity. The Center has decided that on their next trip to Poland in June of 2018, they will bestow an award to Eugeniusz for his family's assistance to Sam, Esther and Chaim. It will not be from *Yad Vashem*, but it will be a beautiful gesture from the Seattle Holocaust Center for Humanity. Our family appreciates the Holocaust Center's effort and kindness.

Buried Treasure

APRIL 21, 2017

"What took you so long?" Idul (Julek) Wilk asked us.

He meant — what took the family so long to find him? This broke my heart. As a six-year-old boy, Idul Wilk had been separated from his family as they ran from the Nazis. He survived using his instincts, brains, and help from some Polish families. One Polish family allowed him to stay in their barn, but in exchange he had to watch their animals in the field. Though the two young daughters were kind to him, their father beat him.

He felt abandoned by his family, left to survive alone for nine years. I say nine years, because his daughter, Magda told me that her father didn't know the war was over until 1948. He stayed hidden an extra three or four years! I have heard and read many stories of Holocaust survival, but I don't have a box to put this one in. A young boy, alone, who stayed hidden until 1948? That is painful.[149]

Esther and I drove to Ossow with Magda, the youngest of the three Wilk daughters. She is a 40-something year old woman with a round face and eyebrows that lift on their own accord. We arrived at her father's home and Idul ushered us into a small sitting room with a TV resting on the ubiquitous lace cloth. Idul is about five feet, eight inches, slim with short, gray wispy hair. His face is not round like his daughter's; his chin defines a rather stern face. His penetrating, dark eyes are set deep, as if his facial bones are protecting them. For our meeting, he wore a button-down, collared shirt and dark pants. At first, he was reserved and didn't talk much. Maybe he just didn't know what to say to us, strangers from America, or perhaps he was trying to make sure we were real.

Sam never knew that his cousin, Idul, survived the war. He must have known him in Bagatele — his family lived just a few houses down the road. Idul had described one of his early memories: he would walk down the dirt road toward his grandparents' home and on the way, some people would come out of their homes, hug him, and say hello. This may have been Sam's family since they were just a few houses away. Now Idul knows that Shmulke Goldberg survived Treblinka and the war and that he had three children, ten grandchildren, and one great-grandson.

After the war, Idul stayed in Poland and put his Judaism behind him. He didn't go back to Bagatele right after the war because he was afraid that his Polish neighbors would kill him. He was baptized as a Catholic and adopted the common Polish name Julek, to blend in with the post-war *Judenrein* population. He served in the Polish army and later, married Ela and had three daughters.

Magda described how life was when she was growing up, others would call her *Jid* – Jew. When she asked her father what that meant, he said, "it's nothing, don't pay any attention." It was as an adult that she learned that her father was Jewish. Her exploration as to what this meant is an ongoing process.

Idul retains only a few other memories of Bagatele: his parents and grandparents; *gefilta* fish; *cholent*; and men wearing *Tefillin*. Esther showed him a photo of Shlomo wearing *Tallis* and *Tefillin*. Idul looked at the photo and blurted out an enthusiastic "*tac, tac, tac,*" shaking his head yes. This was a powerful memory. Idul also described the *Mikve,* where he would go with his father as a small house with steps descending to a pool of water. The *Mikve* was lined with stones and the water was warm. It was a happy memory.

After we had been visiting for an hour or so, Idul's dam of emotion broke. He told us how after the war he had no family and had been waiting all these years for his family to find him. Tears ran down his face as he brought Esther and me close and kissed us on both cheeks and our heads. Esther pulled up a picture of the extended Goldberg family on her phone and whispered:

"We are all your family."

We were all quiet as he looked at the picture for some time, as if in disbelief.

From left to right: Magda Wilk; Esther Goldberg; Idul (Julek) Wilk; Karen Treiger.
Credit: Karen I. Treiger.

Tears welled up in my eyes and I could think of no words of comfort for this tortured man. Meeting Idul Wilk was one of the most tender and happy moments of my two-year journey. What were the chances of finding each other after almost eight decades? It reinforced that this journey was not just about the past; it was about making new history, meeting new people, and discovering novel things about myself and my family. Sometimes when you dig, you find a buried treasure. That's how I felt on this day, like I found a lost treasure.

As we were preparing to take our leave, Magda wrapped her arms around her father and held him close and they cried. I felt those tears release 78 years of existential loneliness. Idul, you are not alone. We are all your family.[150]

Bialystok and the Haunted Tracks

APRIL 22, 2017

What next? After meeting Idul Wilk I felt a tug of war in my soul. I wanted to stay in Poland and explore more, learn more, but I was ready to go home. Esther and I would leave Poland soon, but we had one more day. We decided to take the train to Bialystok for the day. The war years were so terrible, that I yearned for the remembrance of something better than horrific. Bialystok felt like the place to go. Esther lived in Bialystok for a year after fleeing Stoczek in September of 1939.

"I had the time of my life," Esther said of Bialystok.

I wanted to walk the streets of a city where Esther had some fun as a single young woman. During that year, Esther enjoyed the Yiddish and Jewish culture that was around every corner. In 1939, Bialystok had over 100 synagogues, a Jewish Hospital, a Yiddish library, Yiddish theater, Yiddish newspapers, and many Zionist organizations that held events, including speeches and classes. Coming from the *Shtetl* Stoczek to the big city of Bialystok for the 19-year-old Esther was thrilling.

Two weeks from the date of our visit to Bialystok, my daughter, Esther, would turn 19, the same age her grandmother was when she arrived here. I relished the thought. What a crazy set of circumstances has brought me to Bialystok with 19-year-old Esther Goldberg, some 78 years after her grandmother lived here. I did not take the moment for granted.

As we went from the train station towards the center of town, I pictured Esther Wisznia walking this path in 1939. The pre-war buildings, with their stunning adornments and intricate wrought iron balconies were impressive. This was a wealthy city.

On one side of town near the train station, there was a broad white church with a tall steeple, topped with gold. The main street led from this white church to the center of town where there was an even larger church made of red brick with double steeples and three grand doorways in the front — the Stoczek church on steroids. My heart grew heavy as I looked at these churches, standing proud and tall, while the synagogues were all destroyed.

Just before you reached the red church, the white clock tower draws your eye. It's not as tall as the red church, but it has a round cast iron dome. A crown-like appendage sits above the dome like a cherry on top of an ice cream cone. Just to one side of the clock tower is an open square with a fountain in the center. After visiting Rome just two weeks prior, this fountain is modest in comparison, but coming from Stoczek, it must have seemed grand.

In 1939 Esther would have found dirt streets filled with people walking, riding horses, driving horse-pulled carts, and even some cars. There was a "bus station" where Jeep-like cars were lined up to take people to other cities. A picture from the early 1930's showed cars lined up on a dirt road with signs that read "Bialystok — Grodek" or "Bialystok — Lomza." Most of the men in the picture are dressed in suits and the women in dresses and coats, giving the impression of a cosmopolitan city.

A few trees dotted either side of the main road, at the end of which sat the Branicki Palace. Modeled after Versailles, it's a monumental building with an impressive courtyard in the front and a beautiful, manicured garden with naked and semi-naked roman-style, sculptures in the back. In 1939, the Soviets used this palace as administrative offices, but the gardens were open for citizens to enjoy. Just next to the garden, there was a long park that stretched for a couple of kilometers. The walking path in the park was tree-lined and very green, even on a cold day in April (we had snow, hail, and rain all in one day). I imagined the Wisznia family taking a *shpatzir* (walk) on *Shabbat* afternoon here in this lush setting.

As we walked down the main street, just past the big red church, I glanced across the street and couldn't believe my eyes. Through the snow flakes, there stood what looked like German soldiers from World War II. They were standing in a group, talking. There was one especially terrifying looking Nazi smoking a small cigar. I thought — either we are on a movie set — or no one told Bialystok that the war is over. With trepidation, I crossed the street to take a picture and find out who they were. It turns out that they were participating in a World War II reenactment. I thought "that's funny. Here I am, in a sense, doing my own World War II reenactment, retracing Esther's steps in Bialystok. I was not wearing clothes of the era, but I was here to feel what the city might have felt like in 1939." I thanked the actors and left them to their cigars and guns.

There was more to see and learn, but after three hours of walking the streets of Bialystok, we were frozen. I had accomplished my goal. I had walked through a bit of the landscape of Esther's life in Bialystok and felt her presence. We decided to take an earlier train back to Warsaw. Early tomorrow morning we would be leaving Poland on separate planes; Esther would fly to Tel Aviv and I would fly to Seattle. This part of the journey was ending. But, it was time to thaw out. I never thought I would be so happy to get on a train heading towards Malkinia.

❄ ❄ ❄

APRIL 22, 2017

I stared hard at my train ticket when I saw "Malkinia" written on it as one of the places the train would pause between Warsaw and Bialystok. Malkinia was the last train stop before the Treblinka Village Station, before death. Between July of 1942 and November of 1943, trains parked there while twenty cars were unhinged and taken on a separate rail spur to Treblinka whose reception area could not accommodate the whole train. Once these cars were emptied of people and filled with the clothing and valuables of the murdered Jews, the cars moved out and made room for the next group. Approximately 870,000 Jews were brought to Treblinka in this manner from Warsaw, Bialystok, and many other towns and cities throughout Europe.

Our train passed lots of trees — white-trunk birch mingled with brown-trunk pines, low bushes, and lots of farm land — some grassy and some dirt rows of planted crops, stretching as far as I could see and beyond. Scattered throughout the farmland were houses and barns. Closer to the towns, there were industrial buildings, one that scared me because it had a tall round chimney that was billowing white smoke.

When our train reached the Malkinia station, I had trouble breathing. It was because of the train tracks here at the station. These tracks had, in part, been built by Esther's father, *Reb* Shlomo Zalman Wisznia in 1939. On the way to Bialystok, the Nazis pulled *Reb* Wisznia out of the line crossing the border and forced him to spend the day building the rails. The Germans had just taken control of this part of Poland and they were busy creating the wartime infrastructure. Little did anyone know that three years later, these tracks would bring hundreds of thousands to their death at Treblinka. Now, in 2017, as our train reached this gateway to death, I remembered that day in Seattle, when I discovered this fact, when I slowly rose from my chair and walked around the house saying, "Oh my God." I couldn't function for the rest of the day.

Pulling into the Malkinia station, I was still resentful that Shlomo Zalman had been forced to help build these tracks. When I looked out the window, I saw that next to us were at least five parallel tracks. I wondered which tracks Shlomo Zalman, the *Melamed* of Stoczek, had been forced to build. Which tracks sent the cattle cars on to Treblinka? I feel that it should be marked somehow so we could know which track is crying the loudest.

To top it off, I was catching up on my podcasts. This episode of Radio Lab was about the potential use of a nuclear weapon. It told the story of 81-year-old Harold Herring, who was a pilot in the United States Air Force and then a trainee for the job of being an officer who holds the key needed to launch a nuclear weapon. He was learning about the weapons and the elements that must be satisfied before the key is turned to launch a missile.

Harold wondered, "what are the checks and balances that a President must go through before ordering me and my fellow officers to launch a nuclear missile?"

He wanted to be assured that a President could not order a launch on a whim or because he had a bad day. He asked the instructor this question and was told to put his question in writing. He did, and months of hearings and appeals ensued, at the end of which he had gotten no answer to his question and was forced to retire from the military.

Radio Lab obtained documents related to the decision to force Harold's retirement. According to the document, Harold had stated more than once that if he received an order to launch, he would follow the order. The report continued that his assurances were followed by personal subjective qualifications such as: "if he thought the order was legal or if he thought the circumstances required the launching."

When this statement was read to Harold, he was outraged. He said that it was false. He never made any such qualifying statements. Harold went on to say that he had assumed that there had to be some sort of check and balance so that one man could not just on a whim order the launch of nuclear weapon . . . and that we should not put anybody [a military officer in this case] in a position where they are just following orders and throwing their conscience to the four winds. I think it is an affront to play the game that we don't have a need to know for someone who is doing the most serious, grave jobs in the armed forces."[151]

The echo of Adolf Eichmann's defense "just following orders" rang in my ear. Where is the line to be drawn? When is it good and right to follow orders, to uphold "the system"? When is it good and right not to? There have been times in my life when I have made a choice to speak out and to act when I saw injustice or a play for power rather than acts, as the Ethics of our Father's would urge, "for the sake of heaven." I hesitate to compare my choices to those made during the Holocaust, but we each choose how to act and our actions have consequences.

There are many examples. Sam didn't choose to go to Treblinka, but he chose not to kill the *Kapo*[152] when offered the chance and he chose to cook food in his laundry pots to feed the sick. Esther didn't choose to be a hunted animal, hiding in the woods, but she chose to help Velvel and Sam after their escape from Treblinka. The Styś family didn't choose for Poland to be in a war and under Nazi rule, but they chose to hide and feed Jews though that put themselves and their families in danger. The Kavkazer didn't choose to be in a German POW camp, but he chose to give Sam a sugar cube and help him escape. Joanna Millick didn't have to spend her free time translating letters and calling people in Poland in the middle of the night, but she chose to help me. Grzegorz didn't have to spend hours making family trees for us and take two days away from his business to be our guide and mentor in Poland, but he did.

Sitting on the train, I looked around at the people sharing my train car. They were heading to Warsaw — young, old, people on computers, on phones, just living life. What do they know about the Holocaust and how the blood of the Jews saturates Polish soil? Do they even know about the trains to Treblinka? Are they as haunted by these tracks as I am? I wanted to get up and make a speech as we reached the Malkinia station. I wanted to tell them that tonight was the beginning of *Yom Hashoah,* the Holocaust Remembrance Day, and that they should all remember what happened, how many innocent people were lost. But, for the sake of my daughter and my lack of Polish language skills, I held back. I said the speech to myself — that would have to do for the moment.

But I couldn't help but think, "what if I had to fight for my life every single day. What if I had no food or water for days? What if my family was all murdered?" My husband, children and I went on a quest to see, feel, and touch the lives of Sam and Esther Goldberg. But what we found was that it was an odyssey into our own souls. Each of us was forced to reevaluate what it means to live each day and to appreciate the blessings of life, of food, of a warm bed, of a suitcase. Along the way, singular strands of the universe have been woven together to tell this story and to bring the words of Albert Einstein deep into my heart.

"A human being is part of the whole, called by us 'Universe,' a part limited in time and space. He experiences himself, his thoughts and feelings as something separate from the rest, a kind of optical delusion of his consciousness."[153]

When I read this, I said "yes, that's it; the idea that we are separated from each other is an "optical delusion" of our consciousness. That we are all part of a whole is the only explanation that I can fathom as to how it came to be that we found and met Joanna, Grzgorz, Eugeniusz, Jan, and Janina. That because Father Figiel, a Polish priest, was searching the Internet to learn the fate of the murdered

Jews of Bagatele, we were reunited with our Bagatele cousins, Idul Wilk and two of his daughters, Magda and Ola. How else can I understand that my daughter Elisheva thought to tell me about what she learned from Katka Reszke one day after I finished reading Katka's book about today's Polish Jews, or that my day trip to Bialystok would force me to stop at the Malkinia train station — the gateway to Treblinka?

Sam and Esther's story of survival now runs through my veins and forces me to feel the pulse of the universe. Our lives can be extinguished in a moment. But during our lives we can choose how to use our flame — we can use our flame as a destructive force in the world or we can pass the beauty and benefit of our flame to others. We must choose.

By Shlomo Zelig Goldberg

I was born in Maimonides Medical Center[154] in Brooklyn about a year-and-a-half after my parents and sister Fay arrived in New York from the German DP Camp. My parents, in what appears to have been a tradition among survivors, named me for both of my murdered grandfathers — Shlomo Zelig. They also gave me an English name — the most American name they could think of — Sheldon.

When they first arrived, my parents and sister lived with my father's Aunt — the *Tante* Shosha Mischler in Brooklyn. My parents had no money and spoke very little English. Phil Mischler, the *Tante* Shosha's son, gave my father his first job in his lithography business.

My parents and Fay moved to a small, fifth-floor walk-up apartment in Williamsburg, Brooklyn, a building where Benny, another of the *Tante* Shosha's sons lived. My father hated the job at Phil's lithograph company and, instead, took a menial, low paying job (mostly tips) plucking feathers off kosher chickens. This work was dirty and hard, and brought lice into our home. One of my earliest memories is of the tiny white lice comb that my mother would run through our hair. I cannot imagine the impact of lice on my parents. The gas chambers at Treblinka were disguised as delousing facilities. My father described my mother's attire when he met her in the woods as "more lice than clothes."

The first home I remember well is the apartment we rented at 485 Howard Avenue in Brownsville, Brooklyn. This was a neighborhood of poor immigrant families. The dominant ethnicities were Puerto Rican and *Greene* (greenhorn Holocaust survivors), but there was a thorough mix of poor people of every background. My best friends were the Chinese children of the people who ran the hand laundry.

My sister Fay was nine when we moved to Howard Avenue and she attended PS 144, the local public school. She learned English rapidly and well. Her American diction is excellent, no accent. Soon after moving to Howard Avenue, my mother became pregnant with my sister Ray Molly (called Molly by our family). The family lore is that my mother was so worried that they could not afford another child that she arranged to have an abortion. My father returned from work to find someone at our home ready to conduct the abortion on the kitchen table. He threw the man out of the house. When my mother complained that their situation was desperate and that they could not afford another child, my father answered:

The Goldberg family approx. 1959. Back row from left to right: Shlomo; Esther, Fay. Front row: Sam and Molly. Credit: Goldberg Family Archive.

"This baby will bring us luck."

And she did.

After Molly was born, my father's situation improved. He opened his own butcher shop in Bedford Stuyvesant, a poor African American neighborhood, even more impoverished than Brownsville, where we lived. Both my parents worked long hours in the store, especially on Saturday (the Jewish Sabbath) — the busiest day of the week. I remember my father coming home every night and going over the bills using a "reckoning book."

We spoke Yiddish at home, and English crept in over time. We grew up with a mix of Jewish traditions. We kept kosher, we had *Seder* on Passover, we went to *Shul* on *Rosh Hashanah* and *Yom Kippur*. That was the extent of our observance when I was growing up. But *Yahrzeit,* the arbitrary date that a Rabbi in the Föhrenwald DP Camp had given my father on which to commemorate the anniversary of the deaths of my grandparents, was a significant day in the family, as was *Yizkor*, the communal commemoration of the departed souls recited in *Shul* on some holidays.

We had no grandparents or cousins our age. All our parents' friends were Yiddish-speaking Holocaust survivors. It was not until I went to Stuyvesant, a select public High School in Manhattan, that I realized that there were Jewish people who didn't speak Yiddish.

When I was ready for first grade, a distant cousin of my mother, Rabbi Moshe Maidenbaum, convinced my parents to send me to a *Yeshiva* (Jewish school) and (I believe) arranged a scholarship. My sisters attended local public schools. Fay went to an after-school program to learn Jewish traditions. That did not work out for Molly.

Our next move was to East 54th street, in the Flatlands neighborhood of Brooklyn, when I was twelve years old. This was the first home my parents bought. It was a semi-detached, two-family house. The tenants who lived in the lower part of the house were also Holocaust survivors.

There was a story in the family that has followed me for my whole life: When the Soviet Union launched the first satellite, Sputnik, I was six years old. My mother said that I was incensed by this. I had been raised staunchly anti-communist (with a little ambivalence based upon the fact that my parents were liberated by the Soviet army). So, I built my own "Sputnik" in a wicker box and when I plugged it in, it blew all the fuses in the house. My parents were not pleased.

I have strong memories of the trial of Adolf Eichmann in April of 1961. I was ten years old and my mother insisted that I watch the trial on TV every day. My parents cried as the survivors told of the horrors of those years. The final witness in the trial was my father's mentor, Shmuel Rajzman.

I also remember the first time I flew on an airplane. Our family flew to Washington, D.C., so that my father could testify at a deposition for the trail of Kurt Franz, the *Lalka* of Treblinka. We stayed at a very fancy hotel. Franz's trial was held in Düsseldorf, West Germany.

Fay attended two years of Brooklyn College before marrying Irwin Schraga, the son of Holocaust survivors from my mother's home town of Stok (Stoczek) in 1993. I also went to Brooklyn College, majoring in chemistry, followed by Medical School at New York University. My sister Molly attended State University in Buffalo and Boston University Law School. In 1980 she married Fred Erlich, a Boston-born, Yiddish-speaking son of Holocaust survivors. Between the three of us, we gave our parents ten grandchildren. Just over a year ago a great-grandson was born, named for his two deceased grandfathers — Shmuel Zeev (William Samuel).

In 1978, my parents sold the butcher shop and their home in Brooklyn and retired to Miami Beach, Florida, joining a large community of retired Holocaust survivors. They lived there for many years, enjoying the warmth, playing cards, taking walks, swimming in the ocean, and welcoming their children and grandchildren for visits to the Sunshine State. It was during these years that they returned to some of the old rhythms of their early life — my father went to *Shul* each morning and they celebrated *Shabbes* with chicken soup and *gefilta* fish.

Growing up, I heard about Helena Oleshkowa, who helped my parents while hiding in the forest. I remember the packages that my mother sent to the Styś family in Poland. The packages made Poland, the nightmare country, more real — maybe pitiful.

In the fall of 2016 I had the privilege of nominating the Styś family for the *Yad Vashem* Honor of Righteous Among the Nations and had the even greater honor of attending and speaking at the ceremony on January 15, 2018 at the Royal Castle in the Warsaw Palace, where the award was bestowed. I went alone. I was scared to go alone, but I came to feel that it was important to confront Poland, the place where my parents were reared. I was deeply moved as I spoke to a crowd of some three hundred people gathered for the ceremony. As I stood in this ornate post-war replica of the Warsaw Palace, I worked to maintain my composure as I read my speech:

I came to Poland for a ceremony recognizing the Styś family, who helped my parents survive their years of hiding from the murderous NAZIs, as "Righteous Among the Nations."

What my parents were doing when the Styś family bravely helped them is often called "hiding." Hiding does not really capture what my parents were doing. My parents were hunted like noxious, dangerous animals. They could be killed without penalty. They did not have housing, a reliable food supply, or water for bathing. It was a crime to aid or shelter them. These righteous Polish people were, according to the NAZIs, committing a capital offense.

This time of the year, Jewish tradition recalls the Egyptian bondage and Exodus in our weekly readings from the Torah scroll. The story deals with relationships between peoples of different nations. Within the first 20 verses of the book of Exodus, the immigrant Hebrews are enslaved and the cruel Pharaoh has ordered that all Hebrew male infants be drowned. But the God-fearing midwives refuse the order to murder the babies. They are answering to a higher authority.

Belief in God, when mixed with courage, can contain tyranny.

Some commentators posit that these righteous midwives were Egyptian, not Hebrew. This is an appealing interpretation. Perhaps these midwives were the forerunners of the people that helped my parents, and others, during the Holocaust. When the infant Moses is cast into the Nile, the princess daughter of the most evil Pharaoh recognized the contraband Hebrew child. She rescued the child from the water. Here we are certain that an Egyptian, a member of the Royal family, a daughter of the Pharaoh, rescued a persecuted child. Barbarity is not inherited; it is not an inevitable national character, nor a necessary consequence of social class. There were good Egyptians.

This story shows that organized societies can go down the path of evil. It shows that individuals — Shifra, Pua, the daughter of Pharoah — may show courage, help the downtrodden, and become heroes in the light of history. We should continue to celebrate those that answered to the Highest Authority and bravely supported the oppressed, like the Styś family, who helped my parents and allowed my birth.

I have tried to live my life in a way that would make my parents proud. With the publication of this book, I feel the memory of these resilient heroes will live on and be an example to the world. I am proud to be their son. I have a lot to live up to.

תהא נפשו/ה צרורה בצרור החיים

May their souls be bound in the bond of everlasting life.

Shlomo speaking at Yad Vashem Award Ceremony at the Warsaw Palace, January 15, 2018. Credit: Grzegorz Maleszewski.

Dear Sam and Esther: May 2018

How did you do it? How did you go through it all and come out on the other side such nice people? You were like Clark Kent in Superman — mild and unassuming, disguised as retired Jewish New York immigrants living in Miami Beach. But inside, under the thin veneer of skin, you had superpowers in your souls. Your supersized strength, fortitude and resilience were hidden from me and from the world. Maybe you kept your kryptonite in the *schnapps* cupboard.

This book exposes your story and your superpowers. You may be angry. I know that there are parts of your stories that you would rather leave in the past. Please forgive me. Knowing more of your story and walking in your footsteps has made me more courageous and has fortified my commitment to my family and to the Jewish people. I also must ask forgiveness for the parts of the story that are wrong. I have no illusion that it's all accurate, but it's the best I could do without you.

We met the Styś family. They have a deep connection with you. The years that you lived in and around their property are etched into their memory and embedded in their family narrative. This kinship has expanded to include all of us — those of us who met them and the readers of this book.

Sam, you would be amazed to know that your cousin Idul Wilk, survived the war. I can picture your face and hear your voice when I tell you. "Really? Really?" you would say, your eyes widening. You would tell me how you remember him as a boy walking past your house on his way to his grandparents' home. Perhaps our meeting will heal some of the scars on his heart.

How can I understand the world — there is so much hate. Sometimes, I hear your voices in my head — you tell me that yes, we are all capable of Nazi-like behavior. We can kill and torture and then go home to our spouses and children and kiss them goodnight. But God also gave us the capacity for kindness and goodness. We must exist with both impulses in our souls. But, our lives on earth are short, so choose well.

Thank you for all you did for me. I miss you.

Your loving daughter-in-law, Karen

Goldberg family, April 1, 2018. Back Row: Fred Erlich, Jack Goldberg, Judah Pollack, Micha Hacohen, Ray Molly Goldberg Erlich. 2nd Row: Shlomo Goldberg, Karen Treiger, Malka Schraga, Fay (Goldberg) Schraga-Gitnik, Tara Schraga, Steve Gitnik. 3rd Row: Emma Orbach Goldberg, Esther Goldberg, Brandon Hager, Brittany Erlich Hager with William Samuel Hager, Jacob Erlich. Front Row: Leah Schraga, Elisheva Goldberg, Shoshana Goldberg, Jillian Erlich. Credit: Karen Treiger; Photo taken by Ella Tesler.

Thoughts from the Next Generation

ELISHEVA GOLDBERG

When I think back to our family trip to Poland two moments stand out for me: the moment our whole family decided to sing and skip around the tree in Bagatelle, and the reunion with the Styś family at their home. In my memory these two moments are imprinted in my mind; they represent two ends of an experience and contain the contrasting emotional peaks that wrap me up in what it means to be the grandchild of Holocaust survivors.

In Bagatelle, my *Zeyde's* hometown, some strange joy overcame us. We arrived at a place that had one been inhabited — lived in, loved in — by our relatives, and we could see traces! On the farm plot where our *Zeyde* lived, the farmhouse remained outlined by the grass even after all these years. And next to it we saw the tree — a huge, many-branched, very old tree that still grew. The thought that, though the house was gone, and a mere shadow remained, the tree — the thing that was rooted — stayed alive and continued to flourish was what brought us that joy. *Etz Hayim hee Lamachazikim Ba.* "A tree of life it will be for those who grasp it," goes the verse. That tree was our *etz hayim*. And so we danced and sang. We had survived, and we were joyous.

It wasn't sadness that contrasted our joy with the experience around the tree, it was gratitude. In the Styś family we met the blooming kindness that sprang up through the floorboards of that house, so reminiscent of a prior age, so like its inhabitants. These were the people who, now more than seventy years ago, helped shield my *Bubbe* and then my *Zeyde* from the terrible, dangerous winds that were sweeping through every household. They did not let the angel of death take them away. They were the first people to make sure — to care, in whatever way — that my family was safe. So, when Janina sang to us I was again overwhelmed, this time by gratitude. By the knowledge that I was safe, that I could come back to this place and not fear. *Lo Irara ki Ata Imadi.* "I will fear no evil for you are with me." Some had not survived, and we mourned them. But we had, by the grace of God and with some help from these righteous people.

To sing and to cry — these are the emotional expressions of the joy and gratitude that I felt on our family trip to Poland. I am both joyful and grateful that I was able to be on this trip with my mother, who is writing this book that will serve future generations of our family, with my father whose life is indelibly stamped by his parents' stories and with my siblings who, like me, have grown up joyful and grateful to both of them.

JACK GOLDBERG

My family has been on an amazing journey. On the trip to Poland, I bore witness as my father kissed the very hands which kept his parents alive, swam in the river which saved my grandfather's life, saw the pit in which my grandparents were buried alive, fell in love, and survived for over a year. It was heavy. However, it all fit together perfectly, a mosaic of emotions. When I step back, I see the beautiful singular take away I have from the trip, admiration.

Cold, frozen fear was the first emotion that I registered as I landed in Warsaw. It was the kind of fear that only the anticipation of a lightly traumatic experience can make you feel. My family had come together to experience our collective questions and doubts, and slowly, the warmth of my family melted my fear.

As our van pulled into the yard of the Styś home, an overwhelming feeling of gratitude washed over me. Gratitude for their bravery, gratitude for my own life. It was joy and anticipation I will never forget, like when you can't stop smiling regardless of how hard you try. Gratitude was yet another emotion in my mosaic.

However, when I took a step back from the trip and look at the sum of its parts, the combination of the thoughts, feelings and experiences translate to a singular word. Admiration. Admiration for one another within the family and how we handled the difficult issues we faced, admiration for the bravery of the people we met along the way, from the Czyzewski family, to the Styś and Maleszewski families. Whenever I talk about the Holocaust, the question always quietly scratches at the door in the back of my mind "would I be brave, would I save others, putting my family in danger?" It is an impossible question to answer but I hope that the better angels of my nature will smile upon me. I can work to mirror those I admire, specifically my grandparents and family.

The admiration I felt for my grandfather and grandmother and their bravery, their will to live, and their determination to carry on continues to guide me. I hope the day never comes where I am faced with a situation which requires as much grit, determination and willpower as they faced. But if it does, I am proud to say I have their blood running through my veins.

I admire my father, who disobeyed his parents by returning to Poland, but faced his fears. He challenged 64 years of preconceived notions to go on this journey with our family and I am lucky to have a father so brave. Finally, I admire my Mom. Putting herself on the page, subject to second guessing, criticism and judgment, is hard. It is especially hard when you are a self-aware "white Jewish girl from Mercer Island." I am honored to have been part of her process, of her self-exploration and to learn from her example as a role model.

Through this book, my Mom showed that there is no challenge too great and that if you are not afraid to put yourself out there you can do anything. Your example has taught us that we each have the power to write our own legacy. You just have to be brave and willing to work hard. The mosaic of emotions felt throughout this trip allows me to step back in my everyday life and remember to admire the brave and do what I can to continue the story of those courageous ones whose legacy I carry on.

SHOSHANA GOLDBERG

Stepping out of the tour bus from the bubble of my family jokes, a serious yet happy aura enveloped me. I couldn't comprehend the gravity of what was happening. We were meeting the descendants of the people who saved my *Bubbe* and *Zeyde*. The smiles and hugs embraced me, the language I didn't understand but the hearts and the feelings I did. The reunion of family I never knew. The family spoke to us as if we were old friends, yet strangers. They gesticulated wildly, speaking to us like no language barrier, no walls, no cultures and time, no things that we think separate us existed.

They took us to the barn — this is where your grandparents hid in the winter. They took us to the hole, this is the clever hole where your grandparents hid in the summer, using a trap door covered by sticks. It was all so real. The Polish woods, the young trees, the whiff of danger in the air, all the stories we had grown up on were available to be experienced by my five senses and it washed over me, as it simultaneously washed over all of us.

Sitting in the Styś house I was suddenly overwhelmed by emotions. I couldn't believe the gratitude, the connection, the gravity of what had happened in this very house many years ago. I was one with strangers, I grasped the hand of the woman sitting next to me and I began to cry. How can I describe the raw feeling of coming home to a history that I had never lived personally, yet dictated the undercurrent of my very being?

Something as big as surviving the Holocaust doesn't disappear with the survivor. The trauma, the responsibility, the story is passed down through the generations — in an epigenetic spiritual burden that we bear. I felt the burden, pride, kindness and connective energy that I'm sure the Styś family as descendants of righteous Gentiles, felt themselves. Some people there experienced saving my grandparents first hand, and some heard the stories and were in awe of the moment as I was. It was a homecoming.

My father spoke. He thanked our saviors, telling them we wouldn't be alive if it weren't for them. I felt a wave of gratitude, knowing I would never exist, never be the person I am if it weren't for people who were willing to risk their lives to help people in need. We heard from the old man who as a child brought food to my *Bubbe*, pretending it was meant for the dog, all the children deprived of their childhood friends to keep the secret burden of saving lives. Janina told us about her close friendship with *Bubbe* Esther and sang to us from the depths of her heart. She was present in those times as she was in our present. While we sang to our saviors with tears in our eyes, we had gone back in time, crossed bridges and borders, our lives had been touched and touched.

Being in Poland was a whirlwind of emotion, laughter, unbounded love, appreciation, Holocaust jokes and facing our joint trauma. From singing Yiddish songs in rainy graveyards to seeing the marketization of Jewish culture, to meeting the new generation of our saviors, to seeing where my grandfather lived, where he lived in hell, and where my grandmother hid under the cover of lice and stars, I felt like I was in a place both lush and hellish — a place where history was acknowledged yet denied. Where a terrible death camp that housed my grandfather and killed almost a million Jews like a factory, was a simple field with a few misshapen rocks. Jewish graveyards were turned into shopping malls. Jewish culture was misappropriated to some kind of dystopian non-kosher *Meah Shearim,*[*] yet simultaneously being renewed and rejuvenated by the descendants of crypto-Jews and survivors. I felt so much, so connected to my family narrative, and my historical past while creating a new relationship with a new family whose love surpasses cultural and linguistical barriers who understand that we share a common history. Where my heart was full.

---

[*] *Meah Shearim* literally means 100 fences. It is the name of a neighborhood in Jerusalem where ultra-orthodox Jews live.

MICHA HACOHEN

It is common for high schools in Israel to send their seniors on a one-week "trip" to Poland to the camps and memorial sites. As a high school student, I chose not to go on the class trip. It's hard for me to reflect upon the whole range of emotions that influenced my decision eight years ago, but I remember very well the deep conviction that was embedded within me, that it was not yet time. I felt unprepared, not ready to face the shock of leaving my country for the first time, only to face evil in one of its most crude and brutal manifestations.

Fortunately, my gut feeling turned out to be right, and six years later, the Goldberg family gave me the opportunity to join an intimate journey following the miraculous survival of their grandparents, Sam and Esther. I went to Poland with my wife, then my fiancée, Shoshana, with mixed feelings. On the one hand, I felt lucky to have been given a second chance to fulfill the duty of every Jew, to learn to remember and preserve the greatest period of crisis and pain our nation has known since its inception. On the other hand, despite the generous invitation of Karen and Shlomo, I was concerned that by joining, I might disturb the delicate and intimate family fabric that was to be created out of such a journey.

Almost immediately my apprehensions about this or that unpleasantness evaporated. I haven't met many brighter, more cheerful families than the Goldberg family. It's hard not to get caught up in the joy of a group of people who have such an impressive pool of inside jokes in the form of innuendo, quotes and songs up their sleeve. In addition to the marginal fact that the keystone and the family's humor is centered on Holocaust jokes. Throughout the journey, I felt the closeness of the hearts and the power of the family's unconditional and non-judgmental support whenever one members felt overwhelmed by the emotional burden of such a disquieting experience — there was a comforting shoulder beside him.

It is difficult to summarize the entire experience in words, it would be difficult to describe even part of it. Although the whole trip took no more than a week and a half, it was so full of moving emotions, that experiences that lasted only short minutes have been engraved in my mind as long hours and the days seemed like weeks. We often exchanged laughter, tears, and smiles all while confronting deep horror. I will try to reflect on one snapshot of the experience that I wrote while in Poland.

Monday. We went to see the Warsaw ghetto.

There is no Warsaw ghetto. All that remains of the ghetto are milestones, stepping stones that integrate into the city's indifferent sidewalks.

The feeling is that, like the Jews themselves, the Holocaust too has become an archeological artifact, an anecdote intended for tourists.

Although most of the victims of the Holocaust died more than 70 years ago, some people continue to feed the ash mountain at Majdanek with the smut of their memories. What am I doing to change this? Not much.

The taste of bitterness lingers in my mouth, I can't breathe this air. The trees are not green to me, the sky is not blue, the earth is black.

I am grateful that I was privileged to have taken part in this one-of-a-kind journey and to have had the opportunity to try to understand and cherish the unimaginable giants who passed through the Nazi hell and came out alive.

ESTHER GOLDBERG

When we entered the wooden walls of the Styś family home, everyone held their breath. We felt the weight of seventy years pressing down on us. The Styś family sensed the same energy. They were packed together, grandparents and children alike in this Polish farmhouse to meet the descendants of Sam and Esther. There was an ineffable sense of reunion, as if we had met years ago. We touched each other's faces to remind ourselves of how we looked. I was eighteen at the time, around the same age as my *Bubbe* when she hid in the forest. I imagined that the elders of the Styś family saw my B*ubbe* in my countenance. One smiling woman, hearing that I carried the same name as my grandmother, repeated "Estera, Estera," in recognition. It was eerie to occupying the same room as people who knew and saved my grandparents in the war. It was unnerving to see the adjacent barn where my grandparents hid in the winter.

Into this suspended tension, my family gathered in the living room and sang to the Styś family. It was a song of praise that conveyed our indebtedness. While singing eased the tension, the performative aspect separated us from the group, marking us momentarily as outsiders. But then, wonderfully, one women sang back! In an aged and wavering voice, Janina sang a Polish religious song in our honor.

At once I noticed all the labor involved in this gathering. I noted Janina's maroon suit in honor of the occasion, the food carefully prepared with no cooked food — so as to observe the laws of *Kashrut* (with only a few bacon strips going incognito in a cup of pepper slices). Astonishingly, the Styś family matched our enthusiasm. Prior to arriving, I gave no thought to what this gathering would mean for the Styś family. After our song however, the watery eyes meeting mine and Janina's returning voice told me that this reunion was a holy one for both families. Both of us carry this story.

For years we have lugged these stories on our backs. We never rested the weight, never broke it into pieces, never took it into ourselves. Sam and Esther's story lay tacitly at the core of every family conversation but was never cohesive. The Styś family was a myth barely mentioned. This book, in digging out old narratives forgotten and teasing out conflicting truths, has forced our family to look at the past and our present way of dealing with it.

Like when my Mom and I met our long-lost cousin Idu. His stoic face was impassive most of our visit. But when I showed him a picture of our family and told him that this was his family too, his stony exterior immediately crumbled. Stunned by the sudden escalation of emotions, I turned away from his pinched face. His daughter Magda approached him and held his head tenderly. She placed her forehead against his as if they were some warped mirror image — father and offspring, broken and patched, sufferer and the bearer of sufferings past. I watched her crying unashamedly against her father's head, like she was letting out breath held too long.

We, too, are facing ourselves in the mirror. Meeting the Styś family, Idu and Magda, Mr. Załęski. Hugging and kissing their real bodies which exist outside of fable. Complicating myths with real experience. Allowing ourselves to feel gratitude and confront pain and exhale. Forehead to forehead we face this pain and get it down in writing. Then maybe the weight will be lighter living within us, not pressing upon us.

APPENDIX B: FAMILY TREE – ZELIG AND FAIGA GOLDBERG

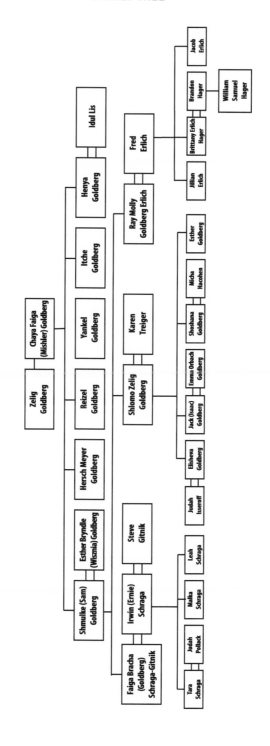

FAMILY TREE — SHLOMO ZALMAN AND BRACHA WISZNIA

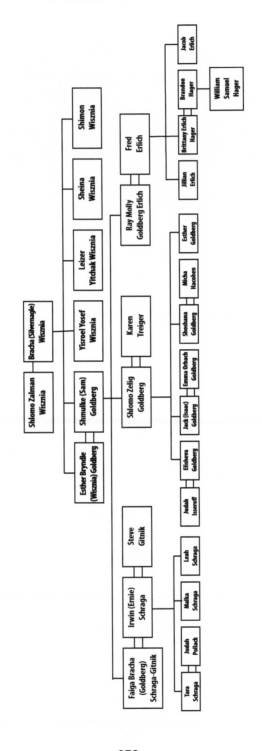

FAMILY TREE – ALEKSANDER AND HELENA STYŚ

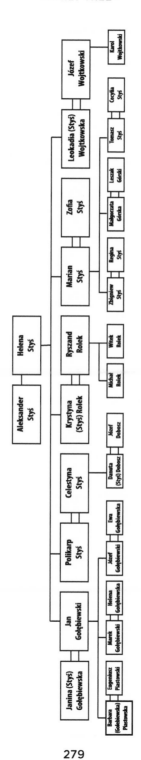

FAMILY TREE – STANISŁAW AND WŁADYSŁAWA STYŚ

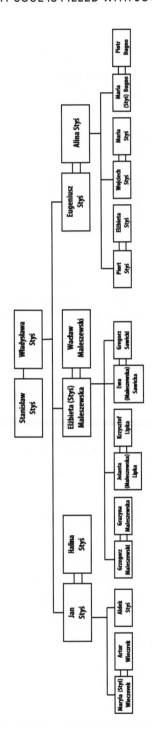

ACKNOWLEDGMENTS

My heart is filled with gratitude to so many without whom this book would not have come to publication.

First and foremost, thanks to Sam and Esther, for being the quiet heroes that they were and loving me in the way they did. To their son, my husband, Shlomo Goldberg, who supported me throughout, even though, at times, it was hard for him to confront the past. The lessons and the trauma of the Holocaust are present in the daily lives of the second generation. Shlomo once made the following comment: "I am in a constant state of escape from Treblinka or of living in a hole in the ground — to survive." This speaks volumes as to why he cares so deeply about his family and his patients — he wants all to survive and live healthy and good lives. I am so thankful that he traveled to (*finstere*) Poland with me and am amazed that he went back — alone — to attend the *Yad Vashem* ceremony when I could not. He is an amazing life partner and father for our four fabulous children.

Our 2016 trip to Poland would have been an entirely different experience were it not for my travel agent and wonderful friend — Joanna Millick. Without her big heart, keen mind and dogged energy, this book and my experience would have been very different. From translating the letters, making impeccable travel arrangements, searching for and reaching out to Jaroslaw Maleszewski, and serving as my translator, she was my partner every step of the way.

The Poland trip would not have been possible without Grzegorz Maleszewski, the man whose heart was full and whose soul was filled with joy. His energy and enthusiasm are contagious, and I am indebted to his hard work to gather the Styś family, make the family trees and be our guide as we met the Styś family and traveled in the area. His friendship is like a precious gem which I will always cherish.

Father Rafael Figiel — the Catholic Priest who served in the Wąsewo/

Bagatele area who found my blog and reached out to me added so much to our family and to this story. Through his efforts we met the Wilk family, including Idul, who survived the war. Having Ola and Marty in the group of Boston Goldberg relatives is exciting and I am grateful to Magda and Farid for being part of our family and *schlepping* me and Esther and later Shlomo, to Bagatele.

Aleksander Czyzewski, the young man with the big beard and sweet smile, who joined us in Warsaw in June of 2016, was my translator in April of 2017 and provided this priceless service to Shlomo in January of 2018. But more than translating for us, he is a dear person whose friendship I treasure. Through Aleks, I was able to meet his parents, Adam and Elżbieta, and hear their story of secrets and the rediscovery of their heritage. I am honored that they shared their story with me.

Shaya (Sam) Schloss was my main advisor regarding Poland before and during the war. He was my "go to" man when I had a question or just needed to clarify facts. He is Sam Goldberg's first cousin and knew him before the war. Shaya lived in Föhrenwald when Sam and Esther and Fay were there. His support and love during this process sustained me and we had many exciting conversations and joyous moments — thank you Shaya.

When it came time to write the book and prepare it for publication, Jennifer McCord, my publishing and editorial consultant, provided invaluable advice and assistance to shape and reshape it. Thank you also to Sheryl Stebbins for being a meticulous copy editor. I am also indebted to Chris Webb, author, historian and founder of the Holocaust Historical Society, who served as my Treblinka expert, helping with facts, maps and pictures. To my dear friend David Naggar, thank you for your help in tightening the story and advising me on how to bring the book to publication.

Finally, a big thank you to all my friends and family who have provided feedback and followed my journey, whether sitting around my kitchen table or following my blog postings. Your love and support were crucial to keep me going.

BIBLIOGRAPHY

Arad, Yitzhak, *Belzec, Sobibor, Treblinka: The Operation Reinhard Death Camps*. Bloomington and Indianapolis: Indiana University Press,1987.

Bartov, Omer, *Anatomy of a Genocide: The Life and Death of a Town Called Buczacz*, New York: Simon & Schuster, 2018.

Bauer, Yehuda, *The Holocaust in Historical Perspective*, Seattle: University of Washington Press, 1978.

Bernstein, Sara Tuval with Thorton, Louise Loots and Samuels, Marlene Bernstein, *The Seamstress: A Memoir of Survival*, New York: Berkley Books, 1997.

Bikont, Anna, *The Crime and the Silence: Confronting the Massacre of Jews in Wartime Jedwabne*, New York: Farrar, Straus and Giroux, 2004.

Browning, Christopher R., *Ordinary Men: Reserve Police Battalion 101 and the Final Solution in Poland*, New York: Harper Perennial, 1992.

Buergenthal, Thomas, *Lucky Child: A Memoir of Surviving Auschwitz as a Young Boy*, New York: Hachette Book Group, 2009.

Cesarani, David, *Final Solution: The Fate of the Jews 1933-1949*. New York: St. Martin's Press, 2016.

Cohen, Henry (director of camp in 1946), "The Anguish of the Holocaust Survivors — Camp Föhrenwald," Lecture given at Conservative Synagogue of Fifth Avenue on Yom HaShoah (Holocaust Remembrance Day) April 13, 1996. [article — http://remember.org/witness/cohen]

Cymlich & Strawczynski, *Escaping Hell in Treblinka*, New York, Jerusalem: Yad Vashem and The Holocaust Survivors' Memoirs Project, 2007.

Dawidowicz, Lucy S., *The War Against the Jews: 1933-1945*. New York: Bantam Books, 1975.

Desbois, Patrick, Father, *The Holocaust by Bullets: A Priest's Journey to Uncover the Truth Behind the Murder of 1.5 Million Jews*. New York: Palgrave Macmillan, St. Martin's Press, 2008.

Desbois, Patrick, Father, *In Broad Daylight: The Secret Procedures behind the Holocaust by Bullets*, translation by Hilary Reyl and Calvert Barksdale, New York: Arcade Publishing, 2018.

Deutsch, Nathaniel, *The Jewish Dark Continent: Life and Death in the Russian Pale of Settlement,* Cambridge: Harvard University Press, 2011.

Donat, Alexander, ed., *The Death Camp Treblinka: A Documentary*, New York: Holocaust Library, 1979 (orig. 1975).

Dressen, Willi, Klee, Ernst, & Riess, Volker, ed., *"The Good Old Days": The Holocaust as Seen by Its Perpetrators and Bystanders*, Old Saybrook: Konecky & Konecky, 1988 (translated in 1991).

Engelking, Barbara, *Such A Beautiful Sunny Day: Jews Seeking Refuge in the Polish Countryside, 1942-1945*, Jerusalem: Yad Vashem, 2016.

Fallada, Hans, *Every Man Dies Alone*, Brooklyn: Melville House Publishing, 2009.

Friedlander, Saul, *Nazi Germany and the Jews 1939-1945: The Years of Extermination*, New York: Harper Collins, 2007.

Fritzsche, Peter, *Life and Death in the Third Reich*, Cambridge: Harvard University Press, 2008.

Gilbert, Martin, *Kristallnacht: Prelude to Destruction*, New York: Harper Collins, 2006.

Goldberg, Esther Wisznia, April 12, 1993, video interview by Ray Molly Goldberg.

Goldberg, Sam, video interview, July 13, 1997, by the Shoah Foundation.

Goldberg, Sam, video interviews in 1991 and 1993, by Shlomo Goldberg.

Goldfarb, Fievel, May 2016 & July 11, 2016, phone interviews.

Goodman, Simon, *The Orpheus Clock: The Search for My Family's Art Treasures Stolen by the Nazis*, New York: Simon and Schuster, Inc., 2015.

Gordon, Aba and Gelbart, M. ed., *Memorial Book of The Jewish Community of Ostrow Mazowiecka*, New York: JewishGen, Inc., 2013.

Gortler, Josh, In-person Interview, August 15, 2017, by Esther Goldberg.

Grabowski, Jan, *Hunt for the Jews: Betrayal and Murder in German-Occupied Poland,* Bloomington: Indiana University Press, 2011, Published in English in 2013.

Gray, Martin, *For Those I Loved,* Charlottesville: Hampton Roads, 2006 (originally published in 1971- Little Brown and Company in French; translated to English in 1975 and published by Seabury Press).

Gross, Jan, Tomasz & Gross, Irena, Grudzinska Gross, *Golden Harvest,* New York: Oxford University Press, 2012.

Gross, Jan, *Neighbors: The Destruction of the Jewish Community of Jedwabne, Poland,* Princeton: Princeton University Press, 2001.

Grossman, Vasily, *A Writer at War,* edited and translated by Antony Beevor and Luba Vinogradova, New York: Random House Press, 2005.

Hays, Peter, *Why? Explaining the Holocaust.* New York: W.W. Norton & Company, Inc., 2017.

Hilberg, Raul, *The Destruction of the European Jews (Student Edition),* Teaneck: P. Holmes & Meier, 1985.

Jablonka, Ivan, *A History of the Grandparents I Never Had,* Stanford: Stanford University Press, 2016. Translated by Jane Kuntz.

Khonigsman, Yakov, "Political Parties and Groups Among the Jews of Poland and Western Ukraine in 1919-1939," in Euroasian Jewish Congress, April 26, 2012.

Kohner, Nancy, *My Father's Roses: A Family's Journey from World War I to Treblinka,* New York: Pegasus Books, 2006.

Konigseder, Angelika & Wetzel, Juliane, *Waiting for Hope: Jewish Displaced Persons in Post-World War II Germany,* Evanston: Northwestern University Press, 2001. Translated from German by John A. Broadwin.

Kronick, Rabbi Lowell, Rybal, Isaak, & Shmulewitz, I., ed., *The Bialystoker Memorial Book,* New York: Bialystoker Center, 1982.

Levy, Naomi, *Einstein and the Rabbi: Searching for the Soul,* New York: Flatiron Books, 2017.

Lichtenstein, Kalman, *Pinskas Slonim (Yizkor — Memorial Book of Slonim),* Tel

Aviv, 1962-1979.

------------, "Marine Jumper (T-AP-200)," Navsource Online: Service Ship Photo Archive, http://www.navsource.org/archives/09/22/22200.htm

McPherson, Alexander, "In the Wilderness of Föhrenwald: Refugees in Occupied Upper Bavaria 1945-1947," in Thesis article, Petersborough, Ontario: Trent University, May 2016.

Ohler, Norman, *Blitzed: Drugs in the Third Reich,* New York: Houghton Mifflin Harcourt, 2017.

Pinkas Stok — Stoczek Yizkor (Memorial) Book, Buenos Aires: Julio Kaufman S.R.L., 1974.

------------, "Poalei Tziyon, Definition," Zionism and Israel, Encyclopedic Dictionary, http://www.zionism-israel.com/dic/Poalei_Tziyon.htm

Rajchman, Chil, *The Last Jew of Treblinka: A Survivor's Memory 1942-1943,* New York: Pegasus Books, translated by Solon Beinfeld, 2011.

Reszke, Katka, *Return of the Jew: Identity Narratives of the Third Post-Holocaust Generation of Jews in Poland,* Boston: Academic Studies Press, 2013.

Ripp, Victor, *Hell's Traces: One Murder, Two Families, Thirty-Five Holocaust Memorials*, New York: Farrar, Straus and Giroux, 2017.

Sands, Philippe, *East West Street: On the Origins of "Genocide" and "Crimes Against Humanity."* New York: Alfred A. Knopf, 2016.

Schloss, Shaya, Multiple Phone Interviews, 2015 — 2018.

Sereny, Gitta, *Into That Darkness: An Examination of Conscience*, New York: Random House, 1974.

Smith, Mark, *Treblinka Survivor: The Life and Death of Hershl Sperling*, Stroud. Gloucestershire: Pellmount, 2010.

Snyder, Timothy, *Bloodlands: Europe Between Hitler and Stalin,* New York: Basic Books, 2010.

Snyder, Timothy, *Black Earth: The Holocaust as History and Warning*, New York: Tim Duggan Books, 2015.

Thompson, Julia Holmlund, "Liberated but not yet Free: Allied Policy, Jewish Displaced Persons, and Identity in Occupied Germany, 1945-1948",

Whitman College, Honors Thesis, Spring 2015.

------------, Treblinka Museum Web Site.
http://www.treblinka-muzeum.eu/index.php/historia/oboz-zaglady/
opor-i-powstanie

Tuszynska, Agata, *Family History of Fear: A Memoir,* New York: Alfred A.
Knopf, 2016.

------------, "Under Soviet Rule (1939-1941)," The Bialystoker Hebrew
Gymnasium,
http://www.bialystokgymnasium.org/soviets.htm

United States Holocaust Memorial Museum, "Föhrenwald," https://www.
ushmm.org/wlc/en/article.php?ModuleId=10007059
August 3, 2017.

United States Holocaust Memorial Museum, "Einsatzgruppen and other SS and
Police Units in the Soviet Union,"
https://www.ushmm.org/wlc/en/article.php?ModuleId=10005518
July 20, 2017.

United States Holocaust Memorial Museum, "Einsatzgruppen (Mobile Killing
Units),"
https://www.ushmm.org/wlc/en/article.php?ModuleId=10005130
July 20, 2017.

United States Holocaust Memorial Museum, "Resistance in the Smaller
Ghettoes of Eastern Europe: Glossary," https://www.ushmm.org/wlc/en/
article.php?ModuleId=10007240
July 25, 2018.

United States Holocaust Memorial Museum, "Hershel Rosenblat," https://www.
ushmm.org/wlc/en/idcard.php?ModuleId=10006765
July 25, 2017.

Wachsmann, Nikolaus, *kl: A History of the Nazi Concentration Camps*, New
York: Farrar, Straus and Giroux, 2015.

Webb, Chris & Chocholatý, Michal, *The Treblinka Death Camp: History,
Biographies, Remembrance,* Stuttgart: Ibidem Press, 2014.

Wilkerson, Isabel, *The Warmth of Other Suns: The Epic Story of America's Great*

Migration, New York: Vintage Books, 2010.

Wikipedia Contributors. "Axis Occupation of Greece." In Wikipedia, The Free Encyclopedia, August 29, 2017. https://en.wikipedia.org/wiki/Axis_occupation_of_Greece

Wikipedia Contributors. "Great Synagogue Bialystok." In Wikipedia, The Free Encyclopedia, July 25, 2017. https://en.wikipedia.org/wiki/Great_Synagogue,_Bia%C5%82ystok

Wikipedia Contributors. "List of Genocides by Death Toll." In Wikipedia, The Free Encyclopedia, August 1, 2017. https://en.wikipedia.org/wiki/List_of_genocides_by_death_toll

Wikipedia Contributors. "Maimonides Medical Center." In Wikipedia, The Free Encyclopedia, April 19, 2018. https://en.wikipedia.org/wiki/Maimonides_Medical_Center

Wikipedia Contributors. "Reichskommissariat Ukraine." In Wikipedia, The Free Encyclopedia, August 24, 2017. https://en.wikipedia.org/wiki/Reichskommissariat_Ukraine

Wikipedia Contributors. "Shiksa." In Wikipedia, The Free Encyclopedia, April 12, 2018. https://en.wikipedia.org/wiki/Shiksa

Wikipedia Contributors. "Slonim Ghetto." In Wikipedia, The Free Encyclopedia, July 27, 2017.

https://en.wikipedia.org/wiki/S%C5%82onim_Ghetto

Wikipedia Contributors. "Warsaw Ghetto." In Wikipedia, The Free Encyclopedia, August 3, 2017. https://en.wikipedia.org/wiki/Warsaw_Ghetto

Winik, Jay, *1944: FDR and the Year that Changed History*, New York: Simon & Schuster, 2015.

Wisse, Ruth R., Ed., *The I.L. Peretz Reader.* New York. Schocken Books. 1990.

Wulf, Linda Press, *The Night of the Burning: A Journey from Despair to Hope,* London: Bloomsbury Press, 2006.

Wyszogrod, Morris, *A Brush with Death: An Artist in the Death Camps*, Albany: State University of New York Press,1999.

Załęski, Mieczysław, In-person Interview, April 21, 2007.

ENDNOTES

1   Sereny, Gitta, *Into That Darkness: An Examination of Conscience* (New York: Random House, 1974), 247.

2   Peyes were and still are worn by some observant Jews. The custom is based on the Biblical verse in Leviticus 19:27: "You shall not round off the *pe'as* (פְּאַת) of your head." Peah (singular) means corner, so this verse is interpreted to mean that a Jewish man should not cut the hairs on the "corners" of his head. The hair on the side of the head is not cut and grows into sidelocks.

3   Interview with Mieczysław Załęski, April 21, 2017.

4   Abe Gordon and M. Gelbart, eds. *Memorial Book of The Jewish Community of Ostrow Mazowiecka* (New York: JewishGen, Inc., 2013), 165-66.

5   For a description of the Ostrow marketplace, see Gordon and Gelbert, 163-168.

6   Gordon and Gelbart, 774.

7   Gordon and Gelbart, 774-75.

8   Gordon and Gelbart, 35-60.

9   On Hitler's order, the SS intelligence service fabricated an attack against a German radio station. They made it appear that the Polish militia attacked the station. This was the excuse used by Germany to cross the Polish border and begin the war. *See* Cesarani, David, *Final Solution: The Fate of the Jews 1933-1949* (New York: St. Martin's Press, 2009), 231.

10   Gordon and Gelbart, 492.

11   Gordon and Gelbart, 493-94.

12   Gordon and Gelbart, 507.

13   The Schloss family was chased out of Jasienitz in 1934, by the antisemitic Poles. With Hitler's rise to power in Germany in 1933, the Poles were emboldened and increased their harassment of Jews. They boycotted their store and picketed outside to ensure that no one would shop there. The family had no choice but to move. They moved to Ostrow Mazowiecka. Schloss, Shaya, Phone Interview.

14   Towards the end of September, Hitler and Stalin negotiated how to split up territory. Stalin wanted control of the Baltic states. Hitler, worried that many German nationals would fall under Soviet rule, agreed to give up the Baltic states if Stalin

would allow all German nationals living in Soviet-controlled lands to be repatriated to Germany. Stalin agreed and the German nationals were brought home. *See* Cesarani, 252.

15 *"Volksdeutscher"* was a term for people "whose native language was German but who lived outside the Reich and were citizens of another country." Debois, Patrick, Father, *In Broad Daylight: the Secret Procedures behind the Holocaust by Bullets* (New York: Arcade Publishing, 2018), 261.

16 At first Hitler gave the military operation the code name, Fritz, likely referring to the King of Prussia, Frederick the Great. Later, he changed the name to "Barbarossa (the common appellation of the twelfth-century Emperor Frederick I of the Hohenstaufen dynasty); the Nazi leader probably wished to evoke Barbarossa's history and legend. The Hohenstaufen emperor had embarked on a crusade in the East against the infidels; and, over time, the Germans had turned Barbarossa into a mythic figure: He was the secret savior, asleep in the Kyffhauser mountain range in Thuringia, who would arise at the time of his people's greatest need and led them to victory and redemption." Friedlander, Saul. *Nazi Germany and the Jews 1939-1945: The Years of Extermination* (New York: Harper Collins, 2007),133-134.

17 Timothy Snyder in *Bloodlands,* explains how the "German prisoner-of-war camps in the East were far deadlier than the German concentration camps. Indeed, the existing concentration camps changed their character upon contact with prisoners of war. . . . The Germans shot, on a conservative estimate, half a million Soviet prisoners of war. By way of starvation or mistreatment during transit, they killed about 2.6 million more. All in all, perhaps 3.1 million Soviet prisoners of war were killed." Snyder, Timothy. *Bloodlands: Europe Between Hitler and Stalin* (New York: Basic Books, 2010), 183-84.

18 Sam's experience was standard Nazi practice with all Soviet POWs. Timothy Snyder describes this phenomena: "The *Einsatzkommandos* could not screen the Soviet prisoners of war very carefully. They would interrogate Soviet prisoners of war in their holding pens, immediately after they were taken. They would ask commissars, communists, and Jews to step forward. Then they would take them away, shoot them, and throw them into pits." *Bloodlands,* 183.

19 Shmulewitz, I., "Bialystok — A Historical Survey," in Rabbi Lowell Kronick, Isaak Rybal, & I. Shmulewitz, eds. *The Bialystoker Memorial Book* (New York: Bialystoker Center, 1982), 4-5.

20 Yoel Lande survived the war and immigrated to Buenos Aries, Argentina. His granddaughter, Julieta, contacted me in December of 2017. She is making a documentary film about her grandparents' lives.

21 In June of 1941, the Great Synagogue was the scene of murder. Over 1,000 men, women and children were locked in the Synagogue, which the Germans set on fire. All those inside burned to death. *See* Rajzner, Refoel, "The 'Action' of February 1943," in Kronick, Rybal and Shmulewitz, 84. Neither Esther nor her family lived in Bialystok when this occurred.

22 Zbar, Awrom, "The Rise and Fall of Bialystok," in Kronick, Rybal and Shmulewitz, 53.

23 Zbar.

24   Nowogrodski, Emanuel, "The 'Bund' in Bialystok," in Kronick, Rybal and Shmulewitz, 23.

25   Zbar, in Kronick, Rybal and Shmulewitz, 53.

26   Zbar, in Kronick, Rybal and Shmulewitz, 54.

27   The word antisemitism is spelled throughout this book as one word, as opposed to the more common "anti-Semitism." I do so after reading Peter Hays' book *Why? Explaining the Holocaust*. Hays states: "[T]he customary insertion of a hyphen and a capital letter in 'anti-Semitism' implies that there is something called 'Semitism' somewhere. The original language of the term, German, doesn't make this mistake; the spelling is *Antisemitismus*, all one word." Hays, Peter, *Why? Explaining the Holocaust* (New York: W.W. Norton & Company, 2017), 5.

28   Dror, Yoseph, "The Wooden *Beis HaMidrash*, Reb Yekutiel Czepelewski's House of Prayer, translated by Gloria Berkenstat Freund, in Lichtenstein, Kalman, *Pinskas Slonim (Yizkor — Memorial Book of Slonim)*, Tel Aviv: 1962-1979.

29   On July 31, 1941, Hermann Göring issued the following order to Reinhard Heydrich: "Complementing the task that was assigned to you on January 21, 1939, which was to solve the Jewish problem by emigration and evacuation in the most effective manner in accordance with the conditions of that time, I hereby charge you with making all necessary organizational, practical and financial preparations for bringing about the final solution of the Jewish problem in the territories within the German sphere of influence in Europe." Donat, Alexander, ed., *The Death Camp Treblinka: A Documentary* (New York: Holocaust Library, 1979), 11.

30   Sam's forced move to Stoczek was likely around the end of 1941. It was around this time, on December 7, 1941 that the Japanese bombed Pearl Harbor and the United States entered the war.

31   Snyder, Timothy, *Black Earth* (New York: Crown Publishing, 2015), 158.

32   Madagascar is an island in the Indian Ocean off the Southeast coast of Africa. The Jews were to remain in Madagascar "in German hands as a pledge for the future behaviour (sic) of the members of their race in America." Cesarani, 300.

33   Snyder, *Bloodlands,* 197.

34   Snyder, *Bloodlands*, 198. *See also* Cesarani, 363-375.

35   It was Nebe's *Einsatzkommando* 8 of *Einsatzgruppen* B that came to Slonim. *See* Cesarani, 370. According to an article on Slonim Ghetto on Wikipedia, the massacre took place on July 17, 1941. *See* Slonim Ghetto, Wikipedia: https://en.wikipedia.org/wiki/S%C5%82onim_Ghetto

36   For a detailed account of the digging of the pits, *see* Debois, *In Broad Daylight,* 47-57.

37   Desbois, *In Broad Daylight*, 67-68. The account of the preparations for the Slonim massacre is taken from a 1947 deposition of Alfred Metzner, a *Volksdeutsche,* who lived in the area. The Nazis often used the *Volksdeutsche* to serve as translators, but some, like Alfred Metzner, also became shooters: "At this extermination,"

Metzner explains, "about 10,000 Jews were liquidated. The night before the *Aktion*, the protection and the sealing off of the ghetto had already been ordered. Protection against the partisans had been ordered by the commander of the town. At four in the morning, the ghetto was surrounded by the local police. All the Jews who tried to escape were immediately shot. The Jews had learned ahead of time about the execution and that is why they had tried to dig holes in the ground at various places in order to escape the encirclement. The ones who did escape were turned in by the local population and shot on the spot. The extermination of the Jews took place as follows: when the Jews refused to leave their houses, they were either forced out and then shot, or shot inside their houses. During the *Aktions*, particularly sadistic people threw lit flares at the living Jews; they caused serious injuries. Men with machine guns were stationed outside the ghetto to counter any attempt to escape. The Jews were not led to graves but shot right on the spot. The night before, women had been raped by police and then shot. The police bragged about the number of women they had abused in this manner and tried to outdo one another. Later, when no one was coming out of the ghetto anymore, the troops were formed up to go inside." *Id.*

38   Desbois, *In Broad Daylight*, 67.

39   Desbois, Patrick, Father. *The Holocaust by Bullets: A Priest's Journey to Uncover the Truth Behind the Murder of 1.5 Million Jews* (New York: Palgrave Macmillan, St. Martin's Press, 2008), 84. For more details about the mass killings in the east, *see*, Desbois, *In Broad Daylight*.

40   Desbois, *Holocaust by Bullets*, 84. See also, Desbois, *In Broad Daylight.*

41   See Holocaust Encyclopedia. United States Holocaust Memorial Museum. Article on Hershel Rosenblat. https://www.ushmm.org/wlc/en/idcard.php?ModuleId=10006765

42   According to Timothy Snyder, construction of the Death Camp Treblinka began on June 1, 1942. Snyder, *Bloodlands,* 261. Other accounts state the construction began in April 1942. See Chrostowski, Witold, Extermination Camp Treblinka (London: Valentine Mitchell, 2004), 25.

43   Thomalla had also supervised the latter stages of construction of the other two Operation Reinhard camps at Belzec and Sobibor. Webb, Chris & Chocholatý, Michal, *The Treblinka Death Camp: History, Biographies, Remembrance* (Stuttgart: Ibidem Press, 2014), 22.

44   *See* "Excerpts from Judgment," in Alexander Donat, ed. *The Death Camp Treblinka: A Documentary* (New York: Holocaust Library, 1979), 298.

45   "Excerpts from Judgment," in Donat, 311. At its height, Treblinka averaged 4,600 murdered each day or 200 people per hour. "It was the most lethal place on earth." Cesarani, *Final Solution* at 508.

46   *See* Cesarani, 503.

47   Webb & Chocholatý, 22.

48   Though Jews were the primary victims of Treblinka, Gypsies were also killed there. "They had *nebach*, an ugly death," Sam later explained. "They burnt them

alive. They put a barbed wire fence around them and they burnt there all the time." Goldberg, Sam, in-person interview.

49   There are differing maps as to the layout of the camp. To describe the layout of the camp, I used the map in Arad, *Belzec, Sobibor, Treblinka: The Operation Reinhard Death Camps* (Bloomington: Indiana University Press, 1987), 39.

50   See Grossman, Vasily, *A Writer at War*, edited and translated by Antony Beevor and Luba Vinogradova (New York: Random House Press, 2005), 289, fn. 5.

51   In their quest for the perfect Aryan race, the Nazis gassed 70,273 children and adults in the Euthanasia Program between 1939 and 1941. The crime deserving such a death was mental illness or physical disability. The Euthanasia Program, called T-4 after the address — Tiergartenstrasse 4, was aimed at Germans, not Jews, though it was fine if some Jews were murdered there. It began with deception — a physical exam by a doctor, followed by an invitation to disrobe and shower, only to have carbon monoxide come out of the spout asphyxiating the patient. Dawidowicz, Lucy S., *The War Against the Jews: 1933-1945* (New York: Bantam Books, 1975), 178-80.

52   "Excerpts from Judgment," in Donat, 299.

53   Arad, 41.

54   The Judges at the Treblinka trials of Kurt Franz and Franz Stangl concluded that there is no way to know how many people fit into the gas chambers at one time. This description and approximate range is from the trial transcript. "Excerpts from Judgment," in Donat, 311. Compare with Wiernik's description: "When I arrived at the camp, three gas chambers were already in operation; another ten were added while I was there. A gas chamber measured 5x5 meters and was about 1.90 meters high." Wiernik, Jankiel, "One Year in Treblinka," in Donat, 158.

55   The carbon monoxide (CO) binds much better than oxygen (O_2) to the hemoglobin in blood, and thereby prevents red blood cells from performing their normal function of bringing oxygen to tissues. Snyder, *Bloodlands*, 256-57.

56   There were either 6, 8 or 10 additional gas chambers built. *See* Donat, 301: Webb & Chocholatý, 55.

57   "Excerpts from Judgment," Donat, 311.

58   Wiernik, in Donat, 161.

59   "Excerpts from Judgment," Donat, 301. This verse is from Psalms 118.

60   "Excerpts from Judgment," Donat, 310.

61   Grossman, 292.

62   The Operation Reinhard death camps were Belzek, Sobibor and Treblinka. The name was in honor of Reinhard Heydrich, who after Hitler and Himmler, was the most important man behind the genocidal plan to kill the Jews. He was injured in an attempted assassination by a man of Czech and Slovak descent employed by British intelligence. Heydrich died on June 4, 1942 as a result of his injuries. Snyder, *Bloodlands*, 262.

63   Arad, 94-96.

64   "Excerpts from Judgment," Donat, 309.

65   "Excerpts from Judgment," in Donat, 312.

66   Rajzman, Samuel, "The End of Treblinka," in Donat, 240.

67   Krzepicki, "Abraham, Eighteen Days in Treblinka," in Donat, 93-96.

68   Cymlich & Strawczynski, *Escaping Hell in Treblinka* (New York, Jerusalem: Yad Vashem and The Holocaust Survivors' Memoirs Project, 2007), 137.

69   Jan Grabowski studied an area of rural Poland, researching the *Judenjagd* as a part of Polish life in between 1942 and 1945. He published his conclusions in *Hunt for the Jews: Betrayal and Murder in German-Occupied Poland*. He states: "There is no doubt that it was not the Germans but next-door neighbors who inspired the greatest fear both in those who rescued, and in those who were being rescued. The Germans only rarely appeared in the villages, and they knew even less about the inhabitants. Neighbors, however, knew a great deal about their immediate surroundings. Many considered Jewish life worthless and felt little hesitation to share their insights and suspicions with the police." Grabowski, Jan, *Hunt for the Jews: Betrayal and Murder in German-Occupied Poland* (Bloomington: Indiana University Press, 2011, Published in English in 2013), 163.

"The [*Judenjagd*] hunts," Grabowski states, "were led by elders, forest rangers, wealthy peasants or simply by anyone who could inspire, threaten, or otherwise mobilize the village collective. The hunts for the Jews did not provoke negative emotions, or moral dilemmas — although some peasants were, quite understandably, upset at wasting a day of work for a basically unfruitful pursuit." Grabowski, 82.

70   Rajzman, in Donat, 240.

71   Webb & Chocholatý, 77-82.

72   Donat, 38.

73   In June of 1941, the Germans took over a gravel pit near the village of Treblinka. They harvested the gravel for military purposes. A penal camp was constructed and "stubborn elements" were sent there as slave labor. This camp was located and functioned as a separate endeavor from the Treblinka Death Camp which was constructed a year later. Webb & Chocholatý, 11-13.

74   Willenberg, Samuel, "I survived Treblinka," in Donat, 211.

75   Webb & Chocholatý, 84-85; Sereny, 182.

76   Neither Sam nor Esther mention Velvel staying after those first few days in hiding. But we recently found a written testimony by Velvel (William) Schneiderman on file at the U.S. Holocaust Memorial Museum, dated September 21, 1994. In this testimony, he states as he ran from Treblinka, he met a man "who lives in Brooklyn — in Miami — yeah" (this was Sam) and that they met a "boy, a young boy with a sister-in-law." The testimony continues to describe how he stayed with them and they dug a hole in the ground, put wood on top and lived in it for 11 months. The Styś children did not remember Velvel, only Esther, Moishe, Chaim and Sam.

77 There were other Jews who dug pits in the forest to hide. For example, Jochewed Kantorowicz, describes being "[t]hrown out from everywhere and robbed, ultimately they decided to dig a shelter in the forest: 'My sister told me: 'Even rabbits make pits for themselves, why should we be worse than rabbits?' We started to dig the pit at night. We worked so strenuously that we dug the whole pit over two nights. We lined it with moss, and covered the opening with spars. We lay for two weeks in this pit. [. . .] One day some peasants discovered us [. . .] We fled to another forest. [. . .] We became skilled at digging pits and over several days we dug several of them, but had to leave them because we were seen every time. We decided to dig a shelter by the river because the underbrush was very thick there. However, this shelter didn't come out as we wanted, because it was too close to water and liable to be flooded. [. . .] We were getting terribly cold; it was already October 9, 1943, and the trees were covered with hoarfrost. We were going helplessly in circles, barefoot and hungry in the forest. We didn't know what to do, and decided to go into a larger forest.'" Engelking, Barbara, *Such a Beautiful Sunny Day: Jews Seeking Refuge in the Polish Countryside -1942-1945* (Jerusalem: Yad Vashem, 2016), 77-78.

Another description of hiding in the Polish countryside and being exposed to the elements of nature was written in a journal of Aryeh Klonicki:

"Heat swallows us during the day, and we suffer from cold during the night. . . . Last night, July 8, I didn't write. There was a pouring rain at seven o'clock and we got wet. We waited until one o'clock in the morning for the rain to stop, as we had been exposed to the downpour for six hours, but it didn't stop. We left the field and went to our peasants. He feared to shelter us in the house and put us up in the potato pit, where we spent the whole day. Darkness didn't let me write. [. . .] Yesterday I didn't write anything. It was fiercely cold. On July 9, in the evening an icy wind began blowing and it lasted for the whole day yesterday. It's terribly uncomfortable. Gusts of wind penetrate our bones . . . last night we couldn't sleep and today too we can barely close our eyes. [. . .] The sky is overcast. A cold wind is blowing. We are waiting for the sun to come out and warm our freezing bodies. [. . .] The unceasing rains flattened the grains in the field. As a result, we were noticed by a peasant who happened to pass by. [. . .] It's been raining all day with short breaks. I don't know whether I'll be able to continue my diary. For all I know these could be my last words. I'm ending now because it's raining." Engelking, 96.

78 To put this date in perspective, the Americans landed at Normandy with 160,000 troops on June 6, 1944 and it was not until early March 1945 that the Red Army reached Berlin and the Germans surrendered on May 7, 1945.

79 Approximately 250,000 Polish Jews tried to evade the Nazis by hiding in the forests or in constructed hideouts, but only 50,000 were alive at the end of the war. *See* Grabowski, 2-3. *See also*, Cesarani, 646, citing Grabowski.

80 This photo is historic, as it shows survivors of the Treblinka uprising. Velvel Schneiderman was from Stoczek and after the war, he emigrated to New York. Chaim Yankel and Lejzer Ciechanowski were from Stoczek and after the war emigrated to Buenos Aires. Zigmand Brothandel was from Wengrow and after the war, he emigrated to Buenos Aires. Shimon Rosenthal, Shimon Goldberg, Yaakov (Jacob) Domb, Gutek (Gustav) Boraks, and Oscar Kudlik, all emigrated to Israel after the war. Shmuel Rajzman was from Wengrow and he emigrated to Montreal after the war. Oscar Strawczynski also emigrated to Canada. See Pinkas Stok — Stoczek Yizkor (Memorial) Book, 427.

81   *See* Wikipedia about these cigarettes: https://en.wikipedia.org/wiki/Belomorkanal

82   See Konigseder, Angelika & Wetzel, Juliane, *Waiting for Hope: Jewish Displaced Persons in Post-World War II Germany, trans. Broadwin, John* (Evanston: Northwestern University Press, 2001), 96.

83   McPherson, Alexander. In the Wilderness of Föhrenwald: Refugees in Occupied Upper Bavaria 1945-1947. Thesis (Trent University, Peterborough Ontario, May 2016).

84   Interview by Esther Goldberg with Josh Gortler, August 15, 2017.

85   Thompson, Julia Holmlund, Liberated but not yet Free: Allied Policy, Jewish Displaced Persons, and Identity in Occupied Germany, 1945-1948. Whitman College. Honors Thesis. Spring 2015 at 121-124. *See also* McPherson.

86   Konigseder, Angelika & Wetzel, Juliane, *Waiting for Hope: Jewish Displaced Person in Post-World War II Germany,* trans. Broadwin, John (Evanston: Northwestern University Press, 2001), 101.

87   Growth in the ORT programs in the American zone was rapid from late 1945 through the next few years, and by mid-1947 ORT alone oversaw 329 different education facilities, 5304 students, and 559 instructors of forty subjects from knitting to welding. *See* Thompson Thesis.

88   One of the camp's theater groups was called *Mapilim* (train blazers) and yet another was called *Bar Kochba*, in honor of the Jewish leader who led an unsuccessful revolt against the Romans in the second century CE. The newspaper was called *Bamidbar* (in the desert). The camp cinema was a busy place. They showed three to five movies per week at first, and later they played a double feature every night. Konigseder & Wetzel, 120-23.

89   "By 1946, the Joint's expenditures had increased more than tenfold to $3,979,500, and in 1947 they reached a maximum of $9,012,000, a staggering amount of money for the time." Konigseder & Wetzel, 62.

90   Konigseder & Wetzel, 69.

91   Navsource Online: Service Ship Photo Archive. Marine Jumper (T-AP-200) http://www.navsource.org/archives/09/22/22200.htm

92   "The etymology of the word *shiksa* is partly derived from the Hebrew term שֶׁקֶץ *shekets*, meaning 'abomination', 'impure,' or 'object of loathing', depending on the translator." Wikipedia Contributors. "Shiksa." In Wikipedia, The Free Encyclopedia, April 12, 2018. https://en.wikipedia.org/wiki/Shiksa

93   Jan Grabowski discusses the fear that arose among Polish Jews around the Christian holidays. He cites testimony given by a Jewish survivor, Joseph Matzer: "[T]he periods of fear were around Christmas and Easter. During Christmas, Poles would blame Jews for the death of Christ, while at Easter the Jewish community would be terrorized with the specter of the blood libel circulating among the gentiles." Grabowski, 20.

94   Before the war there were 3,300,000 Polish Jews. *See* Hilberg, Raul,

Destruction of the European Jews, Student Edition (Teaneck: Holmes & Meier, 1985), 64; Dawidowicz, 544. Approximately three million Polish Jews were murdered. *See* Hilberg, 339; Dawidowicz, 544. This makes the chance of survival .09%. Historians believe that in the summer of 1942, approximately 2.5 million Polish Jews were still alive. Jan Grabowski in his book, *Hunt for the Jews*, he estimates that ten percent of the Jews tried to escape the Nazi deportations. Grabowski, 172. If this estimate is correct, then 250,000 people hid and survived the Nazi roundups. Historians, including Grabowski, estimate that of the 250,000 Jews in hiding, less than 50,000 survived the war. Grabowski, 172.

95   Chris Webb and Michal Chocholatý put the number murdered at Treblinka at 885,023. See Webb & Chocholatý, 193. At the end of the war, approximately 65 of those that arrived at Treblinka, were still alive. Webb & Chocholatý, 232-256. Using these numbers, Sam's chance of survival was .0073%. Webb and Chocholatý's first edition does not include Sam (Shmuel) Goldberg in the list of survivors. The next edition of the book will include Sam. See also, Treblinka Museum Web Site which has a list of 68 Treblinka survivors. As of publication, Sam was not on this list.

http://www.treblinka-muzeum.eu/index.php/historia/oboz-zaglady/opor-i-powstanie

96   The March of the Living is an annual educational trip to Poland taken by thousands of Jewish teenagers from around the world. The trip culminates in a march from Auschwitz to Birkenau, after which the teens fly to Israel for a week exploring the Jewish State.

97   Translated by Joanna Millick.

98   Translated by Joanna Millick. Another letter that was particularly interesting was from Cecyla Borkowska. It was sent from Stoczek and was dated, May 6, 1991:

Dear Mrs. Krysia.
One more time, I allow myself to write a letter and ask for a small favor. I wrote you a letter in 1989 that in our place that is Stanisław Postek, in Stoczek, the Germans killed 17 people including people of Jewish origins and my parents, my father Stawistlaw and other Juliana Postek, they were killed because they were hiding Jews in their home and they were giving them help. They also took my two brothers to the prison Pawiak prison in Warsaw. My mom was killed on the spot and my father was taken to Auschwitz where he was murdered. The rest of the family escaped and survived. As a response to that letter that I sent in 1989, I received your answer and you confirmed that you were hiding in the forest in Dragich and that you remember this tragedy. I showed this letter to the main commission of research on Hitlerite Nazi crimes in Poland and they told me that this is important information and it is important that you write it and take it to the lawyer to confirm the truth. If you can be so kind as to do it and send it to us. We need this in an important matter, so Germans give us reparations for the losses and crimes that were committed on our family. I ask you one more time for your help and I cordially send best regards to your whole family. (Translated by Joanna Millick).

99   Translated by Magda Styś.

100   On August 19, 1992, The Los Angeles Times ran a front-page article profiling a 22-year-old Grzegorz and the town of Lipki. The article can be found: http://articles.latimes.com/1992-08-18/news/mn-5851_1_eastern-europe

101   At Chelmno, the Nazis ran a camp that forced Jews into the back of a truck that was covered with canvas and sealed. Carbon monoxide was piped into the enclosed space asphyxiating those within. The truck would travel to a nearby forest and dump the dead bodies into a pit. Chelmno was approximately 64 kilometers (40 miles) from Łódź and began operations on December 8, 1941. The killing capacity of Chelmno was 1,000 humans per day. Friedlander, 316.

102   After Hitler declared war on the United States on December 12, 1941, he met with his Nazi cronies and stated "that the Jews would have to pay 'with their lives' for the war they had inflicted on Germany — indeed, that they already were doing so. As historian Peter Fritzsche has remarked, 'this is as close to a Hitler order as historians will get,' meaning the closest . . . that we are likely to find to connect Hitler personally with the command to kill the Jews." Hayes, 124.

103   *See* Snyder, *Bloodlands*, 275.

104   Hayes, 181.

105   Yitzchak Arad details a communication between SS *Obergruppenführer* Karl Wolff, Himmler's Chief of Staff and the Secretary of State of Minister of Transport, Dr. Theodor Ganzenmüller about the delay of getting trains rolling from Warsaw to Treblinka. Ganzenmüller reported to Wolff by letter, dated July 27, 1942: "Since July 22, a train load of 5,000 Jews has departed daily from Warsaw via Malkinia to Treblinka, and in addition a train load of 5,000 Jews has left Przemysl twice a week for Belzec. . . . In reply, Wolff wrote Ganzenmüller on August 13, 1942: 'Hearty thanks, in the name of the *Reichsführer* SS, for your letter of July 28, 1942. With great joy I learned from your announcement that, for the past fourteen days, a train has gone daily to Treblinka with 5000 'members of the chosen people.'" Arad, 51.

106   This legend was called into question in a book by Victor Ripp: *Hell's Traces: One Murder, Two Families, Thirty-Five Holocaust Memorials* (New York: Farrar, Straus & Giroux, 2014). He tells of an encounter with a Polish tour guide who explained that the Korczak legend is false: "'It is all because of one man: Władysław Szpilman,' she said. 'In Polanski's movie The Pianist, Szpilman is portrayed as a national hero. After that no one argued with anything Szpilman said. When he wrote in his memoir that he saw Korczak at the train station that day, volunteering to go with the children, that became the truth. But there are many inconsistencies in Szpilman's story — he got the weather of that day wrong, also the time of the train's departure. But you really have to know only one thing. The Nazis did not give anyone that sort of choice. 'They were not so generous.'" Ripp, 58.

107   I.L. Peretz (Isaac Leib) lived 1852 — 1915. He was born in Zamość.

108   Janina told also told us that she was friends with Chaim and Moishe's sister, Chana, from school. Chana told her that she and her mother had prepared a hiding place with a Polish family. They did not want to hide in the attic, so they ran from their home to the hiding place. Janina said that Chana "fell into the devil's arms." Chaim Kwiatek, who settled in Montreal, Canada after the war, left a brief testimony of his wartime experiences. In his testimony, he states that "friends" sent his mother and sister to Treblinka.

109   In my research I found a reference to a man named Marian Styś, who in March of 1943 molested and murdered a Jewish woman and her five-year-old daughter. He was tried and convicted by a Soviet court in 1953. He spent eight years in prison for

his crime. I was worried because Helena Styś had a son named Marian and the murders occurred only a few kilometers from Stoczek. I thought perhaps the Goldberg family legend of a Jew Catcher in the Styś family was true. But after much investigation, I have determined that this murderer is not Helena's son. The murderer was born in 1912 and Helena's son was born in 1933. I was relieved. *See* Engelking, 295.

110   Orders went out throughout Poland to ensure that Jews who escaped the Nazi net would be hunted and caught. An example of one such order was "preserved in the dossiers of the Krakow Appellate Courts. . . .

'Regarding the Regulation issued by the County Authorities on August 14, 1942 and concerning the deportation of the Jews from our areas, I hasten to inform you that the matter is very serious. You are to make absolutely sure that not even one single Jew, Jewess, or Jewish child is left on the territory of your commune. You have to immediately order the hostages to search the entire area, back alleys, bushes, and so on, in order to make certain that no [Jews] are left. Whenever caught, Jews are to be delivered to the nearest station of the Polish Police. I repeat that the penalty for hiding Jews is death. Village elders are also responsible for Jews hidden on the territory of their commune, and — in case of negligence — can face the death penalty. I remind you to make certain that these orders are being followed: you are responsible under the penalty of death — Kosmice Wielkie, August 28, 1942.'" Grabowski, 76-77.

Zygmunt Klukowski, a physician in a small town near Lublin, wrote a diary entry on November 26, 1942, providing an eyewitness report:

"The farmers are seizing the Jews hiding in the villages, out of fear of possible reprisals, and are taking them to the town, or sometimes simply killing them on the spot. In general, there has been a strange brutalization in relation to the Jews. A psychosis has seized hold of people, and, following the German example, they do not consider the Jews to be human, regarding them rather as an injurious pest that must be exterminated using all available means, like a dog sick with rabies or a rat." Hayes, 251.

111   For additional insight into those who aided Jews during the war, see Snyder, *Black Earth*, chapter 12.

112   *See* Snyder, *Bloodlands*, 253-54; 273-75. Snyder describes this shift and explains that although Auschwitz was the site of murder of about one in six Jews, it was not the most efficient killing site. "The most efficient shooting squads killed faster," Snyder explains, "the starvation sites killed faster and Treblinka killed faster. . . . Most Soviet and Polish Jews under German occupation had already been murdered by the time Auschwitz became the major death factory." Snyder, *Bloodlands*, 383.

113   Of the million, 100,000 were non-Jews. Snyder, *Bloodlands*, 275.

114   Snyder, *Bloodlands*, 276.

115   Snyder, *Bloodlands*, viii.

116   Wachsmann, Nikolaus. *KI: A History of the Nazi Concentration Camps* (New York: Alfred A. Knopf, 2016), 100.

117   The Nazi regime had been building concentration camps since they took power in 1933. Between 1933 and 1935, they built camps, most of which were previously unfamiliar to me: Sonnenburg, Brandenburg, Dachau (this one is familiar), Lichtenburg, Emsland, Esterwegen, Columbia House, and Sachsenburg. They were not built for genocide or even for Jews. In fact, the Jewish prisoner population of these early camps was a mere 5%. Himmler explained the national imperative — to imprison "all left-wing opponents" of the Nazi regime, who "threaten the security of the state." Starting with 1937, name recognition goes up: Buchenwald (1937), Mauthausen (1938), Ravensbrück (1939), Auschwitz (1940) and Majdanek (1940). Auschwitz became operational on June 19, 1940. Wachsmann, 46-53, 85, 97.

118   Wachsmann, 267.

119   Most likely September 5, 1941. Wachsmann, 267.

120   Wachsmann, 268.

121   Wachsmann, 269. The bloodbaths referred to were the shooting of Jews into pits in the Eastern lands conquered by Germany beginning in June of 1941.

122   Wachsmann, 269.

123   Wachsmann, 279.

124   Reszke, Katka, *Return of the Jew: Identity Narratives of the Third Post-Holocaust Generation of Jews in Poland* (Boston: Academic Studies Press, 2013), 41.

125   Reszke, 38

126   Reszke, 37.

127   Reszke, 37-38.

128   Reszke, 37-38.

129   Reszke, 23.

130   Reszke, 27.

131   Reszke, 27.

132   Reszke, 27.

133   Reszke, 29. Studies show that the numbers of Jews range from 1,000 to 100,000. See studies cited by Reszke, 28-29.

134   Reszke, 108. The Covenant he refers to is the biblical covenant between God and the Jewish people.

135   Reszke, 121.

136   *See* Polish Polls Reveals Stubborn Anti-Semitism Amid Jewish Revival Hopes, by Don Snyder in Forward on line — Jan. 18, 2014. http://forward.com/news/world/191155/poland-poll-reveals-stubborn-anti-semitism-amid-je/#ixzz4AjPJLqyy

137   Lech Wałęsa, the former President of Poland thinks being Jewish

is cool. He posted on Facebook that he regrets that he is not Jewish and that he "would like to be a part of the Chosen People but [he is] not." Former Polish President Regrets That He Is Not Jewish, By JTA. Forward. MAY 1, 2016: http://forward.com/news/breaking-news/339740/former-polish-president-says-he-regrets-he-is-not-jewish/#ixzz4AjVFweEs

138   For more about the Jedwabne pogrom, see Gross, Jan, *Neighbors: The Destruction of the Jewish Community of Jedwabne, Poland* (Princeton: Princeton University Press, 2012).

139   Krista Tippett, the interviewer of the podcast On Being, expands on this idea:

"I have seen that wisdom, in life and society, emerges precisely through those moments when we have to hold seemingly opposing realities in a creative tension and interplay: power and frailty, birth and death, pain and hope, beauty and broken-ness, mystery and conviction, calm and the fierceness, mine and yours." *See* Krista Tippett and her Civil Conversation Project at: http://www.civilconversationsproject.org/

140   Barbara Engelking discusses the evil she found as she uncovered stories of Jews in hiding: "Darkness thickened in the desert of humanity and terror mounted. As they searched for rescue, Jews began to experience more and more directly the evil inflicted on them by the Poles. This was not simply an absence of good, but real, substantial, and deep evil incarnate. It was an evil whose consequence was mostly death, so it was the final, irrevocable evil, which was also linked with cruelty and violence.

To devote so much attention to evil itself, to concentrate on the dark side of human beings, their evil deeds and to describe them — might be regarded as problematic. However, in my opinion an attempt to understand evil does not in any way indicate forgiveness, or, worse, acquiescence. Furthermore, telling the story of evil creates a strong context for the good, allowing us to appreciate more fully the course of those who aided and saved." Engelking, 175.

141   Wisse, Ruth, R. ed., *The I.L. Peretz Reader*, trans. Hillel Hankin (New York: Schocken Books, 1990), 147. This story was story written in 1894.

142   Wisse, 148.

143   Wisse, 151.

144   Wisse, 151.

145   Wisse, 152.

146   Wisse, 152.

147   Wisse, 152.

148   Gordon and Gelbart, 588-89.

149   Barbara Engelking comments on the fact there were Jewish children who survived the war on their own in the Polish countryside: "[m]any Jewish children who hid on their own survived the war. Arguably their task was admittedly eas-ier because helping children was perceived differently. Perhaps children elicited

greater compassion, were more dependent, and the psychological cost of refusal to help a child was higher?" Engelking, 135.

150   Back in Seattle, Shlomo met Magda and Idul Wilk on a Skype call. This was a tender and emotional moment for all of them. At last, some more Goldbergs are reunited. Shlomo met his cousins Idul and Magda in person when he traveled to Warsaw in January of 2018 to attend the *Yad Vashem* ceremony awarding Righteous Among the Nations to the Styś family.

151   Radio Lab. http://www.radiolab.org/story/nukes/

152   Sam told the following story about a different Kapo: When Sam and Esther lived in Brooklyn, they took a vacation to Grossingers, a kosher resort hotel in the Catskill Mountains of New York State. When Sam came in and saw the manager of Grossingers, he was shocked — it was a *Kapo* from Treblinka. It had been some 20 years, but still, he recognized him immediately, as the "terrible" *Kapo* who "lived with maybe 10 girls." He said to him: "You, you're here?" The *Kapo* said to Sam: "Be quiet, don't say anything." If it had gotten out that the manager of Grossingers was a *Kapo* at Treblinka, he would not have kept his job very long. Sam decided not to "touch him." However, the *Kapo*, feeling the need to add some insurance to Sam's silence, gave Sam and Esther the nicest room in the hotel and sent them a beautiful bottle of champagne and all kinds of delicious food. Goldberg, Sam, Interview. *See also,* soyouwantowriteaholocaustbook.wordpress.com, February 8, 2016.

153   Einstein wrote these words as part of a letter to Rabbi Robert Marcus after the death of his eleven-year-old son. *See* Levy, Naomi, *Einstein and the Rabbi: Searching for the Soul* (New York: Flatiron Books, 2017), 13.

154   Maimonides Medical Center was founded in 1947 as a merger of two existing hospitals in Brooklyn, NY. It was named for Rabbi Moshe Ben Maimon, a 12th Century scholar, philosopher and physician. Wikipedia Contributors. "Maimonides Medical Center." In Wikipedia, The Free Encyclopedia, April 19, 2018. https://en.wikipedia.org/wiki/Maimonides_Medical_Center

READER'S GUIDE DISCUSSION QUESTIONS

My Soul is Filled with Joy: A Holocaust Story, is a memoir about the author's in-laws, Sam and Esther Goldberg, as they survived the Holocaust and her journey of writing the book. The following questions are intended to provide common ground for a shared reading experience for book groups, discussion forums or other events.

1. In her research, the author read or heard different versions of the same event from multiple people. When it comes to events of the past, do you believe that "truth" exists or is there only subjective realities reflecting each person's experience?

2. What do you know about your family's history?

3. How can you dig and find out more?

4. What character traits did Sam and Esther have that helped them to survive?

5. What character traits do you have that would help you survive such hardships?

6. Do you think anyone who survived the Holocaust had as many miraculous things happen as Sam and Esther? Luck, coincidence, God, faith?

7. If you were part of the Styś family – what might you have done? What would have been the factors you considered?

8. When you read about Treblinka and what happened during the Holocaust, how do you respond to what you learned?

9. The author and her family visited Poland, even though Esther told Shlomo never to go back to Poland. Should tourists go to Poland on Holocaust-related trips? Some say – tourist dollars should not be spent in Poland. Others say – we must go – to see what happened, to feel it in our bones, and teach others. What do you think?

10. Both Sam and Esther had dreams which foretold the future. Have you ever had a dream that foretold something that happened? What was it?

11. What would you say to someone who says that Holocaust never happened?

12. What inspiration do you gain from reading Sam and Esther's story?

13. What might you do differently in your life?

14. What lessons can we learn?

ABOUT THE AUTHOR

Karen I. Treiger

https://karentreiger.com
http://starelipkipress.com
https://soyouwanttowriteaholocaustbook.wordpress.com

Karen Treiger is a retired attorney. Since her retirement in 2015, she has been researching and writing this book. She graduated from New York University Law School (order of the Coif) in 1988, where she served as Editor in Chief of the Law Review. She graduated from Barnard College, Columbia University in 1983. Her work experience ranges from a Legislative Assistant to Senator Slade Gorton, business law for a large Seattle Law Firm, and her most recent law practice of fourteen years with the boutique law firm of Thompson, Howle & Vaughn, where she practiced Elder Law.

Treiger's Law Review Note, published in 1987 was entitled *Preventing Patient Dumping: Sharpening the COBRA's Fangs.* New York University Law Review 1987 Dec: 61(6) 1186-223. More recently she had an article related to this book published in Jewish in Seattle Magazine, August-September 2016, entitled, *Sweet Revenge.* In the spring of 2016, Treiger received a Certificate in Nonfiction Writing from the University of Washington Professional and Continuing Education. She is an accomplished and dynamic speaker and has presented at many Continuing Legal Education programs, community events, and is a member of the Seattle Holocaust Center's Speaker's Bureau.